Stetson University
3 4369 00315651 6

D0571621

Managing the Total Quality Transformation

Managing the Total Quality Transformation

Thomas H. Berry

McGraw-Hill, Inc.

New York St. Louis San Francisco Auckland Bogotá
Caracas Lisbon London Madrid Mexico Milan
Montreal New Delhi Paris San Juan São Paulo
Singapore Sydney Tokyo Toronto

Library of Congress Cataloging-in-Publication Data

Berry, Thomas H.
Managing the total quality transformation / Thomas H. Berry.
p. cm.
Includes index.
ISBN 0-07-005071-6 :
1. Quality of products. 2. Quality circles. I. Title.
HF5415.157.B47 1990
658.5'62—dc20 90-39437
CIP

This book is printed on recycled, acid-free paper containing a minimum of 50% recycled de-inked fiber.

8 9 0 DOC/DOC 9 5 4 3

ISBN 0-07-005071-6

The sponsoring editor for this book was James H. Bessent, Jr., the editing supervisor was Olive Collen, the designer was Naomi Auerbach, and the production supervisor was Suzanne W. Babeuf. It was set in Baskerville by McGraw-Hill's Professional and Reference Division composition unit.

Printed and bound by R. R. Donnelley & Sons Company.

To all customer-focused
and quality-minded employees

Contents

Foreword

The first, and probably most natural, reaction to a new book on total quality management is, "Oh no, not another book on quality management! What could possibly be in this book that hasn't been in 50 others?" But this book *is* different. Many other books tell us what we should do, but few tell us how to do it. Many other authors tell us why quality is so important and what spectacular results can be achieved, but few even attempt to describe the steps of the journey to total quality management.

Tom Berry not only describes this journey in detail, he writes with the authority of one who has taken the journey himself. He not only gives us a clear road map, he tells us about the bumps in the road, the ditches, and the railroad crossings.

We have all *read* much about total quality management. Tom Berry provides us with a chance to judge what has been *done* about it. Tom provides proof that total quality management works, works here in the United States, and works in *service* companies! He supplies the concepts and proof and also a road map (with useful warning signs) on how to implement total quality management. From his personal experience in leading the implementation effort at Colonial Penn, Tom discusses:

How and where to start TQM

How to scale-up TQM

How to institutionalize TQM

The role for frontline employees

The role for middle managers

The role for upper managers

Tom gives excellent guidance to the company or organization starting the journey toward total quality management. He provides insights into some of the challenges facing quality leaders in the 1990s. He gives a clear prescription for building quality into the business plans and strategic plans. He shows how to move from a restricted focus on outcomes or results to managing the critical *processes* within the company.

Tom clearly explains the differences between the roles of the cross-functional quality improvement teams and the unit-level quality teams. He shows how the unit-level quality teams use the Deming wheel or Shewhart diagram (Plan, Do, Check, Act) to drive the unit quality process. He explains the use of quality planning and management's key role in planning and in the deployment of plans, goals, and objectives throughout the organization.

But best of all, Tom continuously brings us back to reality with examples of what companies, particularly Colonial Penn and Florida Power and Light, have actually done. He describes in detail what the quality council members do during the first steps of the journey and how they manage the quality improvement process down the road. He stops often to give us specific, useful lists of actions for top managers, quality teams, and quality managers. Tom is not shy with his recommendations. He doesn't miss many opportunities to tell us exactly what to do and how to do it. We suggest you consider all his recommendations seriously.

After finishing the text, we are sure you will find the quote attributed to Sir Winston Churchill appropriate: "It is not the end. It is not the beginning of the end. However, it is the end of the beginning."

A. C. Endres
VICE PRESIDENT

A. Blanton Godfrey
CHAIRMAN AND CEO
JURAN INSTITUTE, INC.

Preface

Managing the Total Quality Transformation describes how an organization can delight its customers and optimize long-term profitability, competitive position, and market share by adopting a customer-focused, total quality management (TQM) process.

A quality management process is a total corporate focus on meeting—and often exceeding—customers' expectations and significantly reducing the costs resulting from poor quality by shaping a new management system and corporate culture. For most companies, the cost of poor quality is estimated to be from 20 to 25 percent of sales revenues!

To many people, including top executives, *quality* is a nebulous word like *excellent* or *outstanding*. If you can't define *quality*, then you can't measure it, and if you can't measure quality, you can't achieve it. If you can't achieve it, the cost of poor quality continues to erode your chances for a profitable future.

A company that can define, measure, and achieve quality, however, will earn and sustain a strong competitive advantage and envious profitability, which are the ultimate objectives of any organization.

This book is intended to provide an easy-to-follow blueprint for achieving quality, particularly in medium to large service businesses, where until quite recently, the faint drumbeat of a growing quality revolution in U.S. manufacturing firms has gone virtually unnoticed. This book can aid the manufacturing revolution as well.

The company that seizes the initiative for constantly catering to the needs of its customers and involves all its people in a quality revolution will emerge victorious in terms of customer satisfaction and loyalty, and in terms of earnings growth and competitive position. There is no better formula for success, and there is no better time to mount a quality offensive than right now.

Step by step and chapter by chapter, this book describes how quality can be defined, measured, achieved, and maintained. It begins by offering a usable definition of *quality* and describing the incentives for achieving it. Succeeding chapters model the journey toward total quality management and guide the reader along the path to a fully realized and totally customer-focused environment, where a reputation for quality products and services can be earned and maintained.

Along the path to achieving quality, the reader is exposed to a total quality model and to such critical ingredients as:

- Developing an approach to quality
- Forming quality improvement teams
- Planning and organizing for quality
- Taking quality to the unit level
- Training people in the use of quality improvement tools and techniques
- Building a knowledge of customers and their needs
- Managing the critical success factors
- Experimenting with the quality process at a test site
- Developing a customer-focused corporate culture
- Improving vendor performance
- Ensuring top management's involvement and support
- Recognizing and rewarding quality achievement
- Measuring and sustaining quality

A vital thread woven through the emerging quality fabric is the absolute necessity for employee involvement at every organizational level and from every corner of the organization. Empowering people to take the quality initiative and inciting management to clear the obstacles that impede the progress of employee involvement are strongly and continuously advocated.

I've included charts, examples, models, and Transformation Checkpoints, which are quality "to-do" lists at the end of each chapter. However, it is not the purpose of this book to provide instruction in the statistical process control tools used by quality improvement teams. I hope that upon completion of this book the reader will feel an impelling need to begin a quality revolution and have the confidence, knowledge, and enthusiasm to get the job done—because it's a matter of corporate survival!

Today we must fight to survive in an increasingly competitive marketplace that is international in scope. We can no longer consider the battlefield to exist only from sea to shining sea.

I believe that our workers are capable of competing and winning in the broader arena. But to do so, we must question some of our long-held and most basic beliefs concerning customer satisfaction and managing for quality. As a nation, we are just beginning to rise to this significant challenge. The recent establishment of the Malcolm Baldrige National Quality Award by the U.S. government provides evidence that the United States is waking up to face the challenge.

Delighting customers is the name of the game in which we are all engaged. Every man and woman in the workplace must be called upon to pitch in—to serve customers as never before. This must be our highest priority, and achieving it must be recognized as a long-term endeavor. Those who walk down Wall Street carrying their shareholder banners while the battle for customer loyalty wages around them must wake up to both the priority and the time frame for improving our corporate competitiveness. They must take pride in their involvement in this quest for quality. After all, what is most important—quarterly earnings per share, price-earnings ratio, dividend declaration? Or should survival next year and into the next decade take the front seat?

The total quality efforts upon which a growing number of enlightened companies are embarking continue to challenge the short-term–earnings mentality. We must believe that an investment in total quality and customer satisfaction today will make all the annual reports look magnificent tomorrow and that the commitment being made now is for greater gain later.

This book encourages adopting a total quality management process now. Each of us, as a consumer, deserves it. Each of us, as a worker, must contribute to it. Each of us must demand it to ensure a bright economic future for the country.

It is my hope that you will read this quality "battle plan" from cover to cover and are motivated to join the quality revolution in your factory, office, or division. If you have already begun to fight, my intention is to smooth the way for you.

If this book doesn't do it for you, then find one that will. And above all, stay the course of quality advocacy.

Thomas H. Berry

Acknowledgments

A number of key people, whether they know it or not, played a vital role in the preparation of this book. Some of them provided personal encouragement or hands-on assistance, which was not only greatly appreciated but was also, from time to time, sorely needed.

First and foremost, I thank Mary Anne, my very best friend and wife of 23 years, for her faith, confidence, love, and encouragement as well as for her editing assistance and insightful comments and suggestions. Her experience and skills as a free-lance copywriter were extremely helpful. I thank my two fine teenage sons, Mark and Adam, for their patience during the hundreds of hours when the house needed to be still and quiet. This was an unusual sacrifice for Adam, who is well along on learning to play the drums. Their cooperation and understanding, as well as their love and encouragement, were a great help.

Two long-time and cherished friends provided substantial encouragement from the very first day (or even earlier) throughout the long haul of producing a marketable proposal and a finished manuscript. John Toedtman clearly recognized my passion for total quality management and pushed me hard to "get the book written." Ferdinand Setaro did exactly the same thing and also introduced me to Patricia Haskell, who became my literary agent. Ferdie and Pat provided technical guidance and much-needed support in marketing my publishing proposal and, later, helped me to manage my own impatience as I floundered in the publishing world for the first time.

Many other people over the past several years were significant contributors to building my knowledge and understanding of total quality.

Dr. Joseph M. Juran worked with me and with Colonial Penn in the initial stages of developing a TQM model for our service organization. Later he recognized that we had a story worth telling and invited me to prepare a paper for presentation at his Institute's 1988 Annual Conference (IMPRO). The presentation received top ranking by the participants.

The people of FPL Group, Inc., and Florida Power and Light Company provided irreplaceable assistance and opportunities for learning as well as encouragement as I worked to develop a TQM process for Colonial Penn. Special thanks goes to Marshall McDonald, former chairman of FPL Group, and John Hudiburg, former chairman of Florida Power and Light Company, and to the following people of these organizations who helped guide the way: Tom Petillo, Carl Stimson, Frank Voehl, Bear Baila, Irwin Weinberg, Barbara Cottrell, Bill Cunningham, Kent Sterret, Sandy Straus, Bill Hamilton, Joe Collier, Jack Woodall, Joe Howard, Bud Hunter, Clark Cook, and Dottie Norton. FPL also provided me with the opportunity to visit Japan and, on numerous occasions, to be exposed to the knowledge of members of the Union of Japanese Scientists and Engineers, including the enlightening Dr. Noriaki Kano.

Many people at Colonial Penn worked tirelessly, diligently, and with a strong passion and an unshakable resolve to develop our TQM process. Sigmund Brody, regional vice president of our Southeast Home Office (our TQM test site) and a good friend for more than 20 years, recognized the "power" of TQM immediately and provided the passionate leadership and personal involvement needed to institutionalize a total quality spirit within his region. Anita Dematos, our first lead facilitator, provided outstanding hands-on guidance in the development of TQM and has been, and continues to be, instrumental in its growing success. The employees of our Southeast Home Office are a spirited and dedicated group. It is they, in the final analysis, who took our rudimentary quality model and plan and transformed it into something of which we are all tremendously proud—something that is making a difference to our customers.

I also owe thanks to the top managers of Colonial Penn, who created the opportunity for our company to pursue TQM and who rolled up their sleeves and jumped in with enthusiasm and confidence. These gentlemen are Richard Ohman, chairman and CEO; Douglas Pierce, president and COO; Ronald Glidden, group vice president, data processing; and Joseph Kaminski, group vice president and CFO. Special thanks go as well to Russell Glicksman, my boss when it all began.

Finally, there is my staff. What a great crew! Their dedication, knowledge, energy, and skill—not to mention their patience with me—represented a critical success factor second to none. My everlasting gratitude and respect goes to Stephanie Dooley, Jean Fendall, Jill Feninger, Dorothy Liggett, and Jerry Gorman. Tracey Schneider and Nancy Calabree deserve special thanks for all the work they did in their spare time to develop and then redevelop the publishing proposal and manuscript. Their word processing skills are truly remarkable.

Thanks to all.

Managing the Total Quality Transformation

1

TQM: What's It Really All About?

This book is about designing, implementing, and sustaining a total quality management (TQM) process primarily in medium to large service corporations. However, it also applies to the manufacturing sector. Other popular labels for total quality management are quality improvement process (QIP) and total quality control (TQC). The company that takes the initiative to adopt TQM can eventually achieve a significant advantage over its competitors with respect to all the key indicators of success: market share, profitability, growth, costs, and so on.

A point I must stress up front is that a TQM process is not a quick-fix strategy. You won't see your competitors fading from sight in your company's rearview mirror a few months after developing TQM. However, if you build a strong quality-focused organization, you will pull away from the field over a several-year period. You maintain this leadership position only by continuing to nurture your TQM approach year after year, forever and ever.

I use the word *process* and avoid the word *program* in order to help make this vital point.

A process is a methodology that is developed to replace the old ways and to guide corporate activity year after year. It is not a special guest. It is not temporary. It is not to be tolerated for a while and then abandoned.

A program, on the other hand, is typically seen by many employees as something with a beginning, a middle, and an end. It is here today and can be expected to be gone tomorrow regardless of how it may otherwise be described by its developer. A program is an overlay on the old ways. It can be tolerated. We can lay low and wait it out.

To serious dieters, a weight-loss strategy should be a process. When it is, overweight people change their eating habits forever, reach their goals, and maintain their desired weight.

Too often, however, dieters will select a program rather than a process, and although they drop the weight, they regain it a year later. Then it's even harder for them to lose the next time.

Florida Power and Light Company manages one of the best QIPs you'll find in the country. Marshall McDonald, president of FPL Group, Inc. (the parent organization of Florida Power and Light Company), until 1989, and now chairman, calls the process a "journey, not a destination." So don't think in terms of an annual drive for quality. Think in terms of establishing a new methodology for managing your business, one which you'll continue to nurture and improve constantly. Florida Power and Light Company has done precisely that. The company began its quality journey in 1981 and in November 1989 was the first company outside Japan to win the Deming Prize, the most prestigious quality award available.

Defining Quality

Before describing what a QIP is, we need to understand what quality is and what it isn't. Quality has nothing to do with how shiny or bright something is, or with how much it costs, or with how many features and gizmos it has. A customer who buys your product or experiences your service has certain needs and expectations in mind. If the product or service meets or exceeds those expectations time and time again, then, in the mind of that customer, it is a quality product or a quality service.

Quality, therefore, relates to the customer's perception. Customers compare the actual performance of the product or the total service experience to their own set of expectations and reach a judgment that is rarely neutral. The product or service either passes or fails. The basic definition of *quality*, then, is meeting customers' needs and expectations.

Most customers are reasonable people. They expect a Rolls Royce to have a leather interior with a built-in refreshment center and television. They don't reasonably expect these features in a Dodge Aries. Customers in the market for each of these products have different sets of expectations; therefore, each car can meet the expectations of its new owner.

So, the enhanced definition of quality is:

MEETING CUSTOMERS' NEEDS AND REASONABLE EXPECTATIONS

Understanding the Quality Improvement Process

A QIP is a systematic method of developing products and services and providing customer service after the sale based on a thorough understanding of customers' needs and reasonable expectations. It involves employees at all levels in the assessment and improvement of quality through the application of statistical process control (SPC) and other quality improvement (QI) tools and techniques.

Many people balk at the word *statistical*, or they experience feelings of anxiety similar to those generated by changes in the tax laws. However, SPC tools are not as complicated as they sound. A little training is all it takes for most applications, and much of it can be done on a PC these days. Many people also believe that SPC only applies to manufacturing. This is one of the most common misconceptions. Quality improvement applies just as well to service businesses as it does to manufacturing. In service, for example, instead of working to improve material variations, you work to adjust process variation such as reducing the time it takes to issue a policy, an ID card, or a claims check in an insurance company. So don't use that old "manufacturing only" excuse for not considering a TQM process.

From the perspective of the customer, we can get another description of the TQM process. Nothing matters more to the success of a business than how customers perceive the product or service for which they've paid. It is the customer's perception that determines whether he or she will buy from the same company the next time. Therefore, everything you do must be driven by what the customer wants. You have to see your business through the eyes of the customer, and you must be constantly aware of how customers are reacting to both the product or service they buy and the way they were treated during each step of the buying experience.

By listening to the customer and by examining your operational methods, you'll find that improvements are needed. As you identify each of these opportunities, you need to train your people—each and every one—in ways to isolate the root causes of problems to gain the improvements needed and ways to lock in the gains they achieve to make improvements permanent, not fleeting. You need to organize your company to empower people to pursue these improvements without letup, and to vigorously support and reward the people who deliver the improvements customers need. A TQM process includes methods for accomplishing all this.

Total Quality Management vs. Quality Circles, Customer Satisfaction, and Productivity Improvement

How does TQM relate to using Quality Circles, customer satisfaction strategies, and the productivity improvement programs we hear about? Total quality management is a powerful strategy that can significantly improve your ability to delight customers day in and day out and, at the same time, send productivity rates soaring.

Productivity programs, first of all, can certainly be effective, but their principal focus is on doing something better, that is, more efficiently. Total quality management not only focuses on doing things right but on doing the right things right. If today we can process a thousand orders for widgets in 2 hours when it took 8 hours previously, that's great! But, it's useless if the customer doesn't need widgets.

Many companies currently utilize or have experimented with Quality Circles but have failed to develop this concept to the point at which it makes a difference.

Most often, Quality Circles consist of several nonmanagement employees from a single department or function. The members of the Quality Circle are volunteers who receive some training in problem-solving techniques, select their own leader, and choose their own problem, which relates to their unit or functional mission, to resolve. Circles typically meet for an hour each week to pursue the problem they have selected.

A TQM process, on the other hand, includes the formation of QI teams. Quality improvement team members are selected by management, and membership on the team is required. A QI team most often consists of employees from any and all organizational levels of the company and from a variety of departments or functions. The problem or project the team will work on is quite often selected by management and always approved by management. In addition, the team leader is assigned by management, and the problem a team is assigned closely relates to a key corporate goal or business priority.

Members of QI teams receive specialized problem-solving training, including the use of SPC tools, and meet frequently to pursue their assigned problem.

In the final analysis, QI teams are a vital part of a TQM system. They are orchestrated by management, include management participation, and are aimed directly at resolving key corporate issues.

If your company uses Quality Circles as I've described them, I urge you to transform this employee involvement program to a TQM process. Utilize the employees now involved in Quality Circles, but don't use the circles themselves because they have a charter that differs from that of QI teams. Former circle members will be eager to participate on the higher plane of TQM, where their efforts will be more directly connected to key corporate goals and where quality team members will include managers and corporate officers.

To summarize this point, using Quality Circles instead of TQM is like planting a few perfectly good seeds in unfertile soil. You'll get a few sprouts if you're lucky, but you'll never reap a profitable harvest. Instead, use your Quality Circle members on QI teams as part of your TQM process.

Customer satisfaction strategies like those presented by Tom Peters, Karl Albrecht, and Ron Zemke, to name a few, are aimed at the same target that a TQM process shoots for: namely, an unwavering focus on meeting customers' needs.

A TQM process is an excellent strategy for achieving a long-term competitive position because it provides specific tools and techniques for doing this. It builds skills and knowledge, involves top management, focuses on constantly gaining improvements, and builds a corporate culture that values customer delight more than anything. Make no mistake about it, quality improvement *is* customer satisfaction and more. Total quality management means building a total customer-focused management system and supporting culture that has, as its driving force, meeting customers' needs the first time and every time. It provides specific tools for accomplishing this goal.

Why Is a TQM Process Needed?

Before deciding to adopt a TQM process, each company needs to answer a very important question. Why bother?

Specific answers to this question may vary from company to company, but generally the answer is this:

BECAUSE IT'S A MATTER OF SURVIVAL!

This may seem overly dramatic, but there are three reasons why I put it in those terms:

1. The business environment today is extremely competitive, not just on a national level anymore but on an international level. More and more foreign businesses are entering U.S. markets, and those businesses are extremely effective. They have to be. They have realized that for them it is a matter of survival. We need to recognize this too, and now!
2. Today's consumer demands quality more than ever before. Recent consumer research shows this. It even makes the news. You may remember the February 2, 1987, *Time* magazine cover story about people in the United States being fed up with shoddy products and services.
3. Research also shows—and your company's own research may verify it—that consumers are more willing to switch from company to company and not just to get a better price. They will switch for better service: reliability, accessibility, courtesy, and so on.

Essentially, if you can't establish yourself as the supplier of choice in your market, your customer base will erode and you'll find it more and more difficult to attract new customers. A certain demise awaits the company losing its customers.

There are reports and surveys to support these claims. More two-wage-earner families exist than ever before. These busy households have little patience for shoddy products and poor services. Research has shown that more people switch companies because of poor service than for a lower price or for any other reason. Today many customers are also willing to pay a little more for quality. Further, it has been shown that dissatisfied customers will relate their story of a poor product or poor service to 10 other people on the average, and those 10 people will rarely be among your future customers. These findings must not be ignored. They must be the incentive for developing a TQM strategy!

What is needed to survive and prosper is a new attitude toward the customer. Each business needs a companywide focus on customers—knowing their needs and meeting or exceeding those needs the first time and every time. I know it sounds like a lofty goal, but isn't it better to shoot for the stars and miss by an inch than to aim for the treetops and make it? Customers are the most important asset any company has, even though they don't show up on the balance sheet. They are an asset which, if nurtured, will multiply and help to ensure corporate survival.

I've found that a well-managed QIP can help a company achieve that lofty goal, and the benefits are real and unbeatable. A QIP can provide you with a sustainable competitive advantage of significant proportions. Some of the benefits to be achieved are:

- Improved profitability
- Increased customer retention
- Reduced customer complaints and warranty claims
- Reduced costs through less waste, rework, and so on
- Greater market share
- Increased employee involvement and satisfaction; lower turnover
- Increased ability to attract new customers

Let's look more closely at the benefits and advantages of TQM.

What Are the Advantages and Benefits of TQM?

The principal advantages and benefits of TQM generally fall under three key headings: improved profitability and competitiveness, improved organizational effectiveness, and improved customer satisfaction.

Improved Profitability and Competitiveness

Improved product and service quality definitely improves bottom-line performance and corporate competitiveness (for example, market share, growth, return on investment). One of the more prestigious and reputable organizations that has studied this issue is the Strategic Planning Institute (SPI). Many of the institute's research findings have been reported in its periodic *PIMSLetters on Business Strategy*.

For example, referring to the benefits of high service quality, *PIMSLetter* 33 reports that

> the advantages of high service quality include (the ability to charge) higher prices, reduced marketing, greater repeat business and higher market share. Data contrasting the experience of excellent quality with poor quality businesses (show that) businesses with excellent quality are more profitable and grow faster.[1]

PIMSLetter 4 states that "product quality is an important determinant of business profitability: High quality and high return on investment usually go together."[2]

PIMSLetter 31 reports: "[O]ur analysis indicates that a customer-oriented, quality-differentiation strategy can often lead not only to customer preference and loyalty, but also to increased market share and lower costs."[3]

Total quality management permits a company to produce more with its current resources by improving and streamlining its work processes (efficiency), and to do more of the right things right the first time through an increased awareness of internal and external customers' needs (effectiveness). This improved efficiency and effectiveness can lower overall costs, reduce customer turnover, increase sales, and even attract new customers at lower marketing costs. A positive bottom-line impacts results—not immediately, but over the long term.

Organizational Effectiveness

Improvements in organizational effectiveness are more difficult to trace to the bottom line, but they, too, can contribute to the overall financial health and competitiveness of an organization. In fact, exceptional levels of organizational effectiveness may represent a strong, unique, and sustainable competitive advantage because they are so difficult for others to duplicate.

Some organizational effectiveness benefits to be derived from TQM are these:

- *Improved teamwork and interunit cooperation as a quality team–oriented modus operandi takes hold.* This also greatly facilitates the strong and effective integration of different work groups. For example, even in the case of a corporate merger, two diverse employee groups that both adhere to TQM practices will merge more effectively and compatibly than two groups that have pursued different work styles.
- *Improved communication through a common language and a strong customer focus.* Total quality management builds a common language and a set of compatible attitudes that greatly improve the effectiveness of a corporation.
- *Increased employee involvement.* Those actually performing the work are in the best position to know what can be done better and how to achieve the improvements. Total quality management provides the setting and tools to more effectively tap this underutilized resource. As involvement increases, so do personal growth and career advancement potential.

- *Lower employee turnover.* As employees find greater opportunities to contribute meaningfully to the company, their satisfaction rises and unwanted resignations decrease.
- *Improved management-employee relations.* Total quality management provides a corporate focus that both managers and nonmanagers pursue in similar ways while speaking the same language. This builds a more effective total corporate team.
- *Improved focus on key goals—the vital few.* Total quality management leads an organization to define its few key priorities better and to communicate these to all employees more effectively. As a result, everyone in the company is pulling on the right oars at the same time and heading in the same direction.

Customer Satisfaction or Customer Delight

In the final analysis, customers matter most. No company can exist without them. Without customers we have no earnings, no market share, no return on investment (ROI), and, of course, no profit.

If TQM is aimed at anything, it is aimed at winning and keeping customers—keeping them delighted. This is certainly a cost issue as well as a revenue issue. Various studies have shown that generally it costs four or five times more to win new customers than to keep the ones you already have.

Total quality management teaches us to "know thy customers"—to know what their needs are, to know how we are doing at meeting those needs, and to know what we must do to improve.

Specifically, TQM can help us achieve great advances in:

- Delighting the customers we have and keeping them
- Attracting more and more customers through the most cost-effective marketing strategy there is: word-of-mouth advertising
- Designing products that meet changing or new customers' needs
- Reducing the costs attributable to dissatisfied customers, such as responding to complaints and processing warranty claims

In addition, TQM provides an expanded view of the customer. Internal customers, for example, are those company employees supported by other company employees (internal providers). This internal partnership or quality chain of events must be highly efficient and effective if the external customer is to be ultimately delighted.

In many cases, others who exist between a company and the ultimate consumer must be recognized and treated as customers too. This includes insurance agents, suppliers, distributors, and so on. Total quality management causes us to focus on this extended quality chain of events in order to serve and delight the external customer.

In summary, TQM definitely affects the traditional measures of corporate health as those on Wall Street see it—revenues, profits, growth, earnings, ROI, and so on. It also affects the internal health of the company in areas such as employee satisfaction, growth and development, and team spirit. Finally, TQM makes a difference to customers and allows us to build and maintain a sizable force of delighted customers.

Ultimately, TQM can help a company to achieve its most lofty goal of enjoying a sustainable competitive advantage—of being, in the minds of its customers, the supplier of choice.

Now, let's just look at costs alone for a minute. Depending on which study you use, the cost of poor quality (COPQ)—costs attributable to not doing it right the first time (waste, scrap, rework, inspectors, complaint handling, fines, defect investigations, and the like)—amounts to between 20 percent and 25 percent of a company's sales revenues. For a company with sales of $500 million, the COPQ ranges from $100 million to $125 million. This is an unnecessary and debilitating cost. If you can cut this COPQ by just 40 percent in 5 years—and it's possible with a good QIP—the result will be a savings of $40 million to $50 million!

The attraction of achieving these gains through a TQM process is that a TQM process is not chiefly a capital-intensive undertaking. It is people and process intensive. Therefore, your ROI will be quite high. Experience has shown, for example, that the typical management-level QI team will deliver a $100,000 improvement result that costs the company $20,000 to achieve—which equals a 400 percent ROI!

Many executives have never thought much about the COPQ, but you can bet it's a sizable sum and worth attention. Think of the COPQ as the erosion of assets. We must consider the customer as a vital asset to protect because losing a customer and finding a replacement is a big part of the COPQ. So it is always better, and four to five times cheaper, to retain existing customers than to attract new ones.

Although a QIP reduces the COPQ, it concurrently leads to significant improvements to the product and the service behind the product. Consequently, the customer enjoys more satisfaction, which leads directly to repeat sales and word-of-mouth advertising. It's like a continuous cycle of improvement or a strategy for competitive advantage.

Maintaining a Competitive Advantage

I've mentioned competitive advantage a few times so far and have proposed that a TQM process can help a company attain it. But what is competitive advantage, and exactly what role does TQM play in attaining it?

Competitive advantage, in the context of business, is a powerful concept; and achieving it should be the ultimate goal of any company. Having the competitive advantage can be defined as being the customers' supplier of choice. Competitive advantage results from the set of characteristics that you build into your company which fundamentally lead customers to elect to do business with you rather than with the corporation down the street or across town, or with any of your other competitors. It's the "magic potion" or "mysterious force" that keeps customers coming to your door again and again.

You achieve a competitive advantage by carefully and constantly analyzing customers' needs and by organizing and operating to meet these needs the first time and every time.

Too many businesses falsely seek a shortcut to gain a competitive advantage, only to find that the advantage switches to a competitor a week, a month, or a year later. These businesses fail to realize that their quick solution to achieving a competitive advantage is built upon a single-focused, one-point-in-time foundation evidenced by the old adage "build a better mousetrap and the world will beat a path to your door."

This "better mousetrap" approach will work only until the mouse gets smarter, or until someone copies the trap and implements a more flexible delivery schedule, or develops a better product-return policy or a better warranty. The point to be made here is that nearly all products or services and nearly all the characteristics of business are commodities in the sense that they can be duplicated by a competitor sooner or later. Most businesses produce commodity products or services so that there is little long-term advantage to be gained through product differentiation. Beyond product, we find that even that great new order processing and billing (data processing) system can be copied by a competitor. Even our guarantee policy, our hours of operation, our delivery schedules, and our speed at answering the phone can all be duplicated.

Because this commoditylike and narrow focus on achieving competitive advantage is destined to fail, we must look at our business from another perspective, the most important perspective, through the eyes of our customers. We need to visualize and analyze every aspect of our customers' journey through our system of service, from the time a customer sees our advertisement or contacts us until the product or service the customer buys has been consumed. Furthermore, we need to do this continuously, not only because customers' needs change over time, but because new customers come into the picture each day.

This constant attention to understanding customers' needs and the total involvement of everyone in the company working to meet these needs is what QI is all about. By implementing TQM, a company can build a unique and dynamic corporate personality or culture involving every employee on every level. This corporate personality will be virtually impossible for competitors to duplicate, and a competitive advantage will be achieved.

Transformation Checkpoints

1. Total quality management is a journey, not a destination.
2. Quality is meeting customers' needs and reasonable expectations.
3. A TQM process is a systematic method of developing products and services, and serving the customer after the sale; it is based on a thorough understanding of customers' needs and expectations. It involves all employees in assessing and improving quality through the application of statistical process control (SPC) and other QI tools and techniques.
4. Total quality management is definitely applicable to service as well as manufacturing organizations.
5. Total quality management is not a Quality Circles program or simply a productivity improvement program. It is a complete management system that builds a total customer-focused culture.
6. Total quality management is about corporate survival.
7. Typically, the COPQ is equal to 20 to 25 percent of a company's sales revenues.
8. Companies that consistently meet customers' needs can achieve a powerful competitive advantage.

References

1. Thompson, Phillip, Glen DeSouza, and Bradley T. Gale, "The Strategic Management of Service Quality," *The PIMSLetter on Business Strategy*

(*PIMSLetter* 33), pp. 8–9, The Strategic Planning Institute, Cambridge, Mass., 1985.

2. Buzzell, Robert D., "Product Quality," *The PIMSLetter on Business Strategy* (*PIMSLetter* 4), p. 11, The Strategic Planning Institute, Cambridge, Mass., 1986.

3. Gale, Bradley T., and Richard Klavans, "Formulating a Quality Improvement Strategy," *The PIMSLetter on Business Strategy* (*PMSLetter* 31), p. 8, The Strategic Planning Institute, Cambridge, Mass., 1985.

2
Setting the Stage for Quality

Establishing an effective TQM process and culture in your organization is a sizable undertaking. Considerable preparation is required to do it well and to ensure its lasting effect. As with any other investment, establishing a TQM process requires up-front effort and a financial outlay. It also requires a firm resolve or commitment to see it through. Often, this commitment is more difficult to attain than the cash needed to get started. Commitment is also more important than cash. Without strong backing and passionate leadership, the cash investment will be squandered because the effort will surely fail. Strong commitment will ensure that you realize an attractive return on the investment made.

This chapter will discuss setting the stage for an effective TQM process and culture. The following points will be covered:

- Organizing for quality and studying TQM
- Assessing corporate culture, employee attitudes, and customer perceptions
- Analyzing the COPQ
- Defining your quality policy

Organizing for Quality

The first step in organizing for quality requires the formation in three phases of a simple and mostly parallel organizational structure as illustrated in Figure 2-1 (see pages 15 and 16). These structures begin to

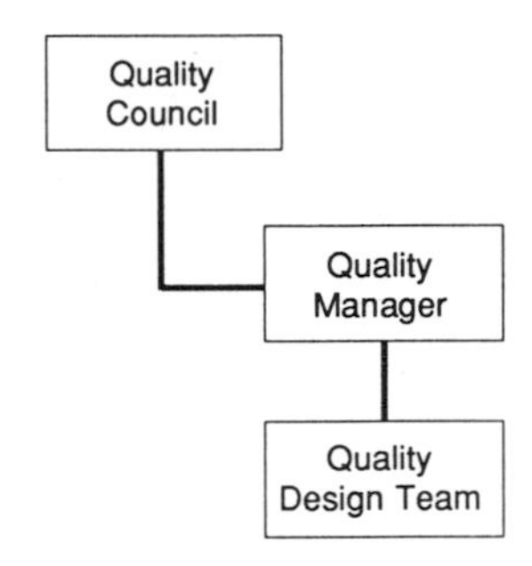

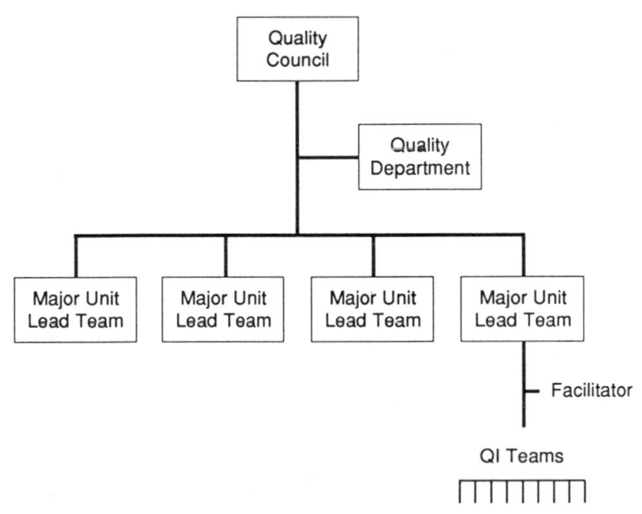

Figure 2-1. Organizing for Quality: Phases 1 and 2.

define the flow of responsibility for the key quality architects and developers, as well as define the hierarchy of support.

The Phase 1 Quality Organization

The phase 1 quality organization should be established quietly and without fanfare once senior management has developed enough interest in

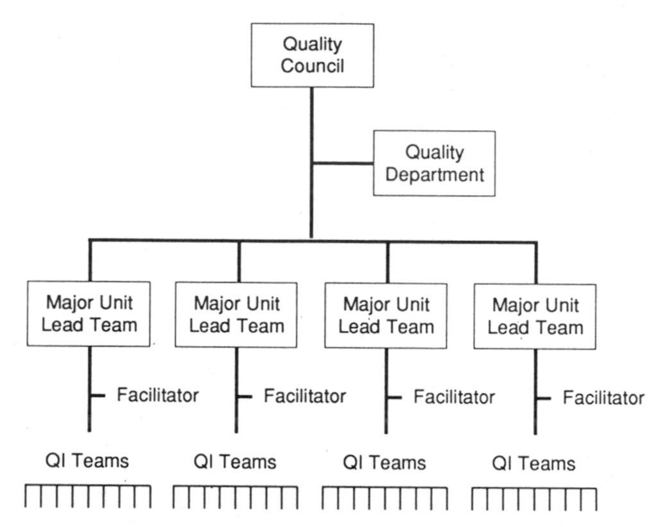

Figure 2-1. (*Continued*) Organizing for Quality: Phase 3.

TQM to warrant a more serious examination of how the concepts may be applied to their particular company. At this point, no commitment to pursue TQM has been made; however, healthy curiosity exists. This initial interest may develop from having read a certain book or set of articles on the subject, from attending a quality seminar, from talking with peers, or from visiting a company that is pursuing TQM.

Essentially, senior management or a particularly influential senior executive is simply thinking that TQM may hold significant benefits and is eager to explore it further.

When this point is reached, a quality council must be formed. The council is the top-level steering group that will make the key decisions and authorize the support needed first to study TQM carefully and later to design, implement, and nurture the process. If a quality process is eventually adopted, the quality council will remain a permanent fixture.

I recommend strongly that the council be chaired by the chief executive officer or chief operating officer and include the other senior executives or officers who report to him or her. This matter is far too important and far-reaching to be delegated to others lower in the organization who may not have the authority to see the project through.

The council should not be viewed as a body separate and distinct from the existing top management group. It *is* the existing top management group, the one reporting, for example, to the board of directors.

Remember, we are not building another structure; we are creating a parallel structure. Quality council business should be conducted whenever the top managers meet to pursue other matters. That is, council business should be a major new and ever-present agenda item for the regular staff meeting.

Council members, both individually and collectively, must commit from day one not only to support TQM, but also to involve themselves personally with the quality process so that it will be successfully implemented. This hands-on, top-level involvement is the most critical factor in the successful development of TQM. The one thing I can guarantee is that without this direct top-level involvement, the effort will certainly fail.

The Quality Council's Mission

The quality council's first meeting should be devoted to developing a mission statement—a list of the key responsibilities the council reserves for itself for the development, implementation, and ongoing administration of the quality process. Figure 2-2 illustrates a sample council mission statement.

The Quality Quarterback and Design Team

With the quality council established, it is now necessary to appoint a quality manager who will recruit a TQM design team from within the company. The design team will devote several hours a week under the leadership of the quality manager and the council to further study TQM and to recommend a TQM development strategy.

The quality manager should be a respected executive currently holding a senior-level position; he or she should also be appointed to the quality council. Ideally, the person selected should be relieved of all other duties for a several-month period; this temporary duty may evolve to a permanent position as head of the company's TQM unit if a quality process is installed for the long term.

The selection of the quality manager is very important. The "right" person must be chosen. He or she must be one of your best executives. The right candidate is someone you really don't want to choose because that person is seen as critical to his or her current function. The right person has an excellent reputation within the company and an out-

Mission Summary:

The XYZ Company's quality council will direct, support, and participate in the development and administration of a TQM process. The council will ensure that key decisions regarding TQM are made and that the financial and human resources needed are made available.

Specific Responsibilities:

1. To formulate, communicate, promote, and guide the TQM process.
2. To establish and direct the activities of company lead teams (lower-level quality councils).
3. To ensure that corporate reward and recognition systems support and reinforce TQM participation and success.
4. To approve quality project proposals to be pursued by QI teams.
5. To monitor and communicate results achieved through the TQM process.
6. To lead the quality planning process.
7. To participate in recognition events that celebrate TQM success.
8. To provide the financial and human resources needed to effectively pursue TQM.
9. To ensure that adequate training is provided in TQM in order to establish an environment of continuous learning.
10. To ensure top management's personal and direct involvement in TQM activities, including membership in a QI team, participation in TQM training, and so on.
11. To set TQM goals on an annual basis.

Figure 2-2. A Quality Council Mission Statement.

standing track record. He or she must have superior leadership abilities and must also be an excellent communicator and a tireless contributor. Finally, the right choice is someone who has demonstrated the ability to manage large, complex-change projects and who has a strong interest in QI and customer satisfaction.

Once a choice is made, the quality manager should recruit the design team. The design team should include six to eight highly respected middle-level managers or other key people selected from a variety of units within the organization. Like the quality manager, candidates for the design team should possess leadership skills, be excellent communicators, and so on. They must also have the explicit support of their respective bosses for participating on the team because some backup for them may be needed for their regular job. Collectively, they should form a compatible group—a cohesive team.

The principal mission of the design team is:

1. To thoroughly study total quality concepts and applications
2. To formulate a recommendation supported by data whether or not to pursue TQM
3. If establishing a TQM process is recommended, to propose a preliminary implementation plan which would include major steps, required resources, time frames, and expected benefits

The design team is extremely important, for the obvious reason that it will make a recommendation to top management on a matter of great, long-range significance. It is also very important for a more subtle reason. By far, people in many companies with whom I've discussed the idea of establishing a corporate quality process have had great difficulty in winning middle-management support. Once top management is committed, most people at the lower levels embrace the quality movement quickly and enthusiastically. The middle levels, however, often feel ignored or threatened. One way to help avoid this is to set up a middle-level design team. Team members will have ideas about how to include the middle levels, and their rising enthusiasm will be transmitted to their peers. As a result, down the road, you'll have an easier time establishing a true, companywide commitment to TQM, and you certainly need middle management's support and involvement to make it happen.

The first activity that I recommend for the design team is a two-day off-site meeting. The quality council should be present only for the first few hours to review its own mission and the mission of the design team. The rest of the day should be devoted to a short seminar on complex-change management provided by an outside consultant. The consultant should also focus on some team-building activities during the day.

Informal socializing should occur at dinner, and that evening...more team building. The second day, with some help from the consultant, should be spent planning how the team will pursue the first part of its mission: studying TQM.

Because the first part of the mission requires a thorough study of TQM, the team may consider available books, seminars, company visits, and the use of a QI consultant. However, in considering a QI consultant, I provide this caution: Don't select one who has a single, specific recipe to sell. Team members need to understand the broad concepts and a variety of approaches so that they can design a TQM process that fits their own culture and circumstances.

Before adjourning from the two-day meeting, the members of the team should decide when they will meet next and how frequently future meetings will occur. Then, get on with it, and keep the quality council advised along the way.

Author's Note:

It will be helpful for you as the reader if we pause here and make an assumption. We'll assume that our design team has completed its mission. It will probably have taken the team from 4 to 6 months. We'll further assume that the team has enthusiastically recommended the pursuit of TQM and, for the most part, has proposed an approach that is compatible with what I am recommending in this book. Whether or not you decide to follow the path I outline in this book, you will still need a design team to customize a strategy for your particular company, as well as to more effectively involve middle management.

Having accepted this assumption, let's look ahead in order to understand the phase 2 and 3 quality organizations.

The Phase 2 Quality Organization

We have now reached a critical point in our TQM development journey. Top management, in the form of the quality council, has accepted the design team's recommendation to develop and test a TQM process. This design and testing phase will take several months, perhaps as long as a year or more, depending on the size of the company, the resources made available, the competition for time and resources within the company, the skill of the design team, and a number of other related factors.

However, at this point, it is time to add two more elements to the phase 1 quality organization structure. First, each major division of the company should form its own quality council or quality lead team and should set a mission similar to that adopted by the top-level quality council. A lead team should be chaired by the senior executive of a division or major unit, and it should consist of those who report to this executive. The primary objective of a lead team is to ensure that TQM is effectively implemented and utilized within its area of responsibility. Initially, this lead team structure prepares the major divisions to learn from the company's early quality efforts.

Second, a suitable unit or division should be chosen as a pilot test site.

It is within this test unit that the TQM process, when it is initially designed, will be plugged in for a trial run. As phase 2 in Figure 2-1 shows, the test site will soon choose a quality team facilitator and will form a number of QI teams.

How to select and utilize a test site will be discussed in Chapter 10. For now, however, we'll discuss all the matters that must be considered in order to provide the test site with a TQM process with which it will experiment. This chapter and Chapters 3 to 9 outline what we need to know before initial implementation.

The Phase 3 Quality Organization

The phase 3 quality organization is put in place once we are satisfied with early results achieved at the test site. The phase 3 organization simply mirrors what we have done at the test site. That is, facilitators are chosen and QI teams are formed. The phase 3 organization becomes the permanent TQM organization for the future.

An important point to be made here is that the lead teams are to feel a strong sense of ownership for TQM within their respective divisions. Total quality management must be line driven. The quality department established in the phase 1 organization should be kept small. Otherwise, this staff unit will be regarded as the driving force, which is okay only in phase 1 and phase 2 organizations. After that, the ownership must switch to the divisions if momentum is to be built and sustained for the years ahead.

Assessing Corporate Culture, Employee Attitudes, and Customer Perceptions

Having taken a peek at the future by reviewing the evolving quality organization structure, we need to jump back to the days of phase 1 to see how the quality manager and the design team set the stage for TQM and offer a TQM model that is right for their company. We begin by assessing the internal people environment and by measuring customer attitudes.

Fundamentally, it is the people of the company, at all levels and in all units, who apply the tools and concepts of quality to meet customers' needs, and it is the customers who ultimately construct the report card that describes the extent to which the company is achieving quality—

meeting customer needs. Therefore, one of the vital first steps to take is assessing the internal human relations environment to determine how ready employees are to accept a significant change in company operations.

We also need to measure customer attitudes toward the company both to set a baseline of satisfaction against which we can compare future results, and also to determine the areas of principal dissatisfaction.

Assessing Corporate Culture and Employee Attitudes

If, for the most part, the employee population has a sour attitude toward management and the company, then gaining their active and enthusiastic participation in TQM will be extremely difficult, if not impossible, without first improving the areas of principal concern.

If you have never conducted a climate (attitude) survey, or if it has been two or more years since you did, I recommend investing in such an activity using a firm that specializes in conducting such surveys. The results should be carefully analyzed and shared with employees, and any changes needed must be developed and quickly implemented to correct the problems disclosed by the survey. Groups of employees should be formed to help develop ideas for improvement based on the survey's results. This employee involvement sends a signal that is compatible with the TQM concepts of involvement and idea generation. However, before utilizing employee groups to identify improvement ideas, consult with your labor attorney to help avoid an allegation later that you have created an in-house, company-controlled union.

The climate survey should consist of two major parts. One part measures attitudes relating to work life and conditions such as satisfaction with pay, communications, benefits, supervision, and appraisals. The other part assesses the company culture. A corporation, through its day-to-day actions and policies, sends signals that define what it thinks is important and proper. Employees then behave according to their interpretation of these signals. For example, the reward system may recognize people for how much they produce and virtually ignore the quality of what's produced. This company will produce a lot of widgets, but the rejection rate will be high.

An assessment of the company culture will help determine changes in company programs, policies, and management behavior that are necessary to support a TQM process. Ignoring this essential stage-setting step of conducting a climate and culture assessment survey would be foolhardy and shortsighted. If management does not possess an accurate and objective view of the climate and culture, then a TQM process could be built on a very weak foundation. The whole thing may come tumbling down long before it can begin to be effective.

When considering a climate and culture survey, don't assume that you already know what employees think. Most of the time you'll be wrong. Also, to assume you know what employees think flies in the face of a basic TQM concept, which cautions us to act on facts and data, not on hunches and guesses. Actions based on objective evidence can yield the right results, whereas those based on hunches yield dismal or fragile results at best.

The general purpose of the survey is to help ensure that the employee population is ready and willing to participate in building a total quality culture—an attitude based on trust, teamwork, objective problem solving, and shared accountability. In this regard, don't ignore the employees in the bargaining unit if you have one. The objective is to get everyone involved, not just the nonunion people. Union leadership should be approached early in the TQM development process in order to win their support and pledge of involvement.

Assessing Customer Perceptions

Ultimately, the objective of TQM is to vastly improve how your customers view the quality of the products and services provided by your company and how they rate the ongoing service behind those products and services. For the most part, when I say "customer," I mean the ultimate, external customer. However, consider internal customers too. An internal customer is the employee or unit that receives work from the previous station in the chain of production or service. If the ball is fumbled as it is passed from one internal unit to another, then the external customer will be adversely affected.

The climate survey can help assess both internal and external customers' perceptions. First, include some questions that will help you assess how employees feel about the support received from other internal units on whom they depend. Second, ask your employees to rate how well they feel the company meets external customers' needs. Your people usually have a very good idea as to how your customers feel. You should also ask your employees to prioritize a list of principal customer needs as they see it.

But, beyond the climate survey, I also recommend that you survey customer perceptions directly and attempt to determine their basic needs and satisfaction levels as they relate to your business. This should be done by professional market research personnel.

The results of the customer survey will provide a baseline or starting point against which you may measure future improvement. Also, the results will reveal areas of concern that should be studied further and addressed through your TQM process once it is established.

This customer survey step is vitally important. If the basic definition of quality is meeting customers' needs and reasonable expectations, then we first need an accurate understanding of what our customers need and expect. Obviously, we also need to see the gap between our performance and what the customer requires if we are going to properly target improvement activities.

Moreover, we need to recognize that the marketplace is dynamic. Customer surveys should be conducted annually and supplemented during the year with focus groups, brief self-mailer point-of-contact surveys (comment cards), and the like.

By all means, stay close to the customers' perceptions. In the final analysis, it makes all the difference.

Paying the Cost of Poor Quality

Too many top managers feel that delighting customers is a nebulous goal. However, if they understand that millions of dollars are wasted getting the product or service produced, delivered, and supported, you'll have their attention.

By measuring the COPQ, you can break through this top management motivational barrier and help propel a company from the status quo to TQM.

As I pointed out in Chapter 1, the COPQ—the cost of not doing things right the first time—can amount to a sizable sum. For most companies, the COPQ is at least 20 to 25 percent of sales revenues, and this usually conservative estimate is supported by extensive research. Even if you are only a $50 million company, we can be talking about $10 million in wasted effort year after year!

Therefore, I recommend a short study to determine at least a ballpark figure for the COPQ. I say a short study because it is difficult and unnecessary to be precise. Good estimates should provide the data that will get top management's attention. In addition, as your TQM process continues, the extent to which you reduce the COPQ represents a satisfying progress report on the most quantifiable results of your efforts.

I recommend that the quality council, upon the recommendation of the design team, commission a group of three or four people from the financial area or from industrial engineering to study the COPQ for about a three-month period. The investigation should include interviews with many people, and these interviews should be strictly confi-

Inspectors	Complaint Handling	Employee Turnover
Product Testing	Warranty Claims	Retraining
Error Correction	Repair Costs	Idle Time
Scrap and Waste	Customer Switching	Late Delivery
Downtime	Rework	Consultants
Redesign	Overtime	Problem Solving
Lost Time Injury	Product Returns	Temporary Help

Figure 2-3. Sources of the Cost of Poor Quality (Partial List).

dential in order to gain useful data. After all, you'll be asking people to quantify what goes wrong in their own department.

The COPQ study group must first develop a list of the categories of poor quality. This list will point to areas and activities from which facts and figures may be collected. Figure 2-3 provides a partial list of categories of the COPQ. Reviewing this list for ideas will help establish one that fits your company.

It is important to realize that any one type of the COPQ will be more or less expensive, depending on the nature and timing of an event. For example, a defective product that leaves the company and ends up in the hands of the ultimate customer will cost far more to fix than a defective product that is discovered before it is shipped. The former scenario contributes more rapidly to customer dissatisfaction as well.

As mentioned, developing an estimate of the COPQ can be helpful in gaining top management's commitment to a quality process. In addition, a COPQ study will begin to identify the most vital, few areas that need improvement. Once TQM is established, these areas become the playing fields for QI teams.

With an estimate of the COPQ, many companies set a goal to cut the COPQ in half within a five-year period. This is a reasonable goal and provides a hard dollar target to which management can really relate. Obviously, of course, if you succeed in addressing many of the COPQ items, customers will be considerably more satisfied. Others, including shareholders, employees, and managers, will be delighted as well.

Defining Your Quality Policy

Companies set corporatewide policies in order to formally commit to and communicate a strong, fundamental belief or goal. Two examples are the Equal Employment Opportunity policy and the 24-hour service policy.

Like these extremely important examples, quality needs to be enshrined in policy initially for internal enlightenment and subsequently for customers. This sequence of communicating your quality policy is deliberate, because a company that advertises quality to its current and prospective customers before it has developed the capability to deliver quality with some consistency will, without doubt, "underwhelm" its customers!

When you have made a commitment to TQM, you must compose a policy statement and share it with your employees. This act will help to demonstrate that the company is firmly committed to the quality process and that it will put top management on the spot to carry out the policy.

If the design team expects to recommend the development of a TQM process, it should draft a proposed policy statement that top management can finalize and approve. Figure 2-4 is a sample quality policy statement.

By the way, once you adopt and communicate a quality policy, stick with it, live it, and protect it. You get only one chance!

Our Quality Pledge

The XYZ Corporation places the quality of its products and services above all else because customer loyalty and satisfaction are our foremost concern. Quality means meeting customers' needs the first time and every time, and we recognize that customers exist both within the company and outside the company.

All company employees will receive quality improvement training and will be involved in meeting our quality goals. The financial resources needed to carry out this policy will be made available, and incentive payments will be directly related to our quality performance.

____

President
XYZ Corporation

Figure 2-4. A Quality Pledge.

Transformation Checkpoints

1. Organize for quality by establishing a parallel structure and evolving it through three phases.
2. Establish a top-level quality council.
3. Select a quality manager and recruit a middle-level design team.
4. The design team's mission is to:
   - Study total quality
   - Recommend whether a TQM process is needed and back up the recommendation with facts
   - Propose a preliminary approach for establishing TQM
5. Provide team-building activities for the design team.
6. Utilize a test site and experiment with your TQM model.
7. Assess the corporate culture, employee attitudes, and customers' needs and perceptions.
8. View customers as both internal and external.
9. Measure the COPQ using a special task force. Set a COPQ reduction goal.
10. Set a strong quality policy and adhere to it with passion and dedication.

3
A Total Quality Management Implementation Strategy

Our design team has made a good deal of progress. The team members have carefully and thoroughly studied total quality concepts and practices, have mapped the evolving quality organization structure, have determined whether the corporate culture and employee satisfaction level are suitable for accepting a TQM process, and have researched customers' needs and perceptions relative to the company's products, services, and performance.

The COPQ has been estimated, and a quality policy has been drafted. The results of the customer research and the COPQ study provide clear evidence of the need for improvement. If we add to these findings what we already know of our competitors' performance and the fact that consumer attitudes are becoming increasingly demanding as far as quality and service are concerned, our assessment of the current situation may be summarized like this:

> We are not doing very well. Our customers know it. Our competitors are gaining, and it's not getting any easier.

A worst-case interpretation—and probably a realistic one—of this current situation is that the survival of the company is at stake. On the other hand, now that we know what we know, there is a real opportunity to mount an improvement effort to ensure long-term profitability and a sustainable competitive advantage.

Whichever interpretation of the current situation you choose, the strategy for the future can only be a strong commitment to TQM—a long-term improvement strategy involving everyone in the company and a strategy driven by customer needs and perceptions. In the final analysis, winning and keeping customers will make the difference.

The top management quality council, having agreed with this interpretation and having begun to see the potential of a TQM process, is ready to consider an approach for implementing total quality.

Chapter 3 will discuss some key implementation strategy points and other matters to consider at this early but critical stage in the development of TQM. We'll cover:

- Knowing what to expect
- Signaling the organization
- Selecting a bottom-up or top-down approach
- Deciding how to begin

Knowing What to Expect

Fear of the unknown or uncertainty as to what to expect can adversely affect both the speed and the quality of the progress needed to attain a goal. Having some idea of what lies ahead, however, better prepares us to make the right decisions along the way and to persevere.

For most organizations, the development of a TQM process represents a major cultural change—the need to turn the company upside down. Although this description may be overstated in some cases, it is wise, nonetheless, to think in terms of massive change at all organizational levels with regard to behavior, attitudes, and emphasis. Eventually, TQM will become a new modus operandi for the company.

People at all levels need to be trained in new skills, and they need to find time to apply their new skills. Customer needs and perceptions must drive corporate activity, interunit cooperation and coordination must prevail, and all corporate policies and programs must reinforce the new culture.

Senior managers must realize that complex change takes years and will never occur as a result of management pronouncement. It happens only as people begin doing things differently. The basic model shown in Figure 3-1 illustrates this concept.

This simple model suggests that a person takes some sort of action, which produces a result. The result is seen and interpreted as either positive or negative. Based on the interpretation of the result, the person modifies his or her attitude and acts differently the next time in order to produce a different result.

If the quarterback acts by repeatedly throwing into double-defensive coverage, the result is a dismal pass completion percentage, few yards gained, and a high rate of interceptions by the opposing team. The attitude the quarterback develops relating to this level of performance is negative. Therefore, an astute quarterback begins to look for more open receivers to produce a better result.

Within a corporation, the attitudes people develop are based on the actions they take and their interpretation of the results. And it is the prevailing attitude of employees that defines the day-to-day corporate culture and, of course, corporate results.

Too often, management tries to change the culture by describing the new attitudes it seeks as "quality first" but fails to take the steps needed to influence the action employees take. This strategy fails because employees act no differently, results of their actions do not change, and, therefore, their attitude remains as it was.

We can affect attitudes and, of course, results only by getting people to do things differently. The arrow in the model in Figure 3-1 points to this key leverage point. It is here that we must intervene in order to accomplish the desired change.

It takes only moments to proclaim new attitudes, but it takes a great deal longer to get hundreds of people to act differently. So, one thing you can expect is that developing TQM is a long-term, culture change process. Planning, patience, and perseverance are needed to do it right and to do it well.

Another thing you can expect is resistance from some people at all

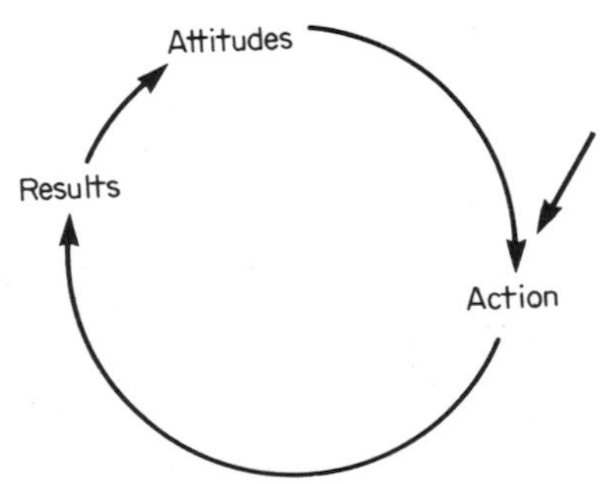

Figure 3-1. Cycle of Behavioral Change.

levels. You'll certainly experience passive resistance and even some active resistance. Resistance to complex change is perfectly normal and shouldn't be interpreted negatively by senior management. It is simply there and must be managed.

Resistance is normal, especially in the early stages of a change effort, because people need time to sort out and understand the meaning as it affects them. Initially, most people see change as adding to the quantity and complexity of their work, and, for a period of time, this is an accurate view, particularly if the change is toward a TQM process. Figure 3-2 illustrates this view as an eclipse.

During stage 1, the new way is first understood and seen as a significantly different way of life. The old way is still in existence and has a comfortable feel. People naturally feel threatened or at least apprehensive at the approaching shadow of a new way.

In stage 2, as the new way begins to overlap the old, people struggle with the need to keep the old ways alive while they attempt to cope with the demands of the new way. It is at this point that people must receive substantial support from management to understand how to manage in two overlapping worlds.

Finally, in stage 3, the new way totally eclipses the old. People accept the new and, for a while, mourn the old.

Management's role during the process of the eclipse is to persevere so that there is no question as to which way will remain for the future. At the same time, management must understand what is happening; it must be sensitive to what people are experiencing and find ways to reassure and support people throughout this difficult time.

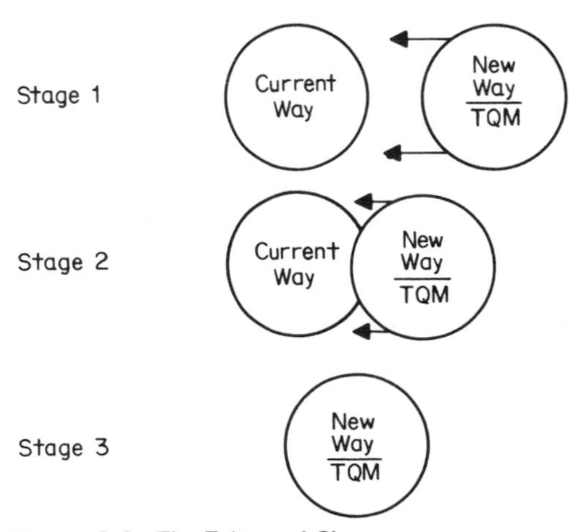

Figure 3-2. The Eclipse of Change.

Clearly, communicating the new way is essential. As we said, fear of the unknown can be harmful. If everyone clearly understands what the new way is, what effects it will have, and the reasons for instituting the change, the process progresses more smoothly.

Also, consider setting some key milestones along the way. Such points will allow the organization to pause and celebrate its progress. The greatest sense of insecurity comes in stage 2 as people begin to let go of the old and grab hold of the new—it's not unlike a circus performer switching from one trapeze to another. Celebration milestones provide the net beneath the big top.

When the new way is dominant, a ceremony to bury the old and celebrate the birth of the new is organizationally comforting.

Dealing with resistance can also be managed by building a critical mass of support and initially bypassing the more heavily fortified bunkers of resistance.

You have a critical mass of support if enough influential people in the organization are solidly behind the change effort to out-muscle the resisters and the uncommitted observers. A critical mass is not a majority of the people, because one particularly influential person is worth three times as much to the support effort as one person whose "weight" is perceived to be typical or average. An influential person can be someone other than a senior manager, although senior managers are invariably necessary for critical mass. People at lower levels who are viewed by their peers as informal leaders or role models, or who are otherwise highly respected, should be looked to as members of the critical mass team as well.

A critical mass of support will help propel the change along its intended path and will gain recruits along the way. However, even a strong critical mass of support cannot and should not initially attack the well-fortified bunkers of resistance. Bypass them at first and, over time, as the number of supporters grows from 30 to 80 percent, the will of the hard-core resistance will be weakened. Then, make it easy for resisters to join the team with dignity.

Dealing with upper-level managers or professionals who are vocal resisters can be significantly more difficult. Therefore, make every attempt early in the process to win them over or, at the very least, to neutralize their negative influence. If you are unsuccessful, the best strategy is to release them to work for your competitor! This action, although severe and a last-resort strategy, will strengthen your chances for success and will also send a strong signal about top management's commitment to the rest of the company.

Finally, with respect to critical mass, don't ignore the union if you have one. By definition, the union, even if it represents only 15 to 20 percent of your employees, is a critical mass in itself. Make every reasonable effort to win the union over to the cause, or at least to have leaders agree to a role of passive observers until a later time.

For union leaders who may be reading this book, I urge you to consider the significant benefits that active support and participation in a TQM process will have for your union and its members. The gap that may now exist between union and management will be narrowed considerably. Grievances will be reduced as people develop a common language and vision. Corporate success and growth, which will result from a total quality effort, will add more jobs and provide more opportunity for members. Management will have a greater incentive for avoiding work stoppages, and you will be modeling a new spirit of cooperation for other unions around the country. Many participants in the total quality effort at Florida Power and Light Company are members of the International Brotherhood of Electrical Workers (IBEW).

Not surprisingly, another thing you can expect as you develop your TQM process is to make a financial investment. There is no such thing as a free lunch.

Training, consultants, materials, research, facilitators, and the like cost money. I can't begin to tell you how much money needs to be invested because the amount depends on so many factors that vary from company to company. A few hundred thousand dollars for the medium to medium-large organization with more than 1000 employees is not unusual during the first 18 to 24 months. This investment, however, is an investment principally in people. It is not a capital-intensive investment, which means that the benefits derived from this cash outlay can extend further into the future than is normally the case with a capital investment. And the payback is significant.

Depending on how well you do at implementing TQM, the initial investment can be won back in a relatively short period of time—in many cases, less than 2 years. From then on, far into the future, you'll realize a handsome return on your continuing investment in TQM. Figure 3-3 illustrates the "crossing of the lines."

Essentially, the benefits realized from TQM will come from increased efficiency achieved through the pursuit of QI projects, many of which will reduce the COPQ. It will also come from increased customer retention and an improved ability to win new customers.

At some point, as Figure 3-3 indicates, your investment in TQM will level off to the point of a gently rising slope, but the benefits being achieved will continue to grow dramatically. This is the road to a sustainable competitive advantage.

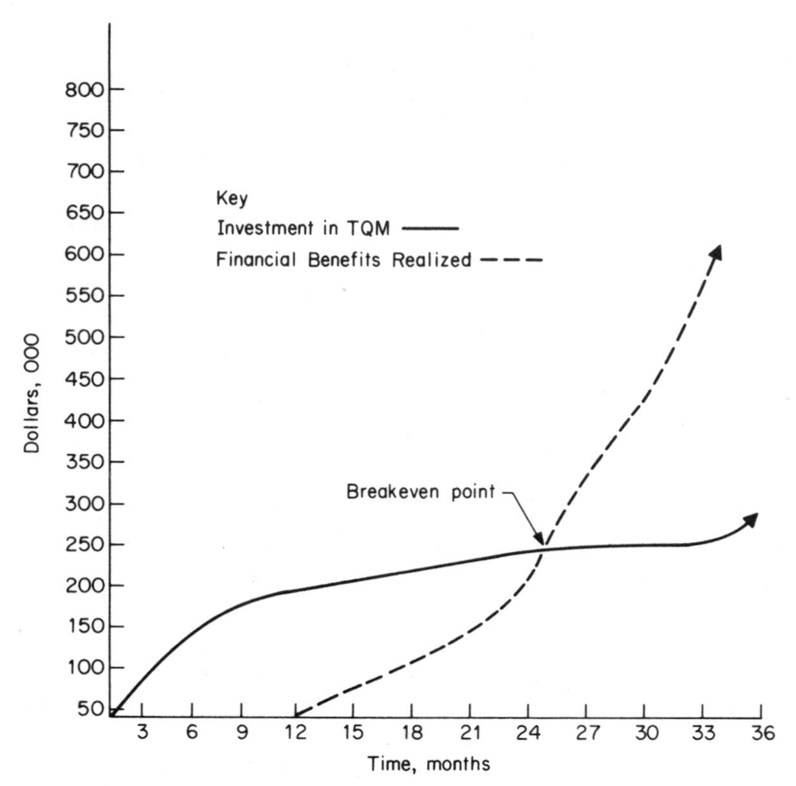

Figure 3-3. TQM Breakeven and ROI Chart.

Signaling the Organization

Consultant and author Tom Peters jokingly describes one way a top executive can signal the organization that he or she is interested in quality management. The advice can be summarized as follows: First go out and buy four or five books on quality improvement and just leave them lying around your office or stacked on your desk. As people enter and leave your office, they'll notice the books and begin to wonder what's going on. Then, about two weeks later, tell your secretary you are going to a conference or seminar on quality and head for your favorite vacation spot for a week of relaxation. By the time you return, the company will know you are interested in quality!

Actually, this approach would probably work at least initially. But, as Mr. Peters well knows, it lacks a very important ingredient. The top executive still wouldn't know what quality management really is.

Something more effective is needed in order to demonstrate management's commitment to quality. I suggest that top managers actually read the books referred to in Tom Peters's description and actually attend a quality seminar. Then, when managers begin talking about their commitment to quality, they'll know what they're talking about!

Once management has decided to pursue TQM seriously, it needs to reveal this fact and the reasons to the rest of the company. If management fails to take the initiative in communicating its intention to develop a QIP, the grapevine will pick it up soon enough. If the grapevine is activated, the message may be distorted, incomplete, and lacking the needed emphasis.

Most climate survey data reveal that employees prefer to hear news that affects them from their supervisor or directly from upper management. Therefore, use the company house organ and other secondary communications devices as backup to more direct means, unless you have strong evidence that a secondary communications channel has an unusually high level of credibility.

Normally, it is best for management to communicate important messages through a series of downward-flowing meetings. This provides an opportunity for two-way communications and ensures a better understanding. This method does take longer and requires more effort, but it is far more effective and builds credibility at the outset. The face-to-face approach also builds a strong foundation on which subsequent communications concerning the developing quality process can rest.

Once the initial communication has been completed, follow up with regular updates; it is not a good idea to surprise people with complex change. A little hand-holding along the way will help the organization to accept the new way as the TQM development process continues.

Selecting a Bottom-Up or Top-Down Approach

One of the first decisions to be made when developing a TQM implementation strategy is whether to involve people at the top of the organization first and then move the quality activity downward through the company—a top-down approach—or to elect the bottom-up approach. This decision has to be made whether or not you utilize a test site. If the test site or the company is small enough—less than a few hundred people—the decision is less important because the quality process will involve everyone soon enough.

For larger companies, I recommend the top-down strategy, which we have already begun to adopt (in Chapter 2) with the establishment of the quality council and lead teams. The reason why a top-down approach is recommended is to help ensure a more effective culture change and to improve your chances of making a more significant positive impact early in the process in terms of dollars saved as well as the extent to which customer satisfaction is affected.

As far as culture change is concerned, nothing sends a stronger message to the entire company than management's action. As the old adage advises, "actions speak louder than words," and managers who model the new TQM process actively demonstrate their commitment to quality improvement. Far too often, management tries to implement a new process, attitude, or program by extolling its virtues and sending the troops down a new path while the executives continue their daily routine. No one is fooled by this approach, and the new way often falls into disuse a few months later because the importance of the new way has not been demonstrated. Management has failed to "walk like it talks."

Even a company with an unusually respected and credible top management group should not try to talk its way into a TQM process. The nonmanagement staff may eagerly learn and begin to use the quality concepts, but later the whole thing will most likely fall apart as those involved adopt a new language and new skills that cannot be understood by those in the executive suite. This communications and experience gap will become wider and wider until the TQM process is swallowed and disappears. In order to support TQM effectively, managers must experience it and learn the language.

Although a bottom-up approach to TQM implementation involves more people more quickly, it may not be the best strategy to adopt—for two reasons.

First, as stated already, managers will not be able to support the effort adequately owing to a communications and experience gap. Second, the early payback will be smaller with a bottom-up approach than with a top-down approach because people at nonmanagement levels are capable of pursuing—owing to their scope of authority—only the less significant quality projects. The extensive quality improvement database of the Juran Institute, Wilton, Connecticut, reveals that the typical quality project pursued by management teams yields a positive financial benefit of about $100,000, whereas the average benefit attributable to nonmanagement teams is $20,000. A primary reason for this, I believe, is in something called the 85/15 rule, which advises that 85 percent of the quality issues are found in faulty work processes, whereas only about 15 percent of a company's quality problems are due to worker error. Of course, managers are the ones who have the authority to set and tamper with work processes, and processes that cross functional lines cause the more sizable quality problems.

The conclusion, therefore, is that it is better to begin in a top-down fashion. Although it can be a little slower, in the long run it ensures a longer-lasting, more effective, and more beneficial TQM process. Cutting corners, especially at the beginning, will lead to disappointing results.

Deciding How to Begin

Now that we've discussed where to begin—at the top—we need to decide how to begin. Later chapters will recommend that a TQM process include three key elements: QI teams, quality planning, and unit-level quality. The question of how to begin is not answered without some debate among knowledgeable practitioners and consultants. However, in the final analysis, I'm not certain that selecting one or the other makes a great deal of difference if you are committed to your choice and persevere. In some companies, it may even be feasible to begin almost simultaneously with both of the popular TQM elements: teams and quality planning.

In 1981 Florida Power and Light Company started with teams. Today people at Florida Power and Light feel that if they had it to do over, they would begin with quality planning, what they call "policy deployment." We at Colonial Penn began with teams at the personal suggestion of Dr. Joseph M. Juran and began implementing quality planning 18 months later. I am recommending the teams-first approach here and urging that quality planning follow closely on the heels of your early QI team experience. Quality improvement teams are described in Chapters 5 and 6. Quality planning is described in Chapter 7, with a discussion of unit-level quality following in Chapter 8.

I recommend a teams-first approach because it involves more members of management early on, and it begins more clearly to affect people's actions, which, as you recall, is the best way to initiate culture change. Team involvement exposes people more quickly to the many concepts and tools of quality improvement and will more rapidly yield some measurable results that can build positive momentum and enthusiasm, particularly among the management group.

However, as I have cautioned, quality planning should follow soon after the introduction of teams. While teams identify and work to solve quality issues such as complaint levels and billing process problems, quality planning helps to improve product development and to focus quality project selection on the issues that make the most difference to a company's quest for competitive advantage—the road to achieving its vision.

Colonial Penn began with teams at the management level, including top management, and utilized a test site employing 350 people. Our experience, a million dollar impact for our company from our first 10 teams, was highly gratifying. The people of our Southeast Regional Home Office in Tampa, Florida, enthusiastically embraced our quality process and showcased their experience for the rest of our company, which propelled us forward with added commitment. Shortly thereafter, a top management team including our chairman and CEO worked on a QI project that yielded a $458,000 improvement in the first year. This amount is not included in the $1 million benefit achieved by our test site!

Begin with teams and stir in quality planning soon after, followed by unit-level quality. Then, hold onto your hat!

Transformation Checkpoints

1. Know what to expect:
   - TQM represents a major cultural change.
   - Effective TQM culture change takes years.
   - Resistance is normal and must be managed.
   - Developing TQM requires a financial investment.
   - The return on your investment in TQM can be quite high.
2. Signal the organization that TQM is coming, and do this in face-to-face meetings involving senior management.
3. Select a top-down approach because:
   - It ensures a more effective culture change.
   - It builds a common language between levels in the company.
   - It pays higher financial returns early in the process.
4. Begin with QI teams followed shortly by quality planning and later by unit-level quality.

4
A Total Quality Model

A total quality process development model I have designed is illustrated in Figure 4-1. If you are not particularly fond of busy models, then we have something in common! However, I encourage your indulgence in familiarizing yourself with this one because it provides at a glance (or at least a 30-second stare) the development of a TQM process in a chronological fashion.

As you probably know, the concentric circles model is meant to depict the evolution of something—it's not unlike a slice or section of a tree trunk. You read this model from the inside out, concentric circle by concentric circle. To oversimplify somewhat, each concentric circle may represent from 6 to 10 months in elapsed time to develop a TQM process. In this case, the model includes five concentric circles and may suggest that to develop the type of TQM process I am recommending will take from 2½ years to nearly 4 years, depending on many factors. Some of the principal factors are the degree of top management commitment, the extent of the resources applied, the size of the company, the state and complexity of the current corporate environment, and the skill with which the various pieces of the TQM process are developed.

It took Colonial Penn 2½ years to complete the model. At the time, Colonial Penn was a billion dollar (revenues) organization employing 3600 people in five principal locations including Pennsylvania (headquarters were in Philadelphia), Florida, Arizona, California, and Rhode Island. The corporate environment during this time was one of maximum change, having just been acquired on December 31, 1985, by FPL Group, Inc., the parent organization of Florida Power and Light Company. This may suggest that a smaller, more centrally located company

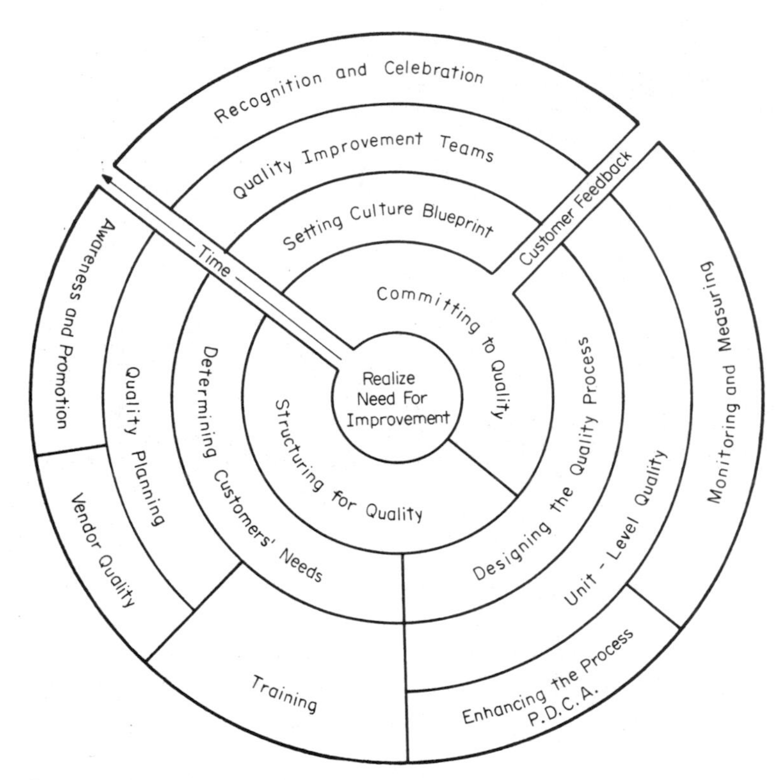

Figure 4-1. The Total Quality Model.

experiencing less distraction may be capable of developing an effective TQM process in 1 to 2 years.

Chapter 4 will briefly explain the components of a total quality model, some of which we've already covered; others are detailed in later chapters. Now that we have started our journey down the road to total quality, my intention is to provide a look at the whole map so that you are properly oriented for the remainder of the trip.

Realizing the Need: Center Circle

Before packing for the trip, management must clearly see the need for improvement. We talked about the issue of survival in a competitive and dynamic environment. Consumers are demanding more, competitors are gaining, we may be slipping in terms of corporate effectiveness and efficiency, and government regulations may be making it more difficult to compete. We also recognize that more foreign competitors are on the road with us or, if not, that their presence is a future threat. An assessment of the current situation and future outlook must concern management enough so that they are driven to consider a far-reaching and fundamentally different way to operate the business. If you are simply looking for a way to cut costs for a while in order to make next year's earnings target, or if you are seeking a way to make employees happy, then I suggest you try something else. There must be a compelling reason for pursuing TQM and an understanding that you need to get into it for the long haul. Anything less and your commitment to TQM will wallow in the choppy seas of uncertainty.

The Japanese were highly motivated to learn the quality approach from Dr. W. Edwards Deming and Dr. Joseph M. Juran. Japan's economy had been virtually destroyed in World War II; so with precious few natural resources as a base for rebuilding, for Japan it was a matter not just of corporate survival but of national survival. A more compelling reason will never exist. The success the Japanese have had with what they call companywide quality control (CWQC) now makes up part of the compelling reason for U.S. auto manufacturers and electronics companies to learn total quality!

So, determine your own compelling need, and let it drive you down the road to TQM.

Structuring, Committing, Setting, Determining, and Designing: Concentric Circles 2 and 3

Structuring for Quality

In Chapter 2 we covered structuring or organizing for quality and committing to quality. In this model, structuring for quality means forming the quality council, choosing a quality quarterback and design team, forming lead teams, and, if appropriate, selecting a test site. An important point to recall is that we are building a parallel organization structure, not a new one. Most organizational effectiveness experts agree that many organizations are far too complex and multilayered today to even begin to tolerate added organizational complexity. The parallel quality organization structure is simple and begins to send an important signal to the rest of the company, a signal which communicates that we are aligning ourselves for something new.

Committing to Quality

Committing to quality comes when the top management quality council reviews the evidence and recommendations brought forward by the design team. We've assessed the current situation, measured the COPQ, investigated customers' needs and satisfaction levels, and measured employee attitudes. We have an idea of what to expect on the quality journey, we realize that there is an investment to be made and a significant return on that investment to be gained, and we've planned how to signal the organization that a new way is approaching.

Now, we commit to quality by setting our quality policy and giving the go-ahead for developing and testing a quality process.

Determining Customers' Needs

At this point in the model, we see the customer feedback "spoke" beginning at circle 2 and extending out into the future. This part of the model reminds us that we must constantly seek customer feedback in a variety of ways so that we may adjust our approaches to the ever-changing marketplace. Because the basic definition of *quality* is meeting customers' needs, we must know what those principal needs are, and we must know how we are measuring up.

The annual customer survey that many companies employ is not enough to enable a corporation to maintain a useful database on customers' needs. An annual survey must be supplemented by a variety of more frequent methods for assessing the needs and reactions of customers. Focus groups, customer visits and interviews, brief, point-of-contact questionnaires like those you find in most hotel rooms (and virtually no airliners), and other methods will all help a great deal in your ability to keep score. Make no mistake about it: The most important score to keep is the one provided by customer perceptions. The customer's attitude is the driving force for all the other scorecard ratings we have all tracked for years, such as earnings per share, sales, ROI, and market share.

Setting the Culture Blueprint

The next segment of concentric circle 3 refers to setting the culture blueprint. As discussed in Chapter 2, this requires measuring employees' attitudes and their view of corporate priorities and values. We must also identify the values that sustain a total quality culture, note the gap between the current and future value systems, and determine what action is needed to close the gap.

Some principal values of a TQM culture are (this is not an all-inclusive list):

- The customer is first.
- Teamwork and cooperation are essential.
- The internal customer is important.
- Customer delight drives all key indicators.
- Long-term improvement is better than a short-term, quick-fix mentality.
- Facts and data matter; hunches and guesses do not.
- Worry about finding solutions, not fault.
- No bench sitting during the quality game.
- Total quality management is not a separate program.
- Total quality management is a people-intensive, not capital-intensive, process.

Designing the Quality Process

Designing the process refers to the need for not just committing to quality by extolling its values and necessary attitudes but by actually designing a process for people to follow. Just as passion without a system will fail, so will a system without passion fail. We must have a system *with* passion. So pick one system or process and stick to it with a religious zeal.

Teams, Quality Planning, Unit-Level Quality, and Training: Concentric Circle 4

Quality improvement teams, quality planning, and unit-level quality are the three basic elements of the TQM process recommended in this book. The QI teams' element—the guts or backbone of TQM—is discussed in Chapters 5 and 6. Quality planning is covered in Chapter 7, and unit-level quality is discussed in Chapter 8.

Teams should involve everyone in the company; quality planning in-

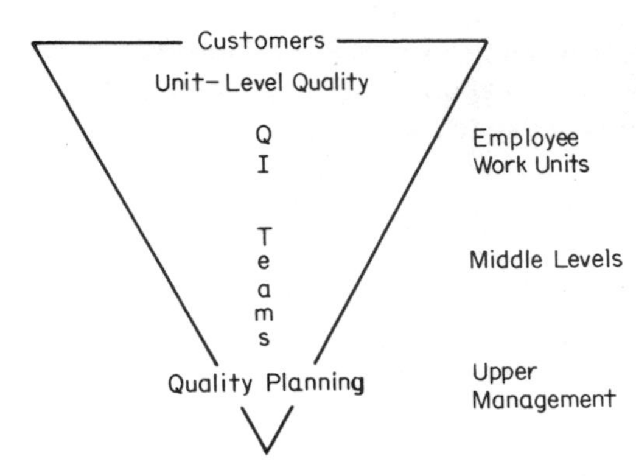

Figure 4-2. The Upside-Down Organizational Pyramid.

volves primarily upper management, and unit-level quality focuses at the office-floor level of the company, the individual department level. However, I prefer to turn the traditional organizational pyramid upside down to illustrate that, at the top of the hierarchy, we have the customers and the front-line employees who interface with the customers. At the bottom, or at the stern of the ship with experienced hands on the tiller, we have top management. This upside-down pyramid is shown in Figure 4-2.

At this point, I'll only briefly describe the three elements of the TQM process: QI teams, quality planning, and unit-level quality. The following four chapters will provide more detail.

QI Teams

Quality improvement teams work to achieve lasting improvements in the work processes of a company. They investigate quality problems utilizing a well-tested, problem-solving process and some SPC tools. Teams typically consist of from five to seven members, sometimes from the same unit or function (functional teams) but more often from a variety of areas (cross-functional teams). In many cases, teams meet an hour or more per week on company time and are guided by a team leader and assisted by a QI facilitator.

An example of a team's problem may be to investigate and resolve customer complaints relating to the billing process or to reduce the time it takes to issue a new credit card to a customer.

Members are assigned to a team based on their knowledge of the issue being investigated and/or their ability or authority to influence the process or issue under study.

Many companies with well-developed TQM processes have hundreds of teams working at any one time.

Quality Planning

Quality planning is the art of setting a corporate vision (top management's realizable dream) and focusing the resources and energy of the organization on the vital few goals that will best propel the company toward its vision. Quality planning also requires that corporate activity be driven by a clear and constantly updated view of customers' needs, that the products and services provided by the company be designed and delivered in such a way as to meet customers' needs, and that all processes and systems in the company are customer-friendly.

By focusing on the vital few priorities rather than using the more common scatter-gun approach, a company can direct the efforts of hundreds of QI teams to those issues that will make the most difference toward achieving its vision. This is done by developing a focused business plan, by communicating it effectively to each person in the company, and by asking all units to determine how they can contribute to one or more of the vital few goals or key emphasis areas.

For the most part, quality planning is the responsibility of upper management. In the dialect of the sharpshooter, it produces a tight pattern of hits in the center of the target.

Unit-Level Quality

Unit-level quality is, in a sense, quality planning, issue identification, and resolution and improvement execution at the unit level. This element of the quality process is built around one of the most basic of the QI concepts or models: *plan, do, check,* and *act* (P.D.C.A.). Popularly known as the Deming wheel or Shewhart diagram, P.D.C.A. is illustrated in Figure 4-3.

In order to have a quality focus, P.D.C.A. suggests that all activity follow a cycle as follows:

1. First, *plan* what you are going to do.
2. Second, *do* what you have planned.
3. Third, *check* on the results of your action.

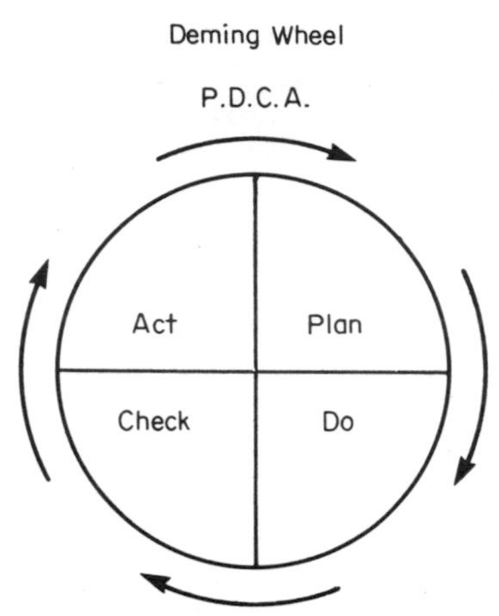

Figure 4-3. Deming Wheel.

4. Fourth, *act* to modify what you do to better ensure the most positive (quality) results.

Then, continue (mentally) turning this wheel in a clockwise direction. That is, replan, redo, recheck, and act again to get better and better.

Chapter 8 will show how we adapt this simple but powerful model to the day-to-day activities of a unit or department. As a unit follows the unit-level quality process, the members discover many incidental actions in which they have been routinely engaged for years and which are found to be time-wasting or that fly directly in the face of quality. They can quickly resolve these. Units might also discover more deep-rooted or chronic problems that they may wish to tackle by forming either a functional or a cross-functional QI team.

Training

As we see from our total quality model, training is a major factor spanning the last two concentric circles. References to the need for training are found throughout this book.

I strongly emphasize that TQM training for employees at *all* levels is absolutely essential. Tom Peters suggests that creating a few good training programs is not enough. We need to develop a continuous learning environment. During a one-day seminar he gave in Philadelphia in September 1988, he put it this way: "Training, training, retraining, then more training, and if I have to say it again then you just don't get it." I'll add this: If you don't get it, then get out of the game! After all, we are changing the culture, which is to say, we are changing attitudes. As Figure 3-1 showed, we do this by getting people to do things differently. This requires training, reinforcement, modeling, and more training—the creation and application of a continuous learning environment.

Awareness, Promotion, Recognition, and Celebration: Concentric Circle 5

Awareness and Promotion

Once your TQM process is in place, it needs to be advertised internally and promoted just like any other major corporate activity. Awareness and promotional strategies should not include too many balloons and streamers. Save these for celebration and recognition, which I'll discuss briefly in a moment and cover more thoroughly in Chapter 13.

Awareness and promotion should be handled in a relatively serious and businesslike manner, but with considerable enthusiasm and a demonstration of long-term commitment. The most effective way to promote TQM and to keep people aware of its benefits and potential is to utilize your most effective communications channels. As was pointed out earlier, surveys have shown that employees most prefer to hear about important matters from their immediate supervisors, from upper management, and through department meetings. Therefore, management has the task of continuously communicating TQM to others in the organization. This is another reason why adopting a top-down approach to implementing TQM is the better choice. Management can't very effectively talk about TQM without having first learned the language and without having personally experienced TQM. Regular staff meetings, management visitations, and other, less formal communications methods must be orchestrated by company managers. If you are a manager, I urge that whenever you find yourself with an audience, even if it is only one or two people, work in some enthusiastic discussion about TQM.

The internal house organ, as well as any other trusted communications vehicles, should also be a vehicle for promoting TQM. Quality-awareness posters, lapel pins, coffee mugs, and other items can be effective supplemental devices, but they can't do the job by themselves.

Also, if your company regularly communicates progress toward achieving important goals, in a company newsletter for example, news of the TQM process must appear here as well. Don't select an awareness and promotion strategy that is different from the approach you now use to communicate important corporate news and results. If you do, TQM will quickly be seen as a "program" separate from the mainstream rather than a "process" aimed at long-term, continuous improvement.

In the final analysis, once TQM is understood and has taken hold, it will promote itself. The many employees who become involved with quality will become your most enthusiastic salespeople, and the positive benefits of TQM will be readily apparent.

At Colonial Penn, awareness and promotion take a multifaceted approach. In addition to managers walking and talking quality, we have or utilize posters, lapel pins (which may also be suspended from a necklace or bracelet), mugs and coasters, T-shirts, our house organ, status reports, a brochure, our in-house video magazine, news center (bulletin) boards, the orientation program, and a quality or customer satisfaction logo and newsletter.

Recognition and Celebration

One of the best ways to promote your quality process is to celebrate your successes and recognize those individuals and teams who distinguish themselves along the road to total quality.

A strategy for recognition and celebration separate from, but linked with your approach to, awareness and promotion is definitely needed. Most people respond favorably to being recognized by their peers and by management. Besides being an effective way to nurture and promote TQM, it's a lot of fun. Chapter 13 will cover recognition and celebration in some detail.

Demanding Vendor Quality, Enhancing the TQM Process, and Monitoring and Measuring Quality: More on Concentric Circle 5

Demanding Vendor Quality

Unfortunately, it is possible for your company to be doing an outstanding job at pursuing its TQM process and to still be experiencing great difficulty in meeting the needs of your customers if your many vendors fall short of meeting your expectations.

A vendor who delivers defective parts and poor service, or who otherwise can't be counted on to perform well consistently, will account for a large part of your COPQ.

Vendor quality will be discussed in Chapter 14. For now, it suffices to say that no quality process can ever be a *total* quality process without involving your vendors. To many people, talk of vendors may sound like a manufacturing-only issue. However, even if you work for a bank, an insurance company, a hotel, an airline, or a university, you have many vendors who play an important role in the quality chain of events.

Some of the larger vendors for service companies include the phone company, computer firms, paper and forms suppliers, and the postal service.

To pursue a TQM process and ignore the issue of vendors is like starting a baseball game knowing in advance that home plate is missing. You can never really score without vendor involvement.

Enhancing the TQM Process

By the time you have reached this point in our total quality model, your TQM process is on its feet, but it is toddling along, still a little unsteady as it advances along the path you've set. As each step is taken, you must continue to spin the Deming wheel (see Figure 4-3) in order to apply your new "Kaizen," or constant improvement, attitude to the quality process itself. That is, you must continuously *check* or evaluate what you have done and *act* to improve it by re*plan*ning and re*do*ing.

Each and every company is unique. My own model and the steps that Colonial Penn has taken have proven to be, for the most part, right for us. However, along the way we did many things that were less effective than they might have been. So, we modified our approach to fit our own needs. This is certainly true of Florida Power and Light Company and any other company that has mounted a drive for TQM.

The message here is to apply the quality concepts to your own developing process—practice what you preach. This is one reason why I so strongly recommend using a pilot test site and why I further recommend testing any and all elements or parts of your TQM process as you proceed. In Chapter 13, I'll describe one example of how Colonial Penn started down the wrong road with recognition and celebration, discovered our mistake before it was too late, and adjusted our course.

Monitoring and Measuring Quality

The last sector of the total quality model urges a monitoring and measuring process. Common sense alone should be enough to sell the need for keeping score. There are a number of factors or indicators that need to be monitored in order to recognize success when we see it.

At the top of this list of key indicators are those important measures that we are accustomed to monitoring such as sales, earnings, and expense levels. After all, a quality process is aimed at achieving a competitive advantage which, in turn, yields an attractive return for investors.

However, we must realize that, over the long haul, none of the key financial indicators will reach targeted levels unless customers are delighted. I know that the more common term is customer satisfaction, but we must really mean customer delight. Customers who are merely satisfied are vulnerable to competitor "rustlers." Because the name of the game is really winning and keeping customers and having them view our company as the supplier of choice, the most important indicator to track is customer perception. More specifically, I recommend that we carefully monitor the growth of our customer base, which is directly related to how delighted our customers are with our products and services.

In addition to tracking the number of customers, I suggest monitoring the number of customers who are repeat buyers or who buy more than one of our products or services. These people are the ones who have selected us as the supplier of choice, and they represent our most precious asset.

The number of customers per employee on the payroll or the dollar amount of sales related to payroll dollars is a useful indicator that helps us track efficiency. Presumably, we could assign two employees to look after the needs of each customer and have a fair shot at delighting these customers. However, earnings would drop like a rock!

Other customer-oriented indicators are the number of complaints and the effectiveness with which we resolve complaints. For example, we must know how quickly we resolve incidents of customer dissatisfaction, how effective the resolution is in the customer's opinion, and, finally, whether the customer who complained will continue to be our customer. Research has shown that a customer who complains and has his or her complaint adjusted fairly and quickly will remain a customer for the future and may even bring friends to your door—additional precious assets. Even an unusual amount of time or money spent to satisfy a complaining customer can be regained and surpassed by the value of repeat and referral business in the future. This point speaks to the long-term attitude we must adopt when it comes to relating to our customers.

We also need to track the results of our customer satisfaction surveys, questionnaires, and other sources of feedback and to isolate and attack the causes of dissatisfaction.

Other indicators help us to monitor how well we are expanding and utilizing our TQM process specifically. We should, for example, monitor the number of QI teams and the number of projects completed by teams. But, we must do this not only in a quantitative manner but also in a qualitative manner. That is, we need to know how many teams are working, and we must also know how effective these teams are. If my company has 400 teams but only 20 percent of the teams have completed a project in the past year, I'd be sorely disappointed.

We've discussed the COPQ. If we have measured the COPQ, found that it approached $12 million, and set a 5-year goal to cut this amount in half, then we will need to measure our progress toward achieving this goal.

Because total quality means total employee involvement, among other things, we may wish to track the number of people and the percent of the population involved in the quality process. This includes people on teams and people involved in unit-level quality. Here, too, remember the quantitative and the qualitative nature of involvement.

Although this list isn't meant to be an exhaustive one, I'll suggest three more indicators: vendor quality ratings, TQM's investment return, and employee perceptions. Depending on the nature of a vendor's business, it is wise to set meaningful quality indicators to track a vendor's effectiveness, such as the number of defective parts per thousand per month.

We also need to track the data that show us when the lines cross, as illustrated in Figure 3-3. That is, when do the financial benefits of TQM exceed the costs attributable to installing and administering the process? And, finally, through continuing surveys of our employees, we need to monitor how they feel about the effectiveness of the TQM process. At Colonial Penn's test site in 1988, an employee survey showed that 83 percent of our employees felt that our quality efforts were having a positive effect on our customers! That's pretty good, but it's not good enough!

All the indicators I've just discussed may be considered macro indicators. But what about micro indicators? Those who usually ask, "How do you measure service quality?" usually refer to micro indicators or transaction-based indicators. This service quality question is a frequent one because, after all, there is no "tangible" product that can break, wear out, or fall apart.

A service is usually something experienced by a customer when it is being provided. The ultimate measure of service quality, then, is the customer's perception of the bank transaction, the claims adjustment process, the hotel checkout procedure, and so on. In the vast majority of cases, each service transaction is as unique as each customer, and the quality score we achieve is directly attributable to the perception of the customer.

The key to being able to measure service quality, therefore, is to be aware of what customers expect from each type of transaction with our company and to develop the measures to track customer perceptions. For example, if our research shows that most customers expect their monthly bank statements to arrive by the fourth of each month, then we need to track the number of statements not mailed by the first of the month. If we know that our insurance customers expect to reach the claims office by telephone on the first attempt, then we need to track the number of abandoned calls coming into claims or, to be accurate, not coming into claims. Measuring service quality is clearly a process of knowing your customers' needs and establishing the means to measure your performance against those needs on a transaction level as well as a macro level.

	Year	Year	Year	YTD Fore-cast
1. Sales Revenues				
2. Total Expenses				
3. Pretax Profit				
4. Number of Customers				
5. Number of Repeat Buyers				
6. Customer Survey Results (composite)				
7. Payroll as Percent of Sales				
8. Number of Customers Per Employee				
9. Number of Customer Complaints				
10. Complaint Resolution Rating				
11. Number of QI Teams				
12. Number of Completed Projects				
13. Number and Percent of Employees Involved				
14. Extent of COPQ Reduction				
15. Employee Survey Results Regarding TQM				
16. Vendor Quality Rating				
17. Return on TQM Investment				

Figure 4-4. Some TQM Success Indicators.

As a Quick Review

To recap this section, Figure 4-4 provides a sample display of TQM success indicators. Of course, this task is more complex than the illustration suggests. However, I urge you to make it as simple as possible and to focus on the vital few indicators rather than creating an excessively large volume of measurements.

There are 15 sectors in my total quality model. Each one must be carefully studied to determine how it may best apply to your company. As a result, your own total quality model, when all is said and done, will probably look different from the one illustrated in Figure 4-1. I may even venture to say that if your final model looks exactly like mine, you probably haven't customized it for your own culture and circumstances.

This is an excellent place to give some well-deserved credit and thanks to the top managers and to all the people of FPL Group, Inc., and Florida Power and Light Company, which acquired Colonial Penn in December 1985. At that time, FPL had been developing its QIP for 4 years under the inspired leadership of Marshall McDonald, now chairman of FPL Group, and John Hudiburg, former chairman of Florida Power and Light Company.

There is no greater understatement than to say that the FPL family was exceedingly proud of and enthusiastic about its QIP. FPL certainly could have directed Colonial Penn to adopt its process as is and tried to manage us through it. Instead, we were given the key to the company and invited to turn the place upside down in order to understand what was happening. To the credit of FPL managers, they left the method of designing our own process to the people who, for years, had worked the soil in which the quality seeds would be planted. They left it to us! Their advice, support, and encouragement along the way were greatly appreciated and indeed were extremely helpful. I have the greatest admiration and respect for FPL's judgment in this matter, as well as a great deal of admiration for what it has accomplished for its millions of customers. FPL's Deming Prize is well deserved.

Transformation Checkpoints

1. The total quality process development model (Figure 4-1) is not intended as your recipe or blueprint for success, because every company is different. However, it may serve as a useful guide for the journey ahead.
2. Find your compelling reason for adopting a TQM process. Otherwise your commitment will dissolve in the presence of other seemingly pressing issues.

3. Organize the company for the quality journey, a journey that never ends.
4. Commit to quality explicitly by setting your quality policy and signaling the organization.
5. Seeking customer feedback is a constant and permanent priority.
6. Measure employee attitudes, identify the attitudes that support TQM, note the gap, and plan to close it.
7. Develop a system with passion.
8. Teams work to resolve quality issues. This is one element of the three-part TQM model.
9. Quality planning focuses energy and resources on the vital few priorities driven by an assessment of customers' needs. This is another element of the TQM model.
10. Unit-level quality is a department-level process for ensuring quality at the factory- or office-floor level. This is the third leg of the TQM stool.
11. Turn the organization chart upside down.
12. Plan, do, check, and act (P.D.C.A.) is a simple but powerful quality concept.
13. Training, training, retraining, then more training. Create a continuous learning environment.
14. Promote your quality commitment and process through the most effective methods. Involvement by managers is a must!
15. Celebrate your successes and recognize your heroes. It's fun too!
16. Vendors need to sign on to quality or it won't be a *total* quality management process.
17. Set and monitor key success indicators with a primary emphasis on customer-related factors. Customer delight drives all the vital measurements.
18. Practice what you preach. Apply P.D.C.A. to the development of your TQM process.

5 Team-Tackling Quality Problems

Quality improvement teams are the guts of a TQM process. It is teams following a structured problem-solving process that identify and permanently fix the costly, inefficient, and ineffective operations of the company.

The use of QI teams is so important that I'll devote two chapters to this vital quality ingredient. This chapter will cover the role of teams in the QIP, the formation of teams, project selection, and stratification. Chapter 6 will cover a structured team problem-solving process and will introduce the seven basic statistical process control tools. I'll also discuss how to adequately support QI teams so that they can succeed in achieving their important mission.

What Is the Role of Teams?

When you really think about it, there is an inadequate amount of corporatewide, organized, and effective improvement activity taking place on a regular basis in most companies. Typically, employees spend their time doing their assigned work—keeping the ball rolling—and when the alarm sounds they rush to their battle stations to control the damage from periodic problems and snafus. Too often this "call to battle stations" approach results in inadequate, short-term fixes—the old quick-fix bandage.

True, the occasional special task force or committee is formed to address the larger and more visible problems, but too often the solutions presented attack only the symptoms of the problem and are the pet ideas of the more influential or powerful people on the task force. These solutions are rarely backed by a thorough, fact-based investigation and a long-range remedial action plan. Therefore, we often find that the grand solution falls apart a few miles down the road.

In contrast, QI teams work within a structured problem-solving process to uncover the root causes of problems, to apply effective solutions, and to ensure that the solutions endure for the long term. Quality improvement team members are those people closest to the problem, so they have a real stake in finding the right solution. They are well trained to follow the structured problem-solving process and are trained in the tools of the process. They work under the guidance of an assigned leader and often with the advice of a specially trained team facilitator. In a QI team, pet ideas or solutions must be proven—backed by hard data regardless of the rank worn by the person offering the idea.

In a company of some size, with a well-developed TQM process, you will find hundreds of teams at work solving key problems—not with quick fixes but with solutions meant to last and supported by hard data—fact-based improvements. Florida Power and Light Company, mentioned earlier, has more than 1600 QI teams, one team for every eight employees on the payroll. These teams have completed hundreds of QI projects. This project-by-project improvement approach is the essential ingredient of a TQM process. It is not achieving improvements per se that can gain the lead for a company in the competitive business environment. Instead, we must achieve a pace of change that is more rapid than that achieved by our competitors in order to realize a competitive advantage.

What Are the Scope and Makeup of QI Teams?

Typically, a QI team consists of from five to seven people, and the members of the team are familiar with the issue or problem the team is to resolve. The concept at work here is that the people closest to the issue will have the most to offer when it comes to analyzing and fixing it. They will also have an incentive to implement the proven solution and to lock in the improvement because, in the long term, it will simplify their own work life.

When a QI team is formed, it is important to make sure that the team members selected for a particular project include a person or two who have the authority, or can easily gain access to it, to implement an appropriate solution. This will facilitate the process of implementation later on by sidestepping the NIH—"not invented here"—syndrome.

Each team also includes a designated leader who has been trained both in the QI problem-solving process and in group leadership skills. An effective leader following a proven problem-solving process, working with people who know the territory and care about it, is a winning combination.

Although a team of dedicated people orchestrated by a talented leader has an excellent chance of achieving sound results, many companies leave even less to chance by also utilizing facilitators. A *facilitator* is an internal quality specialist who serves as a consultant to several QI team leaders. A good facilitator knows the problem-solving process and tools inside and out and possesses well-developed leadership, communications, and group dynamics skills. The more enlightened companies see the use of a few facilitators as a wise investment and rotate them through the job on 2-year assignments. They choose their facilitators from among their best people, those who have excellent work records and the respect of their peers.

So the typical QI team includes about a half dozen dedicated people who care about the project under study. The team has a talented leader and benefits from the counsel of a facilitator.

But, are team members only those who volunteer? Do teams only exist at the lower organizational levels? Are teams organized only by department or function? No, no, and no!

Meeting customers' needs consistently requires everyone's involvement. We cannot afford to have people standing on the sidelines or sitting on the bench when it comes to quality.

Many people will volunteer to serve, but others must be drafted as needed. And the field for the draft must be corporatewide, from top to bottom and from side to side.

Many of the more significant opportunities to achieve improvement are found in cross-functional work processes and cannot be adequately addressed without the participation of people from a variety of functions and organizational levels.

For example, to improve the billing process may require a team made up of people from the accounting area, customer service, data processing, and sales. A team made up of employees only from the accounting area will only be able to adequately focus on one part of the total billing process. And management representation is required if a process that touches several units or functions may need to be altered. As indicated earlier, most QI experts and researchers have found that nearly 85 percent of quality problems are rooted in faulty work processes or procedures, and only 15 percent are attributable to individual worker error. Of course, managers design and control work processes, and many processes cross department lines. So, in most cases, you surely need teams that include managers and cross-functional participation to address quality issues adequately.

There are two more important questions: How long does a team stay in place, and when does it meet? It's the project a team is working on that helps determine the answers to these questions. A team should stay intact until its project is complete, and it should meet regularly, according to the nature and urgency of the project. In most cases, QI teams meet for at least an hour each week, and members may do a little work between meetings. However, if there is a particularly urgent project being tackled, you may need a team to work full time or at least several hours per week until the problem is resolved. The key point is that the project should dictate how frequently a team should meet and how long it should stay in place.

Selecting and Stratifying Projects

Selecting a Project

Selecting the right projects for teams to pursue is a very important matter. If a poor project is selected, the team will become frustrated and ineffective. A project is essentially a problem. A broader definition of a QI project is an effort aimed at gaining a lasting breakthrough or revolutionary result that realizes a quantifiable improvement of a process, product, or service. Results typically include the reduction of cost, waste, process cycle time, errors, variations, or rework. In the final analysis, a problem is solved.

When projects are selected, there are a few criteria to keep in mind.

1. The project should focus on a problem area.
2. The principal aspects of the problem should be measurable.
3. The data pertaining to the problem area should be available in some form.
4. The project should relate to the needs of the customer.

5. Management must be willing to make an investment in pursuing the project.
6. The project should not be so broad or large that a team gets lost in it. Bite-sized projects should be selected. (See the section "Stratifying the Project" later in this chapter.)

There are a variety of sources for project ideas. Some of these are:

1. *Internal measures of performance.* Companies measure a number of performance factors such as product defects, error rates, complaint levels, and the like. Measures that fall below target (the customer's target), either consistently or sporadically, become sources of project ideas.
2. *Customer feedback.* Feedback from customers, both external customers and internal customers (those who receive work from elsewhere in the company), can help to identify quality issues.
3. *The people doing the work.* People actually performing the work definitely know what the issues are. If they are asked, they'll tell you.
4. *Consultants.* Consultants and other outsiders who may have occasion to view your operations can often spot issues that go unnoticed by those closer to the work. The opinions of outside specialists should be actively sought.
5. *Management.* Managers are an obvious and principal source of project ideas. Their broader vantage point permits them to spot issues that affect overall performance and the company's ability to achieve key goals.
6. *Multistep work processes.* Multistep work processes that cross unit lines are invariably inefficient. Look to these overly complex processes as a source for project ideas.
7. *Competitor benchmarking.* If key competitors are outperforming you in certain result areas, these areas are sources of project ideas. For example, if competitor A can process a new order in 4 days, and it takes you 10 days, you need to improve your order processing system.
8. *COPQ studies.* If your company has identified the areas contributing to the COPQ, the result of this analysis is an excellent source of project ideas. Particularly, the vital few areas that account for the majority of your COPQ are obvious targets for QI projects.

Stratifying the Project

In order to avoid selecting too broad a project, I suggest that you first select a project theme, a broad area of concern such as customer complaint levels, product defects, warranty claims, process cycle time, product delivery, or insurance policy issue time. Then the theme must be preliminarily analyzed and stratified by a qualified team. *Stratification* is the process of breaking down a larger project into its smaller (bite-sized) component pieces and subjecting the pieces to Pareto analysis. Pareto analysis reveals which of the project components (the vital few) account for a proportionally larger impact on the broader issue. *Pareto* is generally referred to as the "80/20 rule," which we have all heard about. For example, 20 percent of our customer base submits 80 percent of the complaints, or 80 percent of the warranty claims are attributable to 20 percent of the product portfolio.

The point is that if you break a broader issue down to its basic components, gather some data on each, and analyze the data according to the Pareto principle, you will nearly always find the Pareto effect, that is, a vital few of the parts accounting for a majority of the overall issue. It is a search to separate the vital few from the trivial many. Once you have identified the vital few, you know where to concentrate your QI efforts in order to get the greatest return. You can then assign several teams to further investigate each of the vital few.

Pareto is an extremely valuable QI tool. It is one of the seven basic SPC tools. I won't be teaching you these tools in this book because there isn't time. However, if you mount a QI effort, you must provide training in the various tools and techniques.

Let's try an example from the auto insurance industry—auto insurance application forms incorrectly or incompletely filled out by prospective customers. This would obviously be a quality issue because it may cause you to contact the customer for the correct data or the missing information. This will delay your underwriting and policy issue process, and you may fail to meet a customer need for prompt response or, even worse, you may quote the wrong price for the product.

One way to stratify this issue, or to break it down, is by the type of information missing or incorrect. If you divided your application form into its major sections, took a valid sample, and counted the errors or omissions by section, you might find that 80 percent of the errors are found in 20 percent of the form sections. You might find, for example, that a large percentage of errors are made in the sections where people have to select liability limits and deductibles and where driver data are requested (see Figure 5-1). So, if you can fix these vital few problems,

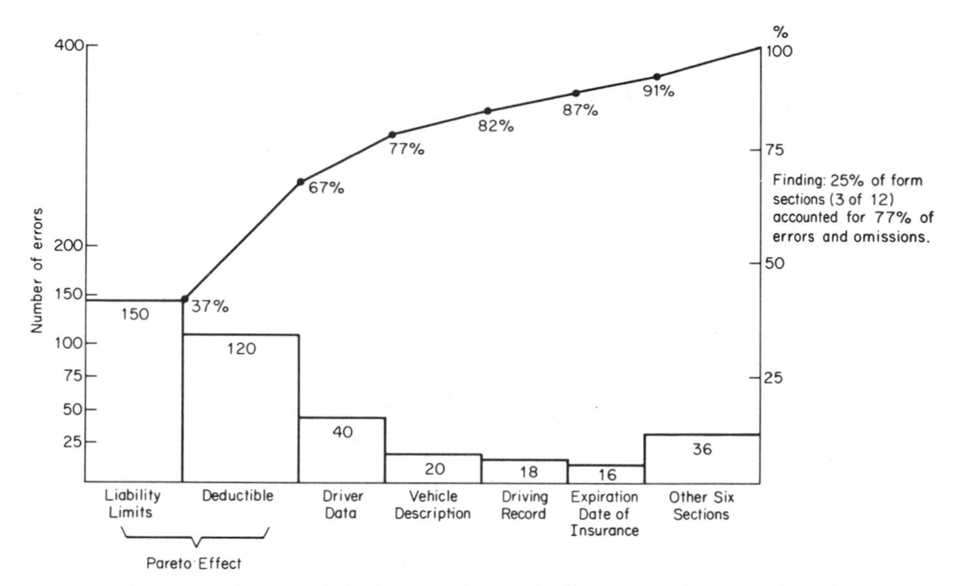

Figure 5-1. Pareto Chart: 1000 Applications Sampled, 400 Errors or Omissions Found.

your percentage of incorrect or incomplete applications will drop dramatically, say from 36 percent to 12 percent.

If you don't find the Pareto effect through this stratification, try another way to break down the issue. For example, you might want to stratify the issue by state of origin and might find that 60 percent of the incomplete forms come from 15 percent of the states in which you do business. A team might later discover that special regulations in these states cause confusion.

The point is that there are usually many ways by which you can stratify. One or more will almost always reveal a Pareto effect. You must keep stratifying and analyzing until you find the vital few subproblems. Then, dig into the issue here for the maximum benefit.

So if you start with a broad theme, stratify it in a variety of ways, and find the Pareto effect, you can then assign teams to work on the vital few subparts, which, in turn, will yield the greatest impact.

Finally, a reminder for those in the service industry. The name of the game in service companies is process cycle time. Service businesses consist of hundreds of work processes, each aimed at creating a result. Quality improvement teams should focus here and try to improve—shorten and simplify—the processes; for example, in insurance, getting the policy issue process down from 8 days to 3 days. Or, in a bank, reducing the loan processing time from 3 days to 1 day. Many processes cross department lines; therefore, managers as team members are especially helpful, even necessary, because only managers have the authority to design or alter cross-functional procedures.

Once a team has stratified a project theme down to one of its vital few components, the team is ready to concentrate its investigation to isolate and counteract the root causes of the problem. The next chapter will discuss how this is done.

Transformation Checkpoints

1. Following a structured problem-solving process, pursuing fact-based investigations, and utilizing some statistical methods to isolate root causes are the functions of a QI team, which in turn is the guts of a QIP.
2. Quality improvement teams should be used at all levels and in all functions of an organization. No one can be exempt from working to improve quality and customer satisfaction.
3. There are eight principal sources for QI project ideas: internal measurements, the people doing the work, customers, managers, consultants or other outsiders, multistep work processes, a competitor's performance record, and your COPQ study.
4. Patience is necessary. Fact-based decisions, the implementation of improvements, and the shaping of a new culture take time.
5. Be aware that 85 percent of quality issues will be in management territory because they involve issues or processes that cross unit boundaries.
6. Inefficient processes and extended process cycle times abound, particularly in service businesses.
7. There is no such thing as too small a QI project.
8. Projects can be easily too broad. However, stratification can be used to identify the vital few, bite-sized pieces of the puzzle. Employ the Pareto principle or the 80/20 rule.

6

QI Teams: The 400 Percent Return on Investment

A trained team working on the right issue and following a structured problem-solving process can deliver amazing results. In most cases, results can be quantified financially, and the ROI can be surprisingly high. However, in the final analysis, customer satisfaction is the outcome from effective teams, and competitive advantage is the ultimate benefit.

A problem-solving process is the path a team should follow to complete a QI project. There can be variations to the one I'll describe here, but the important point is to settle on one, train people thoroughly, and stick to it religiously.

A good problem-solving process is a four-part journey: highlighting the issue, analyzing it, solving it, and following it up.

Part 1: Highlighting the Issue or Problem

In part 1, a team should determine and describe the nature of the issue that has been isolated through stratification. That is, what, in general terms, is the problem? For example, using our incomplete or incorrect insurance applications illustration, we see that the nature of the issue is the inability to process the many application forms in an acceptable amount of time.

We need to describe the present status or state of affairs of the problem by using facts. In our example, 40 percent of the new applications are incomplete or incorrect, yielding an average application cycle time of 22 days.

Finally, in part 1, we need to explain why this condition is unacceptable—why we should devote time to addressing it. For example, this situation delays service to prospective customers by extending our product or service delivery process, resulting in increased costs.

In all cases, we should try to understand what the customers' expectations are with regard to the issue in question and be able to show the gap between actual performance and customer needs. For example, studies may show that customers expect an accurate response to their submitted application in 6 to 8 days rather than in 22 days! Tying quality issues back to customer needs is a must!

The principal output from part 1 of the problem-solving process is a preliminary problem statement. A problem statement should:

- *Be specific;* avoid words like poor, low, or slow.
- *Be measurable;* include facts, numbers, and so on.
- *State the effect;* state what is wrong without presuming a cause or a solution.
- *Identify the gap* between what is and what should be.
- *Focus on the pain;* state why this is an undesirable situation from the customer's point of view.

Remember, a problem well stated is a problem half solved. Here's what our problem statement may look like:

> From July 1 to December 31, 1988, 40 percent or 400 applications for auto insurance were incomplete or incorrect, resulting in an average application process time for this sample of 22 days. Our customers expect a response in 6 to 8 days. Delayed response results in lost sales, increased internal handling costs, and customer dissatisfaction.

This preliminary statement is specific and measurable. It states the gap and the pain. Later, after more analysis, this statement will be improved and will show exactly what the team's focus is. For example, it may later refer to the number of applications missing liability limits data, specify the lost sales in annual revenue dollars, and quantify the added processing costs. A team should constantly work to improve its problem statement through parts 1 and 2 of the problem-solving process.

Part 2: Analyzing the Problem

Once the issue under study has been highlighted and a preliminary problem statement has been written, it is time to collect and seriously crunch some hard data. This is usually the point at which a team needs to see whether it can further stratify the issue as we've discussed earlier. With the help of collected data, we need to look at the problem from all sides and break it down into even more useful subparts if possible, first one way and then another, until we find the Pareto effect—the vital few.

For example, we know that many applications are missing certain data such as desired liability limits. Further investigation may reveal that most of the forms missing these data were submitted by people with older vehicles.

If so, this may suggest a need to provide special instructions for customers who confuse liability limits with the need for collision coverage when they own a vehicle that has a low market value.

Keeping to our example of incomplete and incorrect applications, we may need to survey customers as to what confuses them. We may need to construct a flow diagram, a scatter diagram, and/or a graph or two. All this investigation should, when we step back and look at it for its true meaning, help us write a better problem statement. The problem statement is the emerging picture of what's really going on with respect to the problem.

Analysis marches on and now focuses on a search for the root causes of the problem. Teams need to be careful not to identify symptoms. It's the root causes that need to be isolated. If we end up treating symptoms, the problem resurfaces soon after the treatment. If I treat my headache with aspirin, I may find that the headache lingers on. The root cause could be an improper eyeglass prescription or a dental problem. New glasses, therefore, or a visit to the dentist may be the remedy that permanently cures my headache.

The technique that helps to identify root causes is simple. Just keep asking "why" until you feel you've gotten down to the root cause level. For example, the problem is that our thingamajig motor stopped working. Why? Well, the gizmo part overheated and burned out. Why? Because it wasn't getting oil. Why? Because the oil feed line ruptured. Why? Because the feed line tube was too small. Aha! Root cause. Solution? Replace the oil feed line tube with one of the proper size, add oil, replace your burned-out gizmo, and start 'er up. You may also want to talk with the vendor who supplied the tube. Had we only replaced the gizmo, the problem would return because this was only a symptom, not the root cause.

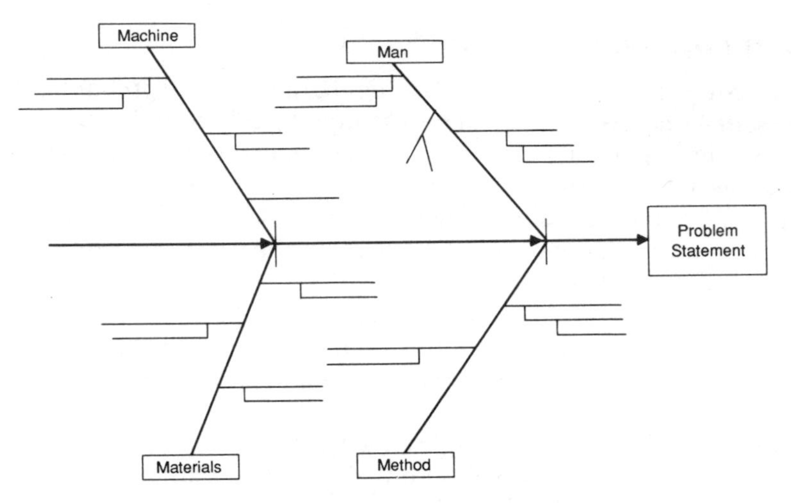

Figure 6-1. Ishikawa Cause-and-Effect Diagram (Fishbone).

A very useful, world-renowned and even entertaining SPC tool to use when determining root causes is the Ishikawa cause-and-effect diagram, popularly known as the fishbone or Godzilla bone graph. I've also heard it called the wishbone! Its structure is pictured in Figure 6-1.

The fishbone is quite helpful in guiding the team from problem statement to potential root causes. You identify principal cause factors or major groupings like the ones shown in the small rectangular boxes, or others that are more suitable to your problem such as communications or procedures. Then you brainstorm all the possible causes and show them as a bone on the fish. Then repeatedly ask why and show this result on sub-bones (see Figure 6-2). Eventually, your attention will center on a few most likely root causes.

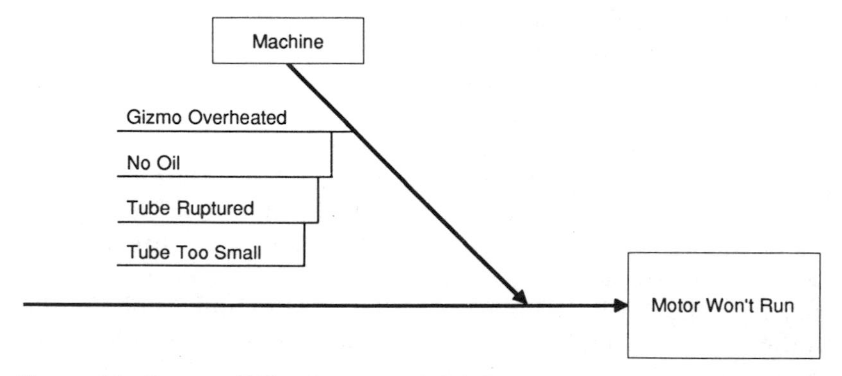

Figure 6-2. Cause-and-Effect Diagram with Sub-Bones.

Once you have isolated what you feel, as a team, are the most likely root causes, you need to verify them somehow. Talking to customers may be a way, but, in any event, try to determine a method to verify whether or not you've identified valid root causes.

Part 3: Solving the Problem

Now it's time to solve the problem by determining the countermeasures that neutralize or eliminate the root causes. But before getting into part 3, you may have observed that our team has spent a lot of time just highlighting and analyzing the issue. It may also seem as if the team has had to work constantly with some statistical wizard—some character who walks around humming Ishikawa cause-and-effect diagrams! Actually, that's both right and wrong. We have an oxymoron of sorts (a combination of contradictory words such as painless dentistry, jumbo shrimp, sanitary landfill, or simplified tax return) working here.

The oxymoron in this case is "on-the-spot problem solving." This is not the case with a QI effort. Fact-based analysis takes some time, but it pays handsome dividends in the long run. A QIP is a long-term improvement strategy that yields long-lasting solutions.

Typically, teams meet an hour or two a week, and it usually takes several months to finish a project when you need to do things like collect data, analyze the data, and reach intelligent decisions. But, think of it this way: A team meeting an hour a week for as long as 10 months has put in 40 to 45 hours or 1 work week! If a team meets twice a week for 1½ hours per session, they'll finish in one-third the time.

Also, you'll be thrilled to learn that the first two parts of the process usually consume 80 percent of the time spent on all four parts. If you do a good job of stratification and analysis, the countermeasures fall in your lap—they become painfully obvious. The challenge, actually, is to not jump to conclusions too soon. Let the facts and analysis guide you all the way to the countermeasures. Finally, as I said before, the SPC tools are fairly simple, and many are doable on a PC. However, it is advisable to have some people around who are particularly competent at applying the statistical tools. They can consult with teams from time to time, but they never have to live with you constantly. They are periodic visitors, not permanent house guests.

Now, on to solving the problem. This part includes two steps: selecting countermeasures and implementing the countermeasures.

As stated before, if the team has done a thorough and conscientious job of analysis to this point, the root causes will have become fairly obvious. I say *root causes* because you rarely find just one. Usually there are two or three. With root causes identified and verified, it is time for the team to discuss what actions can be taken to counteract the root causes. Teams may brainstorm countermeasures and discuss the potential effectiveness and feasibility of each potential countermeasure. It is the judgment, experience, and technical skill of each team member that really come into play here. Sometimes it is advisable to invite someone to a meeting who is especially suited for determining countermeasures for the particular problem under study.

Once the team agrees to a set of countermeasures, it drafts an implementation plan and completes a cost-benefit analysis. Change usually has a price tag and a financially measurable benefit. Management will need to know the investment involved, the potential return (in both dollars and other benefits), and the approximate time period over which the costs must be applied and the benefits realized.

It's important to realize that the initial investment needed to implement a positive change will return benefits over a period of several years. So, don't just think in annual terms; think long-term.

In many cases, a team's problem-solving plan can be tested for effectiveness by conducting a trial implementation. In our insurance application example, we may wish to try a new form in three or four states and analyze the results. If the new form succeeds, we have hard evidence as to the effectiveness of our plan, which will certainly help sell it to top management. If it fails, we need to find out why and adjust our approach. Whenever possible and practical, trial implementation is recommended.

Part 4: Following Up

Following up is as important to the success of the problem-solving process as the first three steps. It is a lot more than cleaning out the conference room and filing our notes.

Following up includes establishing a system to monitor the results of implemented change over time, standardizing the new procedures, and determining whether the countermeasures can be applied with equal success in other parts of the organization. It also includes stepping back to determine what we have learned from our experience, and what we can do with what we have learned. Essentially, part 4 locks in the gains we have achieved and ensures that we apply our new knowledge elsewhere to benefit our customers.

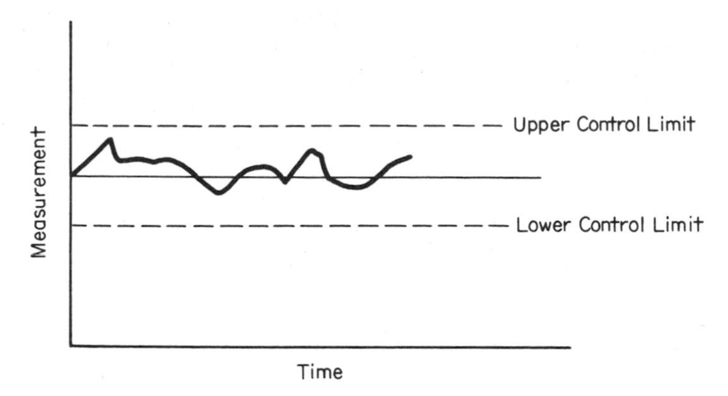

Figure 6-3. Control Chart.

Team members are trained in using control charts. A control chart is an excellent way to monitor the consistency of a process over time, and to ensure that the results are staying within acceptable statistically determined limits, upper- and lower-level control limits. A control chart—and there are a variety of types—is pictured in Figure 6-3. Control charts are somewhat complex. A QI team may occasionally need the assistance of a person familiar with this tool in order to use it correctly.

The monitoring of a well-conceived control chart to track the progress of a modified process is essential. It provides the discipline for knowing whether important processes are running as they should. A process that begins to run out of control is a target for another QI team project. It may mean that the original countermeasures are losing their effectiveness because some other process variable changed. Change, over time, does create new problems.

Now that we've implemented a monitoring system, we need to standardize and routinize the changes we've made and to duplicate them elsewhere if needed. Standardization recognizes the need to adjust procedures and behavior within the organization to ensure that the change which has been implemented is locked in to the operating systems of the company. The team serves as the source of the recommendations for the purpose of standardization.

If the recommended change can be applied elsewhere in the company in whole or in part, replication is needed. For example, even if our team was an eastern region team, its recommendations may apply to other regional offices. Because people are naturally reluctant to use someone else's idea, owing to the NIH syndrome, management support in achieving replication is necessary. Cooperation across organizational boundaries is essential to an effective QIP. If all units are following the QIP, however, cooperation is greatly facilitated because others will be able to quickly see the benefits of another team's work. After all, they are speaking the same language and using facts. It's difficult to dispute hard data.

Finally, the last step of part 4 of the problem-solving process calls for us to step back from the canvas of positive change to determine what we have learned, what else we can do with it, and where we go from here.

The team should review its work and determine whether any further advice related to the recommended changes should be made to others in the company. In most cases, lessons learned are communicated to the managers who planned the original faulty process. This feedback of lessons learned can be helpful when planning new processes, and it extends the team's improvement contribution beyond the original scope of the project. For example, the team may have discovered through its customer survey that most customers find that our forms have too little space for recording required information and would like to have a completed sample form included for their guidance as well. This information may lead to the redesign of a variety of forms, resulting in improved communication of vital information to the company and a higher level of customer satisfaction overall.

Where do we go from here is the last question to answer. More often than not, a team that has completed an improvement journey has discovered a number of other potential projects it may wish to address. Or the team may wish to go back to its Pareto chart and work on the next set of highest bars. Also, a restratification may reveal another issue for the team to address within the same project theme.

The QI contribution made by our fictional QI team is not unusual within a total quality process. Let's review what was accomplished.

The team cut the insurance application process time from 22 days to 10 days in its region. Its findings were implemented in other regions, making this a corporatewide improvement. Sales and customer satisfaction increased. Other company forms were revised on the basis of the team's recommendations; this led to further improvements in efficiency and customer satisfaction. Along the way, the team members honed their problem-solving skills and felt like company heroes, which they are, and top management became even more committed to the QIP.

This project probably took 6 to 8 months. It will probably save the company hundreds of thousands of dollars year after year, retain more customers, and attract new customers. It is not unusual! It can be routine. Quality improvement marches on!

Seven Statistical Process Control Tools

I promised to provide a list of SPC tools. Here it is:

1. Pareto chart
2. Cause-and-effect diagram (fishbone)
3. Stratification
4. Check sheet
5. Histogram
6. Scatter diagram
7. Graph and control chart

To many, the list may be intimidating but, as I've said before, the basic use of these tools is not terribly difficult. Please note that it is also not a complete list of all the tools and techniques a team may find helpful. We've already mentioned a few others, such as brainstorming and flowcharts. I have found that employees at all levels can learn to apply these tools, and when they do, their self-confidence soars.

There is no shortage of firms and consultants qualified to provide training in the use of SPC tools, so when you are ready, just give them a call. Computer-based training (CBT) is also available.

Encouraging Team Support

A well-trained QI team prepared to pursue a carefully selected QI project is an awesome force. However, it must be strongly supported by management or it will self-destruct. This I can guarantee, so we need to talk about team support. Support of teams by management should be considered an essential investment because it will provide returns far beyond the original expectations.

There are 10 kinds of support needed, and each merits equal attention. There can be no shortcutting this list, which includes training, team leaders, facilitators, diagnostic support, management visibility, celebration and recognition, cash, time, open kimono, and limited management interference.

1. *Training.* I can't stress this enough. Team members must be trained, trained, trained, and then retrained. Training cannot be just a few days in the classroom. Instead, it must be a continuous learning process. This is accomplished by bringing people back for refresher training or advanced training. Also, further training can be accomplished by the leader, facilitator, or a visiting trainer during selected team meetings.

2. *Team leaders.* A well-trained team leader possesses excellent communications skills and motivational abilities and is a vital element to success. Good leaders must be chosen.

3. *Facilitators.* Facilitators with advanced QI knowledge and above-average skills in communications, leadership, and group facilitation are a powerful resource for team leaders. They serve as the internal consultants. On the average, a good facilitator can support 12 to 16 teams, or fewer if the teams are new to the QIP.

4. *Diagnostic support.* The availability of one or two statistical "wizards" to help with the advanced application of SPC tools is important to success. Usually, these people have a "regular job" somewhere else in the company but are freed up when needed and can also help train people in the use of the SPC tools. Look for them in the finance, actuarial, engineering, and market research departments.

5. *Management visibility.* Managers must be aware of each team, know when and where they meet, the leader's name, the project being pursued, and so on. An occasional supportive visit to the team is greatly appreciated, and if a manager is called in by a team to help during a meeting, he or she should rush to the opportunity. Also, of course, managers should be regular members of QI teams; their membership is the ultimate expression of visible support.

6. *Celebration and recognition.* I must stress the need for positive reinforcement. Special thanks and recognition when a team completes a project, even if it falls short of expectations, is strongly recommended. Also, publication of the team's efforts in the house organ is important. We'll talk more about recognition in Chapter 13.

7. *Cash.* I don't mean cash for members; I mean cash for projects. We must realize that teams may need financial support to pursue their project and to implement it. If red tape ties them up, they'll back off. However, the facts developed by teams as they pursue the QIP should provide the justification needed for approving the investment.

8. *Time.* Teams need time weekly to pursue their projects. This can be a difficult issue for management, but it must be resolved. Teams also need time to complete their project; and we shouldn't expect re-

sults in three weeks. Many projects take several months. Support the teams, but don't look over their shoulders and stare at the calendar.

9. *Open kimono.* Please pay particularly close attention to the "open kimono" rule. Violating this rule will stifle teams as fast as anything. You'll find that as a QIP is being instituted, people will expose problems you never knew about. They'll do it with pride and enthusiasm. After all, this is what it's all about—exposing and fixing the problems that prevent customer delight and that add to the COPQ.

If managers react as they usually do, by exclaiming "How could we let this happen" and "Who's job was it to prevent this," your QIP will be out the door in a flash. People who identify the problems should be the heroes of the company, even if they had a hand in causing the problem or in never bringing it to someone's attention earlier. Management's response should be "Okay, good. Let's get on it. How can I help?" This attitude will help build a positive problem-solving culture and create a great deal of respect for management.

10. *Limited management interference.* Managers and others often make another serious mistake, but with the best of intentions. When they hear of a problem, they naturally propose their own solution right away. This tendency must be avoided, because the QIP calls for fact-based analysis on which to base permanent solutions. If a manager proposes a solution, a team will deliver it as its own by "backfilling." This entails fitting the manager's solution to the problem rather than following the proper fact-based process to discover the root cause. This doesn't mean management should withhold ideas, but that it should remember to offer them in a nondirective manner. Management's role is to challenge a team to find verifiable solutions.

We've covered ROI before, but it needs another mention. Your investment in teams will not be a modest one in terms of money and management time. The investment must be thought of as a long-term one and considered primarily not as a capital investment but as an investment in people. People applying their energy, knowledge, and QI problem-solving skills will deliver the payback.

Your first year with QI teams could make you question your judgment, but it will pay off handsomely over time, so stick with it and support it like crazy. Remember, over time, the average management-level team will deliver a $100,000 benefit at a cost of $20,000 for the investment, a 400 percent return.

This can all sound great, but because nothing in this life is guaranteed, you'll find that some teams will fail or give up. Don't get discouraged. Learn from your mistakes and persevere. Your customers deserve it, and you'll also be building the most positive corporate culture possible. The long-term payoff of a positive corporate culture will be a powerful, sustainable competitive advantage.

Transformation Checkpoints

1. Select a structured problem-solving process and stick to it with a religious zeal.
2. Consider this suggested problem-solving process.

   Part 1: *Highlighting the Issue or Problem*
   - Describe the nature of the issue.
   - Describe the present status using data.
   - Explain why the condition is unacceptable, relating the issue to customers' needs.
   - Write a preliminary problem statement.

   Part 2: *Analyzing the Problem*
   - Continue to stratify.
   - Identify principal root causes (not symptoms).
   - Verify the root causes.

   Part 3: *Solving the Problem*
   - Select countermeasures.
   - Complete a cost-benefit analysis.
   - Draft an implementation plan.

   Part 4: *Following Up*
   - Set a system to monitor results.
   - Standardize the new procedures.
   - Consider replication.
   - Review lessons learned.
   - Set future plans.
3. Support your QI teams to the hilt through:
   - Training
   - Team leaders
   - Facilitators
   - Diagnostic support
   - Management visibility
   - Celebration and recognition
   - Cash
   - Time
   - An open kimono
   - Little management interference
4. Stick with it. A significant payback in terms of delighted customers, lower costs, and a powerful, sustainable, competitive advantage will result.

7
Quality Planning

Quality improvement teams represent one of three elements of a sound QIP, as illustrated in Figure 4-2. Quality planning, to be discussed here, represents the second element, and in Chapter 8 we'll cover the third element—unit-level quality.

We've begun to see in the preceding chapters that a TQM process generates a lot of activity on the part of people at all levels in the company. All this activity must be focused and directed toward our ultimate goal of meeting customers' needs and achieving a sustainable competitive advantage. Without quality planning, our actions may range far and wide and result in wasted time and energy, followed by dismal results.

Quality planning provides the context within which our quality efforts take place and focuses corporate talent and actions on the key priorities.

Chapter 7 will describe three important parts of quality planning:

1. Quality business planning
2. Quality product and services planning
3. Quality process planning

What Is Quality Business Planning?

Companies that operate according to both a long-range and an annual business plan generally perform better than those that forgo the use of a formal corporate agenda. However, any plan-driven organization must be flexible enough to adjust its focus in the face of changing conditions. A sound business plan that is communicated to all levels of the company also defines what is important to the company and sets indicators or measurements (targets) that help to define and quantify successful performance.

A business plan that doesn't focus on quality, customers' needs, and the importance of continuous project-by-project improvement will not provide a foundation on which a TQM process can be built and from which it can contribute to corporate success. Instead, a TQM process will soon be viewed as an unimportant matter, something that has no legitimate place on the company's agenda. Therefore, the business plan must be constructed and utilized to underscore and enhance the quality efforts of your company. Total quality management must be connected to the corporate battery.

Strategic Planning and Business Planning

Strategic planning provides a broad and long-range view of the company's position and potential within the evolving competitive environment. Once this broad and long-range context is better understood, a company can more effectively determine what fundamental actions it is going to initiate on a year-to-year basis in order to compete successfully within its business sector. These fundamental, shorter-range actions are assembled as its annual business plan.

Essentially, long-range strategic planning involves an internally focused and externally focused assessment to answer some basic questions. Some questions to ask when focusing internally are:

1. What business are we really in?
2. What are our principal strengths and weaknesses for competing in this business, compared to what it takes to compete successfully?
3. What do we wish to become in the future?

The first question is not as easy to answer as it may first appear. We've all heard it said that the railroads should have defined their business as the transportation field rather than defining it as the railroad business. As a result, railroads were never adequately prepared to compete with air transport and trucking companies. Disney, on the other hand, decided that it is not in the amusement park business; it is in the total family entertainment field. The key to answering the question of what business you are in is to think broadly, to consider the viewpoint of customers, and to determine from where your future competitors may come. At Colonial Penn, we are not just in the insurance business; in my opinion, we are in the business of providing financial security, asset protection, and, as a result, peace of mind for our customers. Therefore, our competitors are not just other insurance organizations. We need to compete with banks and with brokerage firms. American Express has determined that other credit card companies do not represent its chief competition. Consumers' use of cash, however, does represent real competition.

Question 2 requires that we determine what it really takes to compete successfully in our business (the critical success factors), such as an effective product distribution system, a rapid and responsive product design process, or an exceptionally skilled work force, and so on, along with an assessment of how we measure up to these vital requirements. The result of this assessment reveals some capability gaps.

Question 3 calls for a company to set a vision—top management's potentially realizable dream for the organization. The vision should be a brief, motivating statement and should be determined after an assessment of external influences is conducted. Florida Power and Light Company's vision is "We want to become the best-managed electric utility in the United States, an excellent company overall, and to be recognized as such."

The external assessment should focus on the following key areas:

1. Consumer demographics and psychographics
2. The emerging economic environment
3. The global competitive business environment
4. The political and legislative environment
5. Advances in technology

After a thorough analysis of the information developed as a result of the internal and external assessments, we need to develop a series of assumptions on which plans and actions will be based. Assumptions may include statements such as: Foreign competition will intensify within 2 years. Government regulation will increase significantly next year. Consumers' demands for quality service are increasing dramatically, and technological advances will represent a unique opportunity to increase efficiency but at a sizable initial cost.

Now, based on our assessments and assumptions, we need to make the transition from strategic planning to business planning. The line between the two is and will remain a fuzzy one. In any event, we now need to determine:

1. How to exploit our strengths and either remedy or minimize our weaknesses.
2. What the critical success factors (CSFs) are for our business and how the capability gaps can be closed. Critical success factors are the few

(3 to 10) things we absolutely must be able to do extremely well in order for our business to survive and prosper.

3. What our key contingency plans will be if some of our basic assumptions are in error.
4. What our goals will be for the midterm (3- to 5-year time horizon), and what annual objectives will be set in order to progress toward our midterm goals.
5. How we will measure success. That is, what are the critical success indicators?
6. How we will fund our activities in order to pursue our plan.

Once we've addressed these six issues, we can draft a business plan that is aimed at achieving our vision, based on an understanding of the external environment, and that recognizes our inherent strengths and limitations.

Weaving Quality into the Planning Process

The previous section briefly described planning with hardly a mention of the word *quality*! So, how do we weave quality into the planning process to support TQM? More important, how can we use TQM to support the goals and objectives of our plan? This section will describe how we turn planning into quality planning for quality results.

Weaving quality into the planning process doesn't mean we reinvent the principles of planning, which we've just discussed. It does mean, however, that we build our plan, adjust our plan, and pursue our plan based on a thorough and continuously updated analysis of customers' needs. It must be clearly recognized, without compromise, that meeting customers' needs is the most important factor in the long-range pursuit of a competitive advantage. Therefore, the plan must contain liberal doses of customer-oriented objectives and measures.

Quality planning must also follow the Pareto principle we learned about in Chapter 5. In the context of quality planning, the Pareto principle advises that of all the objectives we may elect to pursue in our business, there are a "vital few" that will have a proportionally greater impact on our ability to achieve our vision. These vital few must be isolated from the trivial many in order to better focus resources, talent, and energy on the things that make the most difference.

By far, many corporate plans I've seen identify far too many objectives and supporting action plans, and, as a result, the plan itself contains hundreds of pages. No one can figure out what is really important, and no company can really do a good job of pursuing its plan if it contains volumes of objectives. The competition for resources to pursue the plan will, in itself, be a burden that no company can successfully bear. In the final analysis, resources will be squandered as the organization takes a shotgun approach to competitive advantage.

Instead, once a vision is set based on the internal and external analyses mentioned earlier, I recommend that a company define only four or five principal goal areas for the coming 3- to 5-year period. These principal goals should be broadly stated but not so broad as to be vague and meaningless. One principal goal in particular should be in every company's plan: the goal to significantly improve customers' perceptions of the company's products and services. Some other goals may be internal efficiency, vendor performance, employee satisfaction, new market development, and so on.

Once the vital few goals are identified, a company should select only three or four short-term objectives it wishes to emphasize over the next 1 to 2 years for each of its principal, longer-range goal areas. Therefore, if you select four midterm goal areas, you should end up with no more than 12 to 20 short-term objectives in your business plan. Also, once you have identified three or four short-term objectives for each midterm goal area, you need to set an indicator or two for each of these objectives. The indicators will be critical areas of performance you'll measure regularly in order to determine whether or not performance is up to par. (Figure 7-1 shows part of a quality plan.)

It is possible to develop a plan in the form illustrated in Figure 7-1 in fewer than 15 or 20 pages, even when you include your underlying assumptions and a summary of the internal and external assessments that support the assumptions.

Even when you've reached this point, quality planning is not finished. You should include in your plan an objective that aims at expanding and improving your TQM process. Some indicators to track for this objective were recommended in items 11 to 14 of Figure 4-4. The act of including TQM as a plan objective gives your quality process that legitimacy we talked of earlier. It connects it to the corporate battery. Also, as the plan year proceeds and various departments report their progress toward achieving plan goals, they will, at the same time, report on their progress toward utilizing TQM. This helps tie the quality activities to mainstream corporate business plans and activities so that TQM is not viewed as a separate and distinct emphasis.

Now that the plan has been constructed and it includes TQM as a key objective, it must be thoroughly and carefully discussed with everyone in the company because it is now time to execute the plan. First, key people in the company need to draft action steps to be pursued to sup-

Vision: The men and women of the XYZ Corporation are committed to achieving an undisputed national leadership position through the effective marketing of (*product*) backed by outstanding service to the customer before, during, and after the sale.

Critical Success Factors: (We must be extremely good at...)

1. Focusing marketing efforts on the desired customer segments
2. Rapidly fulfilling customers' orders
3. Serving customers through a courteous, knowledgeable, resourceful, and professional customer service staff
4. Processing invoices through a simple, accurate billing process
5. Maintaining a rapid and responsible market research and product development process

Goal 1: Improve customers' perceptions of our products and service.
- Objective 1.1. Reduce the number of customer complaints.
  - Indicator: Number of complaints per month
  - Indicator: Average time to resolve complaints
- Objective 1.2. Improve product and service satisfaction rating.
  - Indicator: Customer survey results
- Objective 1.3. Improve repeat sales and referral sales results.
  - Indicator: Number of customers with multiple XYZ products
  - Indicator: Number of customers referred to us by other customers

Goal 2...

Figure 7-1. The Quality Plan (in part).

port the objectives. For example, what actions should be taken to reduce the number of complaints (objective 1.1 in Figure 7-1).

At the same time, each unit in the company should be asked to review the plan and to determine specifically what it can undertake as a special project or unit-level objective that will directly contribute to achieving one or more of the plan's vital few objectives and to positively affecting the critical indicators. Many of these projects will then be pursued by the sponsoring department or a team utilizing its QIP and QI problem-solving knowledge. This method of deploying the plan within the organization directly ties TQM to the vital few objectives. It also mobilizes the entire company behind the focused plan and brings to bear a tremendous force for improvement. These supporting plan projects should get special attention from upper management throughout the year, and the successful delivery of results should be wildly celebrated.

Earlier we identified our critical success factors—the vital few things we must do well in order to succeed. Although objectives point more to what we should achieve, CSFs point more to how we must operate. Special projects should be aimed at CSFs as well as plan objectives. For example, one unit within the company may sponsor a project to reduce complaints with respect to product A (objective 1.1) in its region; another unit may sponsor a project to simplify the billing process (CSF 4).

As projects are proposed, management should play an active role in reviewing and endorsing the projects and making certain that there is a project or two or three that supports each of the 12 to 20 objectives and each of the 3 to 10 CSFs.

Now you've got a focused plan built on quality, aimed at your vision, and deployed throughout the entire TQM-focused organization! Your competitors better step aside to avoid being trampled in your rush to a competitive advantage. You've unleashed a powerful force that will propel you to the position of supplier of choice in the eyes of your customers. Figure 7-2 illustrates the proposed quality plan format. Florida Power and Light Company's policy deployment process is an excellent application of quality planning.

There is one additional planning activity that involves vendors. Analyze your completed plan to determine where your vendors play a particularly important role in helping to achieve your objectives. Then hold special meetings with them to establish their goals, objectives, and indicators to help guarantee successful performance relating to the goals set forth in your plan.

What Is Quality Product and Services Planning?

Now that we've seen how to establish a quality business plan—one that employs the Pareto principle to focus priorities on the vital few, one that deploys the plan throughout the organization and develops projects to be pursued by units and/or teams utilizing QI problem-solving techniques, and one that includes utilizing and expanding TQM as a key objective—we need to look to quality product and services planning.

Although quality business planning helps us to determine how to run and develop the business, it doesn't adequately address how we plan to develop specific products and services or to improve existing products so that they meet customers' needs and edge out the competition.

What really makes the difference to customers is the quality of the product or service they buy and the degree of excellence they perceive in how the company serves them before, during, and after the sale. These critical customer-company contact points most directly influence

I. **Our Business**: (The business we are really in)

II. **Key Assumptions**: (Underlying our plan)

III. **Data Supporting the Key Assumptions**: (Principal findings from the internal and external assessments that support the assumptions)

   A. Strengths and weaknesses
   B. Consumer demographics and psychographics
   C. Economic environment
   D. Competitive environment
   E. Political and legislative environment
   F. Technological environment

IV. **Vision**: (Top management's potentially realizable dream)

V. **Critical Success Factors**:
   A. CSF
      Project...Sponsoring Unit
   B. CSF
      Project...Sponsoring Unit
      .
      .
      .

VI. **Goal 1**
   Objective 1.1
      Indicator:
      Project...Sponsoring Unit
   Objective 1.2.
      Indicator:
      Project...Sponsoring Unit

   Goal 2
      .
      .
      .

VII. **Contingency Plans**:...

Figure 7-2. The Quality Plan Format.

customer perceptions and determine whether or not your company will emerge as the supplier of choice.

To develop a quality product or service takes a great deal of careful research, planning, testing, evaluating, and replanning. You can find the P.D.C.A. cycle at work again here. The quality product and services planning process is so important that Dr. Joseph M. Juran has written a marvelous book just on this subject alone. The title is *Juran on Planning for Quality*. The process that Dr. Juran describes is an excellent one, tested in 50 manufacturing and services organizations. Because my own discussion of quality product and services planning will be brief, I highly recommend that you consult Dr. Juran's book for a thorough description of planning for quality.

From my experience, most companies design products and services with far too little preliminary research. This is true whether we are referring to a manufactured product such as a stereo receiver or a service product such as an insurance contract. Most product developers may often be too anxious to get something on the shelf or in the catalog of services. However, without sound product planning, the new product is likely to sit untouched on the shelf.

Once a new product idea is conceived or an existing product is to be redesigned, research should begin by identifying who the targeted customers are. That is, who, in the final analysis, will use the product and who will determine whether it is a quality product. Also, unless your product goes directly from your site to the ultimate customer's hands, there are other interim customers along the critical path to the final consumer who must not be forgotten in the product-planning process. For example, you may develop an excellent electric golf cart that meets the needs of the golf enthusiast. However, if you fail to foresee and plan to meet a valid need of the cart rental staff at the course, your carts may never be recommended to the ultimate customer. Or, if your design makes it troublesome for a vendor down the line to install the batteries, the final production cost could exceed your expectation by, for example, $200 per unit!

Having identified the principal customers and any critical path customers, you need to thoroughly research their needs and to interpret those needs carefully enough to identify the principal features that must be built into the product. An auto insurance customer, for example, may voice a strong need for rapidly reporting his or her claim to the company. This may be interpreted to mean that the company providing the product should establish a 24-hour claims hotline with a toll-free 800 number.

Once you have identified the essential product or service features, you need to determine how you will measure the successful application of these features. For example, if your golf cart needs to have a useful range of 20 miles and a battery charge life of 5 to 7 hours, how will you test and measure for success? You should also compare your product's features to what the competition is offering. Superior features, if they don't price you out of the market, can be exploited in advertising. Inferior features, however, will send you back to the planning table.

When you are satisfied with your table of features, you then need to design the process for manufacturing the product or offering the service in the most efficient way possible in order to avoid problems, failure, cost overrun, and the like. Careful planning followed by product testing, evaluation, and modification is the quality path to follow. A noncompetitive or defective product that reaches the customer is much more costly to resolve than one that is honed to perfection before it leaves on its journey to your customer.

Figure 7-3 illustrates a very basic and simple product quality plan worksheet. This worksheet is provided to stimulate your own thinking. It is far too simple to be used as is. If you do enough reading on the TQM subject, you will find other forms, many quite thorough. One of the more thorough methods is called quality function deployment, which I'll briefly describe soon.

For the most part, I believe that each company should design its own process and worksheets to fit its own needs and circumstances.

To complete the form illustrated in Figure 7-3, you will first need to record the data at the top of the form. This calls for us to describe the product or service with which we are concerned and to describe the customer segment we are targeting, as shown in our customer needs research. Note that the form asks us to identify both the ultimate customer (buyer) and the principal critical-path customers defined earlier.

Once we have thoroughly researched and analyzed the needs of the principal customer groups, we can list the most critical needs in priority

Product Description: ____________ Date: ____________

Targeted Customers: ____________ By: ____________

Ultimate, Vital Few (U): ____________

Critical Path Customers (C): ____________

1	2	3	4	5	6	7	8	9
				Competitor Feature Comparison Rating (1–5)				
Principal Customer Needs	U	C	Required Features	Competitor	Competitor	Competitor	Competitor	Competitor
Plan Notes:								

Figure 7-3. Product Quality Plan.

order in column 1. By using a check mark in either column 2 or column 3, we identify whether the need listed in column 1 is attributable to an ultimate customer or to a critical-path customer.

Column 4 provides space to list your product or service features that must be built into the product or service in order to meet the corresponding customer need. Here you may wish to add a rating code signifying to what extent you feel the listed feature will meet the spoken need. For example, an *A* may signify that the feature is expected to fully and definitely meet the need. A *C* may indicate that the feature meets the need partly and indirectly.

Columns 5 to 9 provide space to record the extent to which a proposed product or service feature is also present in a competitor's product. A 1-to-5 rating scale is proposed. A rating of *5* indicates that the competing product feature does an outstanding job at meeting the corresponding customer need. A *3* indicates it does an average job, and a *1* indicates a poor job. You may wish to use a dual rating to see how your own feature compares to a competitor's by listing your own rating first. Therefore, a rating of 4/3 would indicate that your own feature should out perform that of the competitor.

Once this part of the worksheet (columns 5 to 9) is completed, it can be very useful to the people in the marketing and sales departments. The data begin to paint a picture showing how the proposed product stacks up against those of your chief competitors and which product features may be highlighted in advertising. On the other hand, the completed form may prove to your product planners that if they want this product to sell, they need to find a more effective way of meeting customers' needs! It is far better to discover product shortcomings in this paper-and-pencil planning exercise than to have the competitive market point out the deficiencies.

Another method for transforming customers' needs into the product and the product development or product improvement process was first developed in Japan about 18 years ago. This method is called *quality function deployment (QFD)*. Quality function deployment is just beginning to be utilized by some U.S. manufacturing firms, such as Ford Motor Company. However, QFD can be applied to developing services as well.

Quality function deployment is a somewhat complex and tedious process. However, it can be highly effective, and it is definitely customer-needs driven. Space does not permit a detailed description of QFD, but I will provide a brief review of the workings of this unique process.

The QFD process results in a sophisticated matrix diagram that resembles a house. Some refer to it as the house of quality (see Figure 7-4). The left side of the matrix displays expressed customers' needs de-

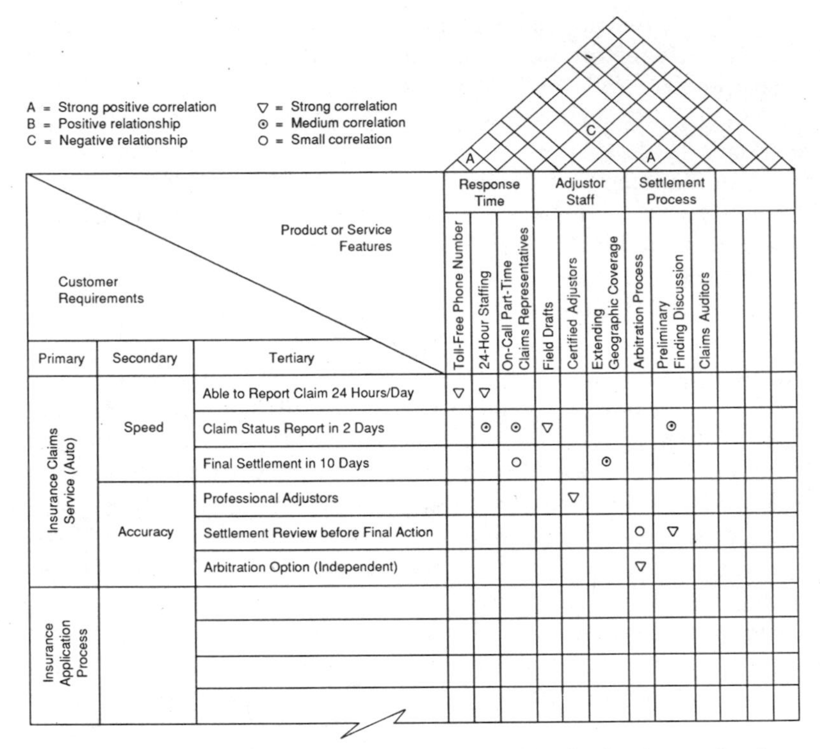

Figure 7-4. Quality Function Deployment's House of Quality (partly completed).

termined through consumer research in primary, secondary, and tertiary levels of specificity. The right side of the matrix shows the product or service features that correspond to customers' requirements. Symbols placed at the points where customers' needs intersect with product or service features judge the degree of correlation between these critical factors. The "roof" of the house points out the relationship that exists between two product or service features and indicates whether a positive or negative relationship exists. For example, the rigidity of a television cabinet has a strong relationship to the overall weight of the TV. So, what is more important to the customer? Should the TV be lightweight or unbreakable? Quality function deployment points out such key questions. When a QFD diagram has been completed by people in a variety of functions such as consumer research, product design, and sales, it provides information that can be translated by designers into a finished or improved product or service which closely corresponds to what the customer really wants. In addition, this detailed level of planning can avoid midproduction design changes that delay the introduction of a new product and increase the costs related to product design and development.

After your product or service has been well planned and produced, and it is ready to enter the competitive and unforgiving market, there is a final and very important step that must be taken. We need to unveil the new or redesigned product or service for the entire organization. Seemingly, to this point, only the product planners, engineers, market research staff, sales and marketing staff, and managers are familiar with it. However, when it reaches the customer, anyone in the company, particularly the customer service staff, telephone operators, and others, will play a vital and continuing product and service support role. These key people need to be intimately familiar with the product or service in order to support its introduction and sale. I recommend strongly that detailed information be communicated to these people and that you not wait until the last minute to accomplish this. If your support people know of the product's development during the planning process, they may be able to provide input or even to presell it for you as they talk with existing and prospective customers. Product planning should be a companywide event!

What Is Quality Process Planning?

We've discussed quality business planning and quality product or services planning. Now, we need to cover quality process planning in the macro sense.

At a micro level, QI teams will be working to improve the internal processes that provide services to external customers and internal customers, and they will investigate and resolve problems that prevent customer delight and high levels of efficiency and effectiveness.

However, at a macro level, management has to view its total corporate system through the customer's eyes rather than through only its own internally focused eyes. This customer view of the organization must dictate how we basically structure our company and design our processes so that any customer who enters our system or maze will not experience unnecessary detours, roadblocks, and a confusing or frustrating network of service paths.

For example, if my insurance company is so compartmentalized that I need to speak with four different units in order to transfer my auto coverage from my old vehicle to my shiny new pride and joy, I'll quickly become frustrated. If my bank makes me jump through several different hoops in order to process a loan application and then two days later

I get a call from yet another "officer" who needs additional information, I'm going to think of switching banks.

Far too many companies structure and organize themselves after considering only their internal view of what is corporately effective. Instead, we must put ourselves in the shoes and minds of our customers and design our overall service system to be customer-friendly.

To do this successfully requires careful thought and analysis as well as a strong commitment to making the changes needed.

One way to proceed is to first identify all the reasons why a customer may contact or visit your company. Then, with respect to each of these customer or potential customer motivators, we need to conduct research with customers to determine what they need and expect from each contact or visit. Once we have taken these steps, we can determine what changes are needed in order to meet the needs of customers when they enter our corporate world. We must realize that each and every time a customer has contact with us, a perception is formed in the customer's mind as to the quality of the service. This perception is shaped by both the employees who directly serve the customer and the path or process the customer must take to complete the transaction. Chapter 15 will cover more on the quality of our customer-contact people. Here, we are more concerned with the paths available to our customers.

Let's try a banking example to illustrate this vital point. Customers visit a bank for many reasons. Some of the more common ones are:

- To deposit or withdraw funds from a checking account
- To apply for a loan
- To order new checks
- To open a savings account

Customers have numerous questions or concerns in mind as they think about visiting the bank—questions or concerns that also translate to needs. Some of these are shown in Figure 7-5.

A careful examination of customer concerns and expectations relating to the purpose for a customer's visit will reveal some clear indications of what should be in place in order to meet customers' needs. Taking the appropriate action will help to ensure customer delight through customer-friendly systems.

I still vividly and fondly remember arriving at the Los Angeles International Airport on March 10, 1969, having just gotten off a flight from Danang, South Vietnam, after completing a tour of duty with the Marines. I was tired, a little confused at the bustling airport scene, and, as

Question or Concern	Need
1. Where do I park?	1.1 Free, convenient parking
2. Are the bank's hours compatible with my schedule?	2.1 Weekend/evening hours
3. Who do I see to complete my transaction: Teller, loan officer, new account manager?	3.1 Knowledgeable customer representative to guide me 3.2 Clear signs to direct me
4. Will I have to wait in line a long time?	4.1 Responsiveness/flexibility
5. What information will I need to bring to apply for a loan?	5.1 Clear, concise pamphlets and telephone service representative
6. Can my local branch meet all my needs?	6.1 Full-service branch banks
7. How long will it take to complete my business?	7.1 Rapid, responsive, hassle-free service

Figure 7-5. Questions and Concerns Translate to Need (for a bank).

you may imagine, terribly anxious to find a flight to Philadelphia to rejoin my wife. Within a minute of entering the main area of LAX, I was approached by a woman in a bright blazer who identified herself as a passenger service representative. She asked me very politely where I needed to go, consulted a master flight schedule she was carrying, and escorted me to the proper ticket counter. I was on a flight home within 90 minutes!

So, a thorough analysis of your corporate scene as viewed through the eyes of customers will reveal numerous opportunities for creating more customer-friendly systems and processes. However, don't complete this analysis entirely on your own. Involve customers in some way to help you. For the past 7 decades, Northwestern Mutual Life Insurance Company has, on an annual basis, invited a group of policyholders into the company to conduct an "audit" of its operations. The findings from this visit are taken very seriously and used to improve the operations of the company. Involve your customers too.

Finally, with regard to this element of quality process planning, we also need to take periodic trips through our own system to spot the little things. Many companies employ "mystery shoppers" for this task—people who are paid to act as customers and evaluate what they see.

Going back to our bank example, this kind of analysis may reveal the following:

1. The pens are chained to the table. Don't you trust the customer?
2. The trash can near the front door is always overflowing by 1:30 p.m. The physical environment makes an impression too!
3. Signs in the parking lot say "15-minute parking only." This is inadequate for someone applying for a loan.
4. The signs in the bank use too much jargon—words like *disbursement* or *loan origination*.
5. The manager's door is *always* shut.

The point is, sweat the small stuff too. It can make a difference.

As a Quick Review

To briefly review, quality business planning will tie your TQM process to the corporate plan and provide it with a legitimate role in running the business. The recommended planning process focuses the organization on the vital few goals and objectives essential for achieving the mission and provides indicators to measure success. It is developed based on a thorough understanding of customers' needs and mobilizes the entire company to contribute to achieving corporate objectives.

Quality product and services planning ensures that what we plan to sell is developed based on an analysis of customers' needs and an understanding of our competitors' strength in the particular product area.

Quality process planning ensures that we see the company through the eyes of our customers so that we will design and maintain processes and systems that are customer-friendly.

A good plan, well executed, is hard to beat. Products or services designed on the basis of customers' needs will be successful products, and customer-friendly processes will ensure a hassle-free experience for customers.

Transformation Checkpoints

1. Total quality management efforts must be supported by the corporate plan. In fact, quality planning is one critical element of TQM.
2. Strategic planning provides a broad and long-range view of the company's position and potential within the evolving competitive environment.

3. The business plan outlines shorter-range goals and objectives to be pursued in order for a company to realize its longer-range potential.
4. To plan strategically:

   Focus internally:
   - What business are we really in?
   - What are our principal strengths and weaknesses for competing in this business, and what does it take to compete successfully?
   - What do we wish (dream) to become in the future?

   Focus externally. Study:
   - Consumer demographics and psychographics
   - The emerging economic environment
   - The global competitive business environment
   - The political and legislative environment
   - The technological environment
5. Generate a series of assumptions based on your internal and external analyses. Base business plans and actions on your assumptions. Make contingency plans.
6. Establish a vision, critical success factors, four or five midterm goals, three or four short-term objectives for each midterm goal, and set measurement indicators.
7. Select customer-oriented goals and objectives.
8. Ensure that the utilization of your TQM process is listed as a corporate objective every year.
9. Thoroughly communicate the business plan and invite each unit to identify a project to pursue that is related to one or more of the plan objectives or critical success factors (CSFs).
10. Determine where vendors must support the plan.
11. Remember that quality product and services planning requires extensive customer research.
12. Identify the product's ultimate and critical-path customers. Research their needs carefully.
13. Identify product features based on customers' needs.
14. Determine how to measure the successful application of the product features.

15. Carefully plan how to efficiently and effectively develop the product or service.
16. Develop a product planning worksheet to display data on customer needs, corresponding product features, and competitor comparisons.
17. Unveil the new product or service internally before it is marketed.
18. Develop customer-friendly processes and systems.

8
Unit-Level Quality

One hundred percent participation is what turns quality management into TQM. Quality improvement teams, quality planning, customer satisfaction, and a continuous improvement attitude and set of actions come together for the entire organization in what I call *unit-level quality*—the third element of a TQM process.

In Chapters 5 and 6, we discussed QI teams, the guts or backbone of a TQM process. I pointed out that management-level QI teams, in particular, are needed in order to tackle the more substantive quality issues, and that management teams deliver a more significant improvement in terms of scope, magnitude, and dollar savings. Nonmanagement employees must be involved in QI teams as well. But teams come and go, so you rarely achieve 100 percent participation through the use of QI teams.

Quality planning was discussed in Chapter 7, and, as indicated, this element of TQM primarily involves upper management. So, we find that the QI teams and QI planning elements of TQM can really keep managers and some nonmanagers quite busy. The need for this heavy or extensive management participation is an undeniable quality fact of life. A company that fails to accept and act on this fact of life will not develop a workable TQM process and shouldn't waste its time trying—for two reasons. First, without management's day-to-day participation, significant improvements focused on the company's key goals simply will not materialize. Second, employees at lower levels will not participate effectively and continuously in quality improvement unless the total quality culture is anchored by management action. Sure, you may get a seemingly good start, but TQM will not be sustainable and will not be effective enough to achieve a competitive advantage if managers are not truly involved.

If management involvement is one quality fact of life, then 100 percent employee participation is another. We cannot afford to have spectators and bench sitters when it comes to quality. No one is exempt, and no one can be excused from playing in the competitive-advantage game. Unit-level quality is the way to get everyone else involved.

This chapter will describe unit-level quality. Specifically, we'll cover:

- The quality chain of events
- Unit-level quality and P.D.C.A.
- Unit-level quality: *Plan*
- Unit-level quality: *Do*
- Unit-level quality: *Check*
- Unit-level quality: *Act*
- The benefits of unit-level quality

(Plan, Do, Check, Act: P.D.C.A)

Defining the Quality Chain of Events

Whatever business you are in, be it banking, transportation, insurance, energy, health care, manufacturing, retail sales, or education just to name a few, a chain of events—transactions between departments and between people—exists within your organization. Make sure that this chain of events is a quality chain of events.

Every company is made up of an extensive number of individual departments and individual responsibility areas, the basic cells of the corporate organism. Each cell has a function to perform, and other cells are affected by how well a neighboring or adjacent cell does its work. In addition, vendor cells connect to the corporate organism at key points to support the overall mission of the company. The extent to which each internal or vendor cell supports others—meets their needs—determines the quality of the finished product or service offered to the ultimate, external customer. This network of events or employee work activities is the quality chain of events. Any cell, unit, or person that fumbles the ball on the critical handoff to another it must support ends up being a statistic in the COPQ. In the final analysis, the customer suffers, rates our quality as poor, and then either complains or, more likely, goes quietly to a competitor.

There are particularly critical points in the quality chain of events.

These critical points are found where, for example, an internal department hands off its work to the department or person that has direct contact with the customer.

A simple example of this quality chain of events concept is found in a restaurant. The cast consists of the diner (customer), the server, and the chef. See Figure 8-1.

The diner, of course, is the external customer, and the server and chef are internal customers and internal providers with respect to one another. That is, the server and the chef need to meet one another's needs if the external customer is to be satisfied.

Much can go wrong within this simple chain of events. For example, the server may deliver a poorly written meal order to the chef. The chef may then prepare the wrong meal. If the wrong meal is delivered to the customer, the customer is not satisfied. Even if the server notices that the prepared meal is not the one ordered by the customer prior to presenting it, the meal has to be discarded (waste) and prepared again (delay). The customer is still dissatisfied, and the COPQ rises.

In this case, the chef, an internal customer of the server, had a reasonable need and expectation for a legible meal order. The server had a reasonable need and expectation for a correctly prepared meal. But something went wrong, resulting in waste, delay, frustration, and an unhappy customer who may never return—a classic case of the COPQ.

In reality, even this simple example is a lot more complex than it appears. Add the busperson who hadn't cleared and set the table properly, the maitre d' who failed to greet the customer promptly and courteously or failed to provide a menu, a dishwasher who provided soiled silverware, a salad chef who used wilted lettuce, a poultry vendor who delivered spoiled chickens, and so on, and you have the makings of a culinary disaster as far as the diner is concerned. Each party in this quality chain of events needs to know who his or her internal customer is, what the needs of the customer are, and how those needs can be met each and every time.

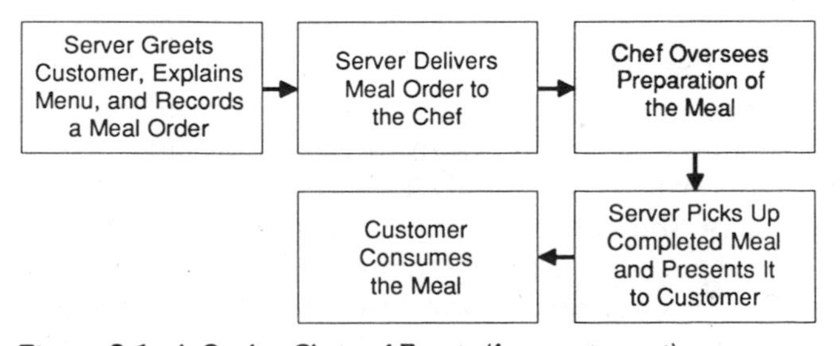

Figure 8-1. A Quality Chain of Events (for a restaurant).

However, each party in this chain must also look beyond his or her internal customers and be sensitive to the needs of the ultimate customer, in this case, the diner. That is, each party involved in this chain of events must understand the total service transaction and the role each plays in the complete service delivery process.

Now think about your own company and think about a total corporate flow diagram depicting each and every corporate activity and where it connects with the next activity. Picture this diagram with boxes drawn around each set of activities handled by a company department or by a vendor. You can now visualize the vital interrelationships that exist within your company—the quality chain of events. Now ask yourself these key questions:

- To what extent do these departments or units recognize the importance of their respective roles in supporting the units to which they are connected through the quality chain of events?
- Is there room for improvement?

Regardless of how you answered the first question, the answer to the second one is yes for the vast majority of companies. The fact of the matter is, in most organizations, units neither cooperate nor communicate effectively enough with each other. Instead there is much internal bickering, turf protecting, spotlight grabbing, and blinder wearing. A unit-level quality process can put an end to this!

So the quality chain of events concept introduces the subconcept of the internal customer. The late Dr. Kaoru Ishikawa introduced this "next process is your customer" (internal customer) concept in his famous book *What Is Total Quality Control? The Japanese Way*. He advises that each employee and each unit within a company must consider the people and units that they support as customers. We need to identify our internal customers and recognize their needs. We also need to monitor our performance in order to ensure a quality chain of events. An *internal customer* is defined as any unit or person within a company that receives work, in any stage of completion, from another unit or person within the same corporation or from a vendor. The unit or person supplying the work is the internal provider, and, in most cases, people wear both hats—internal customer as well as internal provider. Consider our restaurant example. The chef is an internal customer of the server and needs a legible meal order. The chef is also an internal provider to the server because the chef must meet the server's need for a correct meal properly prepared in a timely manner.

In my former company (insurance), the word processing department is an internal provider for the customer service unit. Word processing prepares typewritten letters for external customers from dictated material produced by customer service representatives. The word processors, conversely, are internal customers of the customer service unit because the word processors need clearly dictated tapes rather than garbled tapes from the customer service representatives in order to prepare the letters correctly and quickly. We surely found that communications between these vital units needed some improvement, and they quickly rose to the challenge.

The internal customer concept is extremely important; however, I offer this caution in applying it. An internal customer focus may be too short-ranged or narrow in its application if people fail to look beyond their internal customers and if they fail to remember that the ultimate customer is the external customer. Said another way, the external customer is the reason why we are focusing internally at all! An internal customer focus is fine, but we don't want to find ourselves falling all over our fellow employees while the paying customers wait for the dust to settle before their needs are met. In addition, blind obedience to the initially expressed needs of your internal customer may not be advisable or efficient for the organization. There must be a two-way dialog between internal customers and providers as well as some effective negotiation in order to reach a mutually agreeable, reasonable, and fundamentally efficient set of needs that are ultimately based upon a clear view of the needs of the external customer. An internal customer focus can easily breed inefficiency and off-target results unless it is managed wisely.

Unit-Level Quality and P.D.C.A.

A properly managed internal customer-focused attitude is helpful and, in fact, extremely important. Fine, so what do we do to achieve it? As pointed out earlier, we change attitudes by getting people to do things differently. To accomplish this, we need a prescribed process or road map—a unit-level quality process—backed by training.

The concepts of the quality chain of events and the internal customer are put into practice in unit-level quality. Also, as mentioned, QI teams, quality planning, customer satisfaction, and a continuous improvement attitude and set of actions all come together in this process as well.

In Chapter 4 we discussed the simple QI concept of plan, do, check, and act, or P.D.C.A. (see Figure 4-3). The process for unit-level quality is built around this Deming wheel as described in the following sections. To preview the unit-level quality process, please review Figure 8-2. As you do, consider this process (or something similar) as the one you want each basic corporate unit to follow continuously. Consider this the way you want each department to manage itself. This process also fits, I believe, what Dr. Joseph M. Juran calls the *concept of self-control,*[1] which advises us to:

1. Provide people with the means of knowing what their quality goals are
2. Provide the means to know how well we are meeting our quality goals
3. Provide the means for adjusting our work process—improving our results—in order to meet our quality goals

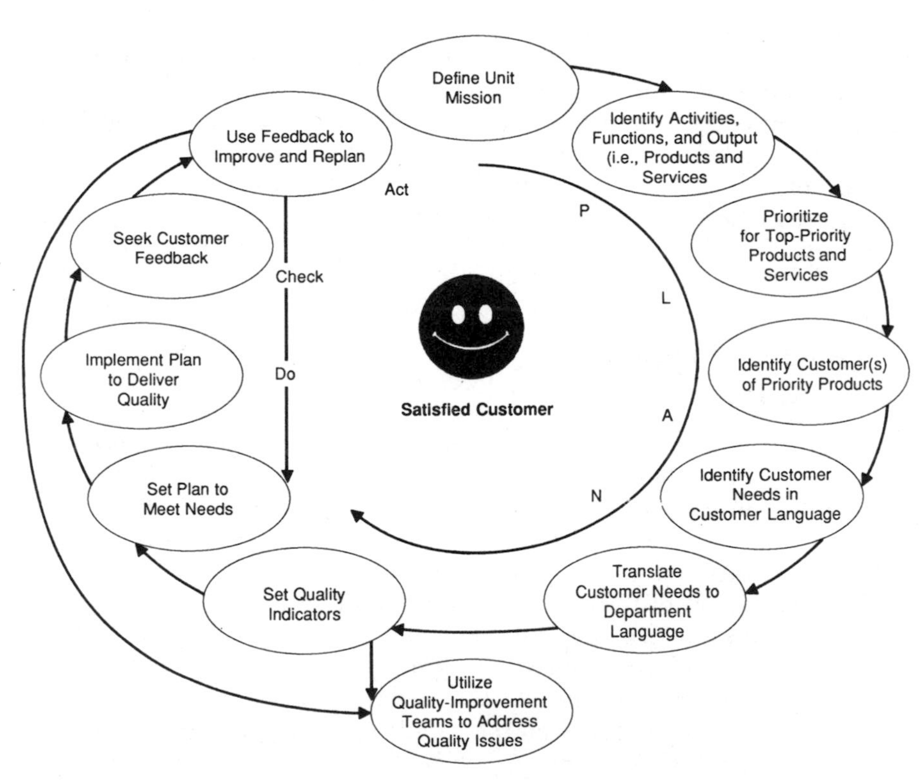

Figure 8-2. Unit-Level Quality P.D.C.A. at the Unit Level.

In addition, consider this process as quality business planning and execution at the unit level. It consists of 11 important steps plus an improvement step (bottom oval of the process model).

Most important, this process is intended to be carried out by all the employees of a unit working together with their supervisor and with the support of, and some participation from, higher-level management. It is not just a supervisory exercise, the result of which is handed down to the employees. Instead, it recognizes the fact that the people actually doing the work are the best ones to influence the outcome and achieve quality in their own units. It may not be easy, but find a way to meaningfully involve all employees of the unit.

Plan: P. D. C. A.

Eight of the 11 process steps in the unit-level quality model make up the *plan* portion of the P.D.C.A. The eight steps are as follows.

1. *Define the unit's mission.* Step 1 is rather simple. It warms the unit to the more difficult steps ahead. The unit needs to write a mission statement. The mission statement simply answers the question: Why does our unit exist? The statement should be brief, no longer than about 25 to 30 words, and it should focus on the basic, essential reason for the unit's existence.

   To revisit our word processing department discussed earlier, its mission might be:

   > To produce accurate and presentable typewritten letters for customers on a timely basis.

   By confining the mission statement to the essential purpose for the unit's existence, we begin to focus on the vital few (the Pareto approach) rather than the trivial many. Too often, units spend far too much time sweating the small stuff at the expense of the major emphasis areas. The small stuff matters too, but there is a proper balance to be struck.

   Many units frame and post their mission statement in their department with pride. This is a great idea.
2. *Identify unit output.* In this step, the employees of the unit brainstorm and list all activities that are performed. For many, the list will be surprisingly long and should cause people to begin to question whether or not they really need to be worrying about all items.

   With the list of activities displayed in front of them, they begin to identify those activities that are considered to be the vital few—that is, the activities which relate most closely to achieving the unit's defined mission. Then, the vital few items are examined to define the principal outputs which result from the vital few activities. Output refers to the products or services produced.

3. *Prioritize products and services.* The products or services produced are then prioritized vis-à-vis the unit mission.

   The outcome of step 3 is a prioritized list of the principal products or services, produced by the unit, that closely relate to the unit's mission. Some may be partly completed products or services that are only fully completed by a unit further down the chain of events.

   It is also useful at this point to diagram the internal work flow for the vital few activities and principal products and services. This flow diagram is helpful in step 4.

4. *Identify customers of priority products.* With the unit's principal products and services identified and prioritized, and with the help of a flow diagram, it is rather simple to list all the customers (internal or external) who next receive the product or service in question. In many cases, the customers of a unit's products or services will be internal customers. However, the list of possible types of customers may include the following:

   a. Internal customers (within the same company)
   b. External customers—ultimate, paying customers
   c. External customers—company vendors
   d. External customers—government agencies and regulatory bodies

   For example, in items *c* and *d*, a unit may produce purchase orders for parts or materials that are sent to a vendor. Or, a unit may produce reports sent to government agencies.

   The result of step 4 is a list of the unit's prioritized products and services and, for each, a list of the recipients by type of customer (that is, internal, external vendor, and so on).

5. *Identify customers' needs in customers' language.* The definition of *quality* is meeting customers' needs. At this point, we have agreed as a unit on our principal products or services, we have prioritized them based on our mission statement, and we've identified the customers. Now, obviously, we need to do some research on what our customers need with respect to the product or service in question.

   We must now decide how we will go about investigating the needs of our principal customers. There are a few basic methods to use, and some training should be provided in each. Some methods are:

   a. Customer interviews
   b. Customer focus groups
   c. Surveys and questionnaires

   Selecting just one method may not be a suitable strategy. Depending on the complexity of the situation, a variety of methods may be appropriate. For example, if the customer base is extensive, a unit may wish to conduct a written survey that reveals what its customers think, followed by focus group research or selected interviews to determine why customers feel the way they do.

In most cases, however, customers are going to be the gang of fellow employees in the next unit. In this instance, valid sample interviewing or a short questionnaire will do just fine. This customer-needs research is an important step and should be taken seriously, whichever method is selected. In your own company, assistance or advice from your market research staff may need to be provided. In reality, of course, the typical unit is not trained in sophisticated customer research techniques and cannot be expected to produce a result that would be the envy of the pros. You'll find, however, that the members of a unit will discover some very useful information upon which they can act. You'll also find that this research marks the beginning of a new and more positive relationship between units, which must support each other on a day-to-day basis.

If a unit deals directly with paying external customers, the unit probably shouldn't single-handedly contact the customers without first reviewing its intention with senior management. Any contact with external customers must be well coordinated, not haphazard. Also, research findings may already exist within the company from recent surveys and the like.

6. *Translate customers' needs to department language.* Step 6 is somewhat subtle but, nonetheless, important. Most units operate using their own jargon as well as with their own view of what is important. In order for a unit to act properly on the researched customers' needs, the members must be able to interpret or translate these customer needs into language the people in the provider unit can understand and act upon—quality product and services planning at the unit level.

   Once a unit has collected data on the needs of its customers, this key question should be asked: If our customers say that they need this, how can we go about providing it? The answers to this question begin to form rudimentary action plan ideas for the provider unit to consider in order to do a better job at meeting customers' needs.

   For example, if customers say they really need 100 percent accuracy on certain types of transactions, the provider unit may need to think about assigning a unit "specialist" to oversee these types of critical transactions.

7. *Set quality indicators.* Now that the unit has researched customer needs with respect to their principal products or services, a set of measures need to be established. These measures—quality indica-

tors—will help the unit to continuously monitor how well the needs of customers are being met.

A quality indicator is simply a statement of what will be measured. Indicators should be specific. Some examples of quality indicators are:

a. The number of items delivered to the customer with errors or defects per week
b. The number of items delivered to the customer after the fourth of the month
c. The number of complaints received from the customer per month
d. The number of days required to fix errors and defects

You'll notice that the quality indicator examples provided include a reference to numbers rather than percentages. This is no coincidence. *Percentages are false satisfiers*! They create a false sense of security—a false sense of quality. Almost any unit with reasonably alert people can do things right 90 percent of the time. We all learned in school that a grade of 90 is pretty good. I know when my sons tell me they received a grade of 90 on a math quiz I ask some follow-up questions like: How many questions were on the quiz? How many did you get wrong? Do you know why you got wrong answers? Do you know how to do those problems correctly the next time?

In business and within a TQM process, seemingly acceptable percentages tend to provide a false sense of security. They don't stimulate action to improve. For example, if my unit needs to produce 2500 items per month and my indicator shows that 92 percent were free of errors, I may pat myself on the back and leave for the golf course. After all, I earned a grade of *A*. But wait! Although I got an *A* this month, 200 items were delivered with errors! Now, I'm not so happy. Within the context of a TQM process and with my quality training, I should, for example, set a goal to cut the number of errors in half within 2 months and to reduce them to no more than 25 within 6 months. I'd form a QI team to investigate the causes of the errors and to suggest actions to improve.

The grade of *A* was satisfying. The thought of 200 errors in one month or 200 dissatisfied customers was terrifying! Which view of the situation stimulated positive QI action? Stay away from percentages! It is acceptable to use them only when you combine a percentage with an action-stimulating number; for example: Quality rate = 92% (200 errors).

Step 7, then, is to set quality indicators that call for numbers, not just percentages. A half dozen primary indicators for a unit may be about right, depending on the circumstances. Too many may cause a lack of focus. Find the vital few that help to track performance for the priority products and services and that are tied to the principal customer needs revealed in your research.

Construct indicator charts and post them visibly within the unit so that all can see the score on a day-to-day basis.

The type of indicators we've just discussed are most useful in determining how a unit is doing at meeting the needs of its customers. It is also useful to revisit the internal flow diagram that was constructed earlier and to set in process indicators that measure the effectiveness and efficiency of key intra-unit transactions. That is, how well are two sections within the same unit doing at meeting each other's needs?

8. *Set a plan to meet customers' needs.* Step 8 will complete the *plan* part of the P.D.C.A. cycle within the unit-level quality process.

   Having defined our mission, identified and prioritized our output, products, and services, identified our customers, researched and translated their needs, and set up our score card with number-oriented quality indicators, we need to assemble all this work into a unit plan. A sample format is found in Figure 8-3.

   The plan should be brief, customer-centered, and action-oriented. It should outline key actions the unit expects to take based

I. Unit Mission ______________________ Unit: ______________________

Date: ______________________

II. Key Products and Services	Customers	Key Customer Needs	Quality Indicators
A.			
B.			

III. Improvment Actions Planned	Relationship to Corporate Plan	Person Responsible	Resources Required	Completion Date
A. B. C. D.				

IV. Special Corporate QI Project	Supporting Goal or CSF	Team Members	Completion Date

V. Signatures: ______________________

Figure 8-3. Unit-Level Quality Plan.

on its unit-level quality planning work to date, and it should include goals for the indicators we've set, for example, fewer than five errors per month on item *A*. In addition, remember what was covered in Chapter 7, "Quality Planning." The unit-level plan should also be aimed to support the key corporate goals, and, if our unit has selected a special QI project to support a corporate objective or critical success factor, this QI project should be listed in our unit plan.

Everyone in the unit should sign the plan, and it should be updated as circumstances warrant, but no less frequently than once a year.

Do: P. [D.] C. A.

9. *Implement the plan.* Now that we've *planned*, it is time to *do* while we also prepare to *check* and *act*. *Do* simply means putting our knowledge and our plan into action. We now settle down to run the unit with close attention to our principal products and services and to the expressed needs of the customers of these products and services.

Check: P. D. [C.] A.

10. *Check the results.* As the unit goes about its daily work, it needs to continuously *check* on how it's doing. We accomplish this checking in two ways. First, we monitor our quality indicators. The indicators will show us where we are falling short of meeting the needs of our customers, at least in the areas monitored by our indicators. Second, we should frequently check back with our customers and simply ask them: How are we doing?

    These two methods of checking will reveal what is not conforming to the plan. In addition, this checking keeps us in touch with our customers so that we can continue to build a positive relationship with them and quickly learn of any changing circumstances which may suggest that our plan needs to be modified.

Act: P. D. C. [A.]

11. *Use feedback to improve and replan.* Monitoring our indicators and talking with our customers provide feedback on how we are

doing at meeting our quality goals. We must *act* on this feedback to modify our plan and our actions to meet our customers' needs.

We may discover two kinds of problems from time to time. We'll find the simple, sporadic problems that the unit can pounce on quickly and fix. But, we may also find the more deep-rooted, complex, chronic problems that will require assigning a QI team to investigate. Hence, the oval at the bottom of Figure 8-2.

Whatever we find, it is up to the unit to act on the feedback it receives in order to continuously improve. This is the essence of TQM.

The Benefits of Unit-Level Quality

The benefits of unit-level quality are significant in terms of quality, employee growth and development, and organizational effectiveness.

Organizational Effectiveness

Organizations are effective when everyone is pulling together, speaking the same language, pursuing meaningful goals that relate to expressed customers' needs, and doing all this with a strong sense of teamwork, cooperation, and pride. Unit-level quality provides a consistent process for planning, doing, checking, and acting—P.D.C.A.—to improve results. Results are targeted to researched customer needs, and results are measured objectively.

Once unit-level quality is in place on a companywide basis, managers at all organizational levels should be asking a standard set of 10 questions whenever they visit a unit to monitor performance. The standard 10 questions are these:

1. What is the mission of this unit?
2. What are the principal products or services this unit provides?
3. Who are the customers of these principal products or services?
4. What are the needs of these customers?
5. How were their needs determined?
6. What indicators do you track that will tell you how well you are doing at meeting the needs of your customers?
7. How does the work you do benefit the ultimate, external customer?
8. How well are you actually doing at meeting the needs of your cus-

tomers? That is, what do your indicators reveal about performance, and what are your customers saying about your performance?

9. What have you done or what are you doing to improve?
10. What can I do to help and support your improvement efforts?

Finally, my good friend Ferdie Setaro, managing director of TLE Consultants of Haddonfield, New Jersey, correctly observes that "the ultimate quality teams are the in-place units of the organization." Unit-level quality represents the way to structure the day-to-day activities of these ultimate quality teams so that they can focus on meeting customers' needs the first time and every time.

Quality

Meeting customers' needs is the definition of *quality*, and with unit-level quality we find each basic unit of the company defining its principal customers' needs, measuring its own performance in relation to those expressed needs, and acting to improve its performance both through quick, decisive action and through more sophisticated QI team techniques. We find units charting their own destiny and following their own prescribed path to excellent, focused results.

Employee Growth and Development

Employees expect and deserve the opportunity for meaningful involvement in meeting the goals of the company and the opportunity to grow professionally and to develop themselves as increasingly competent contributors. Unit-level quality lets each person in the company take a role in managing his or her part of the business instead of simply doing a specific set of assigned tasks each day. People will learn to develop planning skills, research skills, performance measurement skills, communications skills, and problem-solving skills.

As employees apply their new knowledge and the skills that result from unit-level quality, they develop a strong sense of ownership for unit results and corporate results. They feel more valued by management and more important to the business. You'll find that employees who previously were marginally satisfied "switch throwers" develop into dedicated thinkers—real businesspeople. What more can we ask?

Transformation Checkpoints

1. One hundred percent employee participation in TQM is essential. Unit-level quality is a way to involve everyone.

2. A quality chain of events exists in all organizations. If the ball is fumbled during any handoff from one link of the chain to another, quality suffers—customer satisfaction suffers.
3. An internal customer is any person or unit within a company that receives work, in any stage of completion, from another unit or person within the same company (internal provider) or from a vendor.
4. Most of us wear the hat of both an internal provider and an internal customer.
5. It is important to look beyond the internal customer all the way along the chain of quality events to the ultimate, external customer.
6. Unit-level quality is designed around the P.D.C.A. cycle: *plan, do, check, act.*
7. Unit-level quality is an 11-step process for a unit to follow—all employees working with their supervisor—as shown in Figure 8-4.

Plan	Do	Check	Act
1. Set mission 2. Identify products 3. Prioritize 4. Identify customers 5. Determine needs 6. Translate 7. Set indicators 8. Set unit plan	9. Implement plan	10. Monitor indicators and check with customers	11. Act to improve

Figure 8-4. The Eleven Steps to Unit-Level Quality.

8. Benefits of unit-level quality include
   a. Quality achievement
   b. Employee growth and development
   c. Organizational effectiveness:
      - Ask the 10 standard questions.
      - Recognize that in-place units are the ultimate quality teams.

References

1. *Quality Improvement for Services Training Manual,* Third Printing, Juran Institute, Inc., Wilton, Conn., August 1986, p. 7-1.

9
A Transformation to TQM and the Critical Success Factors

We have covered a great deal of material in the preceding eight chapters. We've discussed what quality really is, we've set the stage for implementing a TQM system, we've determined an implementation strategy, we've familiarized ourselves with a total quality model, and we've discussed three critical elements of a TQM process: teams, quality planning, and unit-level quality.

Before continuing our QI journey, it may be helpful to pause and take a side trip to a fictitious company both before and after it has successfully installed a TQM process.

Later in this chapter we'll focus on the vital few CSFs for developing and nurturing an effective quality process. These CSFs are:

1. The commitment and involvement of top management
2. A supportive corporate culture
3. Training
4. Customer communications

Our quality tour, or side trip, will take us to a totally fictitious catalog sales organization. I have chosen this type of organization for our example because I think we can all relate to the catalog sales experience and because catalog sales involves hundreds or thousands of transactions between the company and its customers each week. For simplicity, we'll assume a cloak of invisibility while on the side trip.

Before TQM

Our tour begins in the president's office in a lavishly decorated corner of a large, single-story building. The president is there alone talking on the telephone. We can quickly determine that he is talking with one of the company's major vendors as we overhear him saying, "Look, Don, this is the third year in a row that you've sent us large quantities of defective merchandise. We try to sell the stuff, but an awful lot of it is returned. I hope you can do better next year." While the president is talking, he is also leafing through a large notebook labeled *Annual Plan*. The book looks as though it contains over 400 pages of material. A single chart hangs on the wall to the left of the president's desk. The chart depicts trend lines for sales and costs over the past 3 years. The sales line is sloping downward at what appears to be a 30 degree angle while the cost line is climbing. Within 6 months it appears as though the lines will intersect.

We leave the president's office as he is arranging a golf date for the following afternoon with his vendor. As we walk toward the main part of the building, we notice the entrance to a room which, according to a hastily repainted sign, was formerly a training room. Apparently, the department next door—customer complaints, adjustments, and refunds—needed expansion space. This department now occupies the training room, and what little training is still conducted occurs in the cafeteria. We try to listen in to determine what is happening, but the sounds of ringing phones and raised voices make this impossible.

Further down the hall we enter the main part of the building, which is occupied by the telephone order processing unit and is adjacent to the merchandise warehouse. Two employees on a coffee break are chatting in an animated fashion, so we stop to listen.

One employee, obviously a veteran, is offering some advice to a recently hired person. The veteran is saying, "...so the most important thing to remember is, that if we are out of the item the customer wants, try to get the customer to accept a substitute that's in stock. With our systems, there is no way you can provide an accurate prediction of when their first-choice item will be available. But always adhere to our standard of getting the customer off the phone in 3 minutes because bonuses are partly based on how many calls you handle. There's no way anyone will ever know how many sales you yourself actually make or how happy the customers are that you speak to."

We continue on to the order form processing unit and pause to observe an employee working at her desk. She has a modest stack of order forms in front of her, a rack of rubber stamps, and a large ink pad. While we watch, she grabs one of the stamps, pounds it on the ink pad, and slams it onto the order form in a machinelike fashion. The slightly smeared message advises the customer:

Your order is incomplete. Please reorder specifying the size you desire.

She then remarks to a fellow employee, "I wish I could just call this person on the phone. I hate to make the customer submit a corrected order when I could straighten this out in two minutes with a simple phone call." Her friend responds, "Why don't you suggest that to the supervisor?" The order processor replies, "I'm still waiting to get a response to the six ideas I offered two months ago."

As we continue our tour, we find ourselves in the order picking, packaging, and shipping department. One order picker is standing near the stacks with a fistfull of order tickets and complaining to a friend that "I told them two days ago that we were out of the large-size burgundy sweaters. What do I do with all these orders for that item?" "I don't know," replies the friend. "It's not our problem. Just send them back to the order processing unit. Let them worry about it."

We continue to wind our way through the building. Soon we come across a conference room with a sign warning that there is a meeting in progress. So, in we go. The meeting consists of the marketing director and her staff. Marketing is deciding how to improve the catalog. Specifically, they are engaged in a heated discussion on how to improve that part of the catalog containing the "How to Place Your Order Instructions" so that customers can properly order merchandise. There is no one in the meeting from the order processing unit or from the customer complaints, adjustments, and refunds staff. Brenda, a marketing assistant, inquires, "Shouldn't we ask others in the office what they've found to be ineffective with the instructions and forms we currently use?" "No," replies the director, "it's our job to produce the catalog. I don't need advice from a bunch of clerks to do that."

Our time is about up. We can make only one more stop. We decide to search for the customer relations director and eventually locate her office a few doors from the president's. No one is in the office, but we overhear her secretary advising a caller that Ms. Dematos has left for a luncheon meeting with a QI consultant.

So, feeling somewhat depressed at what we've seen, we drive off to await a more enlightening future visit.

Witnessing a TQM Transformation

We return to the catalog sales company after 2 years. We decide to retrace the path we took before, so we head for the president's office. He isn't in his office when we arrive, and his secretary's desk is vacant as well.

We step into the president's office and immediately notice some significant changes. The old sales and cost trends chart is still there but the sales line, which 2 years ago was heading in a southeasterly direction, began climbing toward the northeast about 14 months ago. Somewhat more recently, the cost line leveled out and is now trending down at an increasingly rapid rate.

In addition to this chart, however, several others occupy wall space in the president's office. There is a chart that tracks the number of employees and managers who are trained in and involved with the company's seemingly new quality process. Another chart measures the number of customer complaints, product returns, and average order processing time. Still another chart monitors the quality performance of each vendor. Finally, a chart resting on an easel compares the president's company to six competitors, and a chart resting against a wall in a state of partial completion will apparently measure the total number of customers and the number of customers who are repeat buyers.

Sitting on the president's desk are three framed documents. One is a certificate showing that the president has successfully completed the company's QI training program. Another displays the company's vision statement and quality policy; the third is a listing of customers' needs and expectations that apparently was derived from the well-worn customer research study lying on a side table.

We notice the company's annual plan right in the middle of the president's desk. It now contains about 25 pages, compared to the 400 pages we saw earlier, and is titled "Plan for Customer Satisfaction and Competitive Advantage." We can begin to tell just from this stop on our trip that the company has begun a significant transformation from its old ways to a strong, new environment centered on customers' needs and employee involvement. Is this company under new management?

As we walk down the hall, we notice that the training room is back in business. It is brightly decorated and larger than it was 2 years ago, having taken some space from the neighboring customer complaint unit, which is now called the customer services team. Stepping into the training room, we find the president awarding graduation certificates to 15 employees who have just completed the company's quality training program. The president's secretary is one of the proud graduates and is seated next to the vice president of marketing.

As we leave the training room, we observe that it is well situated within the building because the unit next door, the customer services team, is an unusually quiet spot—few ringing phones and no raised, impatient-sounding voices.

Upon entering the main part of the building, we are immediately struck by how different it looks. It has been completely reorganized into small work teams. Apparently, each team now specializes in a geographic section of the country and consists of telephone order representatives, order form representatives, stock specialists, and word processors. Overhearing a few conversations, we soon learn that work teams are rewarded principally on the basis of growth in their customer base and on customer satisfaction. Each team has a set of charts for its respective region, similar to those we saw in the president's office. Obviously, these people are all speaking the same language. They are all shooting at the same targets, and the targets themselves are customer-oriented.

Continuing our tour, we soon find that the marketing department now plays a supporting role to the work teams, as do other staff and professional units. It appears that people who deal directly with the customers are the center of attention. In addition, the marketing department apparently added a new unit called customer research. Members of this unit are drawn from the customer-contact forces on a job-rotation basis and conduct special surveys of customer needs and satisfaction. However, the work teams also seek customer feedback on a day-by-day basis through the use of simple postcard questionnaires and telephone surveys.

As we continue the tour, it becomes obvious how all these positive changes developed. We notice the addition of several small conference rooms and find that they are perpetually occupied by employees from *all* levels who are identifying improvement opportunities and putting their quality training to work—to resolve problems and implement their solutions. The conference rooms are also used by all units to set their own plans based on the needs expressed by customers and the needs expressed by other areas within the company that they support.

Finally, as we leave, we notice a construction crew preparing to add a wing to the building to accommodate the real and anticipated growth. This company is on the move! This company is gaining a competitive advantage, and everyone from the president to the newest employee is directly and actively involved. The same people who were here 2 years ago are still here today. But this company *is* under new management!

The type of transformation we've just witnessed is what quality improvement is all about. It is about training, as well as involving and empowering, every person in the company to constantly question the status quo, to identify problems and improvement opportunities, and to tackle them enthusiastically in a spirit of teamwork. It is about putting customer delight above all else because delighted customers are absolutely essential to sales and profits. You can unleash this force for a positive quality transformation within your own company if you are willing to take the total quality journey. As you do, pay close attention to the critical success factors.

The Critical Success Factors for TQM

The chapter on quality planning introduced the concept of CSFs and explained that CSFs are the vital few things that must be done extremely well in order for a company to achieve its goals. We saw how helpful CSFs are in the business planning process. However, the CSF concept can also be applied to the development of a new corporate program or process such as TQM. In this case, CSFs represent the vital few things that absolutely must be present and must be effective for the new process—in this case, a TQM process—to succeed.

CSF 1: Top Management Involvement

I have touched on the need for the involvement of top management before, and I'll reemphasize it here because the single CSF that is clearly most critical to effective quality management is the involvement of top management.

My observations confirm that there has never been a successful TQM effort without active participation and support from top management. Therefore, I conclude that there can never be a successful TQM process without this vital ingredient.

Top management's commitment alone, no matter how enthusiastic, is not enough to sustain a TQM process for very long. Direct and active participation, which clearly demonstrates that commitment, is the essential factor.

Why is top management's involvement so critical, and how can we go about securing it?

It is a corporate fact of life that management's behavior shapes the corporate attitude and defines what is important to the success and survival of the company. It is not what management *says*; rather, it is what management *does* that is most influential on the company and its people. Organizations that are highly successful over a period of many years boast a top management team which "walks like it talks." Words are important, but they must be backed by top-level action in order to create and stimulate the desired corporatewide response.

The degree to which a corporate policy or process is sustained is directly related to the degree of management's involvement with the policy or process at all stages of its enactment. Management may say, for example, that training is important, and it may demonstrate a conviction that training is important by increasing the number of training programs offered by the company. This outlay of money does send a positive signal about training to the employees and will positively influence the organization, but probably not for the long term. However, if management people involve themselves in training by helping to select the training programs, by becoming both students and instructors themselves, and by graduating with other employees, then the emphasis on training will be sustainable for the long term. It is the *behavior* of management, much more than the *language* of management, that leads to success.

After all, management controls the corporate purse strings. Over time, resources will be available only to the extent needed for those things that are strongly endorsed by top managers. However, resources will eventually be wasted unless the people of the organization utilize the resources wisely. It is management's behavior that can ensure that the people of the company maximize the use of the resources made available.

Therefore, management behavior on both a policy-approval and an action-oriented level is needed in order to sustain long-term, positive change. First, put in place what is needed by devoting the required resources. Then, ensure that the benefit is realized by personally demonstrating the wise use of the investment.

Because TQM requires an investment, because it requires people to do things differently, and because it is a long-term strategy, it will not happen without active managerial participation.

The managerial levels just below the executive suite are the most watchful of top-level behavior. They have front row seats. This level of management is particularly vital to a successful TQM process—for two reasons. First, as was pointed out earlier, middle managers serving on QI teams significantly raise the level of benefit returned by the team. Remember the finding that a typical management-level QI team will typically return a $100,000 benefit at a cost of $20,000 to produce the benefit. If the front row managers question top management's sincerity for TQM, this significant benefit will not materialize. Lip-service quality is all you'll get, and it is not worth the effort or expense.

Second, middle-level managers more directly influence those people at lower organizational levels. If the middle levels are not convinced, you can bet that lower-level participation and effectiveness will be dismal.

If top management's involvement is so critical, how can we secure top management's participation? First, of course, before top managers will participate, they need to be convinced that a TQM process is needed. Much has been said in previous chapters of this book that can help to convince top-level managers that a new approach is necessary. First, however, you need to get their attention and interest. If this can be done, they will discover excellent reasons for a corporatewide quality process all by themselves.

I believe that the attention getter can be the COPQ analysis that was discussed in Chapter 2. If the language of top management is the language of money, then knowing the COPQ can definitely get top management's attention. As I mentioned earlier, the COPQ for most organizations is conservatively estimated at 20 to 25 percent of sales revenues. For some, this may be as high as 30 to 40 percent!

Try to estimate the COPQ as suggested in Chapter 2. Then, drop the report on the CEO's desk and stand back!

Finally, another barrier to top management involvement can be indecision as to what to do or how to behave. Guidelines for management behavior needed to support a TQM process will be provided in Chapter 12.

CSF 2: A Supportive Corporate Culture

Corporate culture was discussed briefly in Chapters 2 and 4. Corporate culture is a company's value system, its collection of guiding beliefs and daily beliefs backed by its policies, programs, and top management's actions. This fabric of beliefs covers the whole organization and influences how people behave. The employees of a company don't need a culture brochure to figure out what is important. Their collective understanding of policies, programs, and the like guides their own actions and beliefs. The result is a corporate personality. It is possible to define the current culture through special studies as suggested in Chapter 2.

We must define the current culture and the desired culture—one supportive of TQM—and take action to close the gaps. A culture that does not support TQM will eventually destroy a quality process. As mentioned previously, the seeds of quality must be planted in fertile soil in order to yield a bumper crop of quality improvements, and in order to harvest a competitive advantage.

Chapter 4 provided a list of some of the principal values of a TQM culture. This list is repeated in Figure 9-1. Next to each cultural value is an example of the actions a company may take to send the signals necessary to support the culture value listed. This illustration may be helpful as you assess your current culture and work to build or adjust one that will more directly support TQM.

As you read down the right-hand column, some common threads within the quality fabric become clear. These are:

- Management involvement
- Supportive managerial actions
- Continuous learning and training
- Rewards, recognition, and celebration
- Constant, on-target communications
- Tracking of the right indicators
- Utilization of QI teams, quality planning, and unit-level quality

CSF 3: Training

Training, training, more training, and then retraining as mentioned in Chapter 4 are essential to an effective TQM process. Quality improvement teams are the guts or backbone of total quality. The employees of a company come together with the process for achieving improvements and solving problems in the QI team approach. But teams cannot be effective unless the team members know how to identify improvement opportunities and investigate problems.

Also, employees will not develop a quality, customer-first attitude without modifying their actions. Actions will not be altered without training. Our cycle of behavioral change model (Figure 3-1) illustrated this. If we want to shape attitudes, then we must alter behavior. Differ-

TQM Value	Actions Necessary to Support TQM Value
1. "Customer-first" attitude.	1.1 Share customer survey results with all employees. 1.2 Include customer satisfaction scores as a key plan measure. 1.3 Recognize and reward individuals for exceptional service to customers.
2. Teamwork and cooperation.	2.1 Utilize QI teams extensively. 2.2 Reward team members via the appraisal system and special recognition events.
3. Internal customer support is vital.	3.1 Utilize unit-level quality. 3.2 Encourage interaction among supporting units.
4. Customer delight drives all other indicators.	4.1 Communicate this clearly. 4.2 Show customer satisfaction and retention ratings as top-of-the-list indicators of corporate performance.
5. Long-term improvements are better than quick fixes.	5.1 Train teams to follow fact-based problem solving. 5.2 Reject quick fixes not supported by data.
6. Facts and data are better than hunches and guesses.	6.1 Train teams to follow fact-based problem solving. 6.2 Provide diagnostic support, and help teams find needed data.
7. Worry about solutions. Don't concentrate on finding fault.	7.1 Praise those who discover problems and work to fix them. 7.2 Don't kill the messenger.
8. No bench sitting. Total involvement is key.	8.1 Closely monitor the number of people involved in TQM. 8.2 Make it easy to join the quality effort. 8.3 Recognize involvement in appraisals. 8.4 Require management's involvement.
9. TQM is not a separate program.	9.1 Create a parallel organization structure. 9.2 Set long-term goals and plans for TQM. Set a vision. 9.3 Refer to TQM as the "new way."

Figure 9-1. A TQM Corporate Culture: Values and Actions.

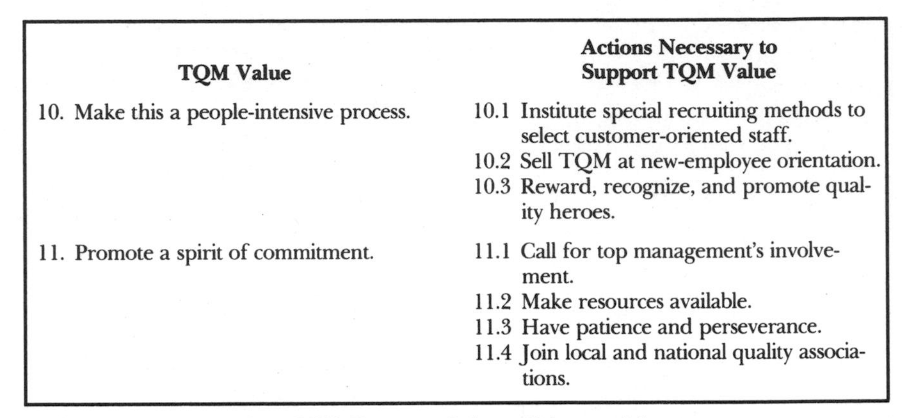

TQM Value	Actions Necessary to Support TQM Value
10. Make this a people-intensive process.	10.1 Institute special recruiting methods to select customer-oriented staff. 10.2 Sell TQM at new-employee orientation. 10.3 Reward, recognize, and promote quality heroes.
11. Promote a spirit of commitment.	11.1 Call for top management's involvement. 11.2 Make resources available. 11.3 Have patience and perseverance. 11.4 Join local and national quality associations.

Figure 9-1. (*Continued*) A TQM Corporate Culture: Values and Actions.

ent actions yield different results, and different results shape new attitudes. And so it goes.

One criticism of many training programs is that there is little structured opportunity for trainees to put their new knowledge to work soon after they've acquired it. Using what we've learned soon after we've learned it is the best way to fully develop new skills and to hone them to perfection.

With TQM and specifically through the use of quality teams, we find that training can be put to effective use immediately. Training for QI team members, in particular, is far from being a warm and fuzzy experience. Team members learn specific tools and techniques, many of them statistically based, for analyzing problems and for identifying the root causes. Teams learn how to stratify an issue, and they learn about Pareto analysis, cause and effect analysis, and flow diagramming. Moreover, they learn to construct control charts, histograms, scatter diagrams, check sheets, and the like. Teams learn sampling, surveying, data collection, and other useful skills. It's not easy but, on the other hand, it's not all that difficult either.

Quality improvement team training has a double payoff, too. Those who complete the training will be prepared to serve on a QI team and can work effectively to solve quality problems. In addition, you'll find that your trained people will begin to use their new skills and knowledge in their day-to-day work activities. They will become more effective workers whether they are serving on a QI team or not! You'll also find that their confidence will grow significantly. People who were so-so performers will improve dramatically. I've seen it happen again and again.

Quality improvement training surely builds within the organization a common language, which is a positive and powerful corporate tool or virtue. This common language spans organizational levels and functional boundaries. A customer service representative and a vice president of finance can actually hold a conversation on a matter of great importance to their company and understand each other. Their conversation would be liberally sprinkled with phrases and words such as:

Vital few	Sampling table
Cause and effect	Pareto effect
Survey data	Stratification
Customers' needs	Root causes
Standard deviation	Countermeasures

Structuring the training experience is as important as what goes into the training. For QI teams that will pursue a particular project for several months, I recommend a modular approach—what I call *just in time training*. Consider splitting your training into three modules and training teams together, all members sitting at one table, ideally after they have selected a QI project theme.

Module 1 should consist of an overview of quality improvement, the underlying concepts and beliefs and the process for stratifying a potential QI project. Module 2 may cover data gathering and analysis and conclude at the problem statement phase of a QI journey. The final module may cover analyzing to identify root causes, selecting countermeasures, developing an implementation plan, completing a cost-benefit analysis, and tracking results.

Start with the first module, and bring the team members back together when they have reached the right part of their team journey. This way the knowledge they'll need will be fresh in their minds. I also suggest producing or buying a team members' handbook, which members may use to refresh their memories as they work on their respective projects. Such a handbook is available by writing to GOAL/QPC, 13 Branch Street, Methuen, Massachusetts 01844. It is called *The Memory Jogger: A Pocket Guide of Tools for Continuous Improvement.*

Several different training programs are needed. Here are some of them:

- QI Team Member Workshop
- QI Team Leader Training
- QI Facilitator Training

- Advanced Statistical Techniques for QI Teams
- Managing for Quality (for the management levels)

Supplement training with a newsletter to go to all team members. The newsletter can communicate common mistakes and misunderstandings experienced by others.

The point is, a training program is not enough. You must create a continuous learning environment for quality results in order to sustain a TQM environment for the long term.

CSF 4: Customer Communications

The simple quality formula is:

$$Q = CP$$

Where Q = Quality
CP = Customers' perceptions

Continuous communication with your customers is needed in order to identify issues of poor quality, customers' principal needs, and incidents of (good) quality. As I've said before, an annual survey is fine, but it is not nearly enough.

There are a variety of ways to monitor customers' perceptions and changing needs. All or most of these techniques are needed if you are to truly have an accurate understanding of what is going on in the minds of your customers. Figure 9-2 provides a short list of techniques to use.

A company that is sincerely interested in meeting the needs of its cus-

1. Formal in-house survey
2. Personal interviews
3. Customer focus groups
4. Debriefing of customer-contact personnel
5. Consultant-run surveys
6. Rate-our-service cards (postage paid)
7. Special research studies completed by universities, think tanks, and so on
8. Review of customer correspondence
9. Customer visits to your location

Figure 9-2. Sources and Techniques for Tracking Customers' Needs and Satisfaction.

tomers will use any number of the techniques shown in Figure 9-2. Instead of just administering the annual survey, a company whose focus is on quality will supplement this with additional customer needs and satisfaction research every 60 days. A continuous learning environment applies not only when discussing training but also to knowing your customer.

If you have internal customers, apply this continuous learning and research emphasis to them as well. After all, the quality chain of events eventually affects the external customer.

Finally, when you collect data pertaining to customers' needs and their level of satisfaction or frustration, by all means don't lock these data in the executive suite or the market research unit. Share what you learn with all employees, and do this continuously. The employees at all levels who are actually working to improve quality need these data more than the research professionals. Also, widely sharing the customer research findings helps support the "customer-first" TQM value shown in Figure 9-1.

Transformation Checkpoints

1. Take a quality tour or side trip. Note the transformation from the status quo to TQM.
2. *CSF 1: Top management's involvement.* Actions speak louder than words.
3. *CSF 2: A supportive corporate culture.* What is it now? What should it be? Close the gaps!
4. *CSF 3: Training.* Take a continuous learning approach. Try modular training for QI teams.
5. *CSF 4: Customer communications.* Take a continuous learning approach. Use a variety of research techniques. Share the findings widely within the company.

10
The Quality Kickoff: Turning on the Burners

There are many similarities between playing golf and developing a TQM process. In both, it's important to learn about the game in a broad sense, to take some initial lessons, and to familiarize yourself with the basics. Then, before hitting the big course, it's wise to spend some time practicing on a driving range and a putting green. Finally, when you are ready to advance to the course at the country club, you will be able to apply what you've learned, concentrating on your target while avoiding the traps.

This chapter will discuss using a test site for experimenting with your TQM process. It will cover selecting the right site, getting quality improvement started at the test site, keeping the ball in play, and providing the support needed. Finally, it will summarize what to expect.

Picking a Test Site

In our quality analogy, we're about to go to the driving range—in this case, a test site at which to practice. I always recommend using a pilot test site, particularly for large companies, followed by a phased rollout to the rest of the organization. Somewhat smaller companies (fewer than 600 or 700 employees located in one area) can usually jump right in without a test site. However, consider your initial experience with

TQM to be an experiment that should be carefully reviewed and then improved.

Using a pilot-test approach to setting up a QIP has a number of advantages:

1. Your early efforts will be focused on a smaller, more manageable section of the company. This is advisable because at this early stage you won't have organized the resources needed to permit an orderly start-up in a more sizable part of your organization. The resources required include money, training, administrative support, and facilitators.
2. A test site will allow you to make mistakes and to correct them quickly without distracting the whole company.
3. Because the test site is relatively small, you can more easily evaluate results through frequent meetings with small groups of employees.
4. Usually a test site will limit your involvement to a few corporate functions rather than the full range of corporate functions, making the test simpler to manage.
5. It will be easier to generate enthusiasm among the test site employees because they will feel special at having been selected to begin something new. They'll also feel special because of all the attention they'll receive from headquarters and test site management.
6. Using a test site will permit you to better manage the rumor mill and any initial confusion.
7. Once you have realized some successes at the test site, you can model them for others using employees from the test site. They will be your best salespeople.

Selecting the *right* test site is critical. Here are a few suggestions for making the best selection.

1. Use the right manager. Select a part of the company that is managed by a person whose style and values are compatible with those needed to manage an effective employee involvement effort. This manager must respect people, be an excellent communicator, be willing to get involved at a "shirt-sleeves" level, and demonstrate a strong interest in improving customer perceptions. I hope you have many from which to choose.
2. Select a part of the company that is separated physically from the rest, if possible. A branch office or plant of 100 to 300 employees

may be ideal. This will isolate your pilot test and permit you to take full advantage of all the benefits a test site can provide.

3. Choose a site where mainstream company functions are performed rather than a site with specialized, one-of-a-kind functions to which others outside the test site area may not easily relate.
4. Finally, try to choose a site where there are no other major projects or distractions occurring, such as the installation of a new computer system, the testing of a new product, or the negotiation of a union contract. You won't need the competition.

The Kickoff

Okay, you've picked your site for the big TQM experiment. It is removed from the rest of the company, it's managed by the right person, it performs mainstream functions with which most employees are familiar, and it is relatively stable—no new computer system being installed, no union negotiation, or the like.

So what now? Well, it's time to grab your clubs and head for the driving range. We'll assume that we've decided on a top-down strategy and that we'll begin by getting some experience with the guts of quality improvement—teams.

It is time to train the management staff from the first-line supervisor to the test site's senior manager. No one in management is sidelined for this one. Training should begin with a broad overview of quality improvement so that everyone sees the big picture. The commitment and support of top management must be demonstrated so that everyone realizes the importance of this early QI effort. Therefore, invite the top management group from headquarters to participate in this training at the test site.

Start with an overview of quality improvement and a thorough question-and-answer period. Then train the management group in the selected problem-solving process. If training is less than 4 or 5 days, you are probably skimping on the effort. Don't cut corners on training, which is a vitally important event.

But what about all the nonmanagement people? They don't even know what's going on yet. Shouldn't it be announced to them? My advice is: Not yet, at least no details. Remember, I referred to this training not just as training but as an event. An event is noticed, it has impact, and it sends a message. Think of it. For several days all the brass are at "school," preferably on site. Word will begin to leak into the vacuum of curiosity, and people will get excited or at least very interested. Now I said no details at first, but I do recommend putting out a brief announcement simply saying that "this office has been selected to test a new and exciting effort for our company which should yield significant benefits for our customers and, therefore, for all of us. More information will follow soon." This announcement is needed just to avoid undue fears of a company takeover or the like.

After management training is completed and headquarters management has departed, let the QI graduates meet with their own people to explain what will be happening. This serves to emphasize that managers will be the first to be involved. A discussion outline should be provided for each manager who has completed QI training to ensure some consistency in the message.

This procedure itself sends a powerful signal. Typically, when a company introduces a new program (but remember, always consider TQM to be a process, not a program), it is the workers who are asked to change and who are given the new direction through exhortation and training. Management endorses the change initially, but because top managers are not actively involved in the new program, they often ignore it later.

However, with the TQM process, the managers are "doing" it first. Their training, before others, sends a strong message of commitment to the quality process to the whole company.

Later, during the week following training, hold a short graduation ceremony that will include all employees, and have the management graduates receive a quality certificate and a short kickoff pep talk. This begins to build the quality spirit with a little hoopla. A few balloons are okay, but don't go crazy. Your employees have seen it all before.

Turning on the Burners

All the managers are trained, and we've gotten the attention of the work force. It is now time to get increasingly serious. The top managers of the test site should designate themselves as the test site quality council or QI steering committee.

The first order of business for the test site's quality council is the formation of QI teams composed of all who were trained. Next, some bite-sized QI projects should be selected and the process begun to solve these problems by applying all the problem-solving steps and QI tools.

The selection of projects for new teams is very important. The first projects should be real and meaningful, but please, avoid going after "world hunger." Select bite-sized projects. Real and meaningful projects are those that definitely relate to a pressing issue or problem that management already recognizes as a pressing issue and that can be related to external customer needs. Themes such as complaints, defects, rework, waste, extended process cycle time, and customer turnover are real and meaningful issues. Also, be as certain as possible that your first projects are ones that can be successfully solved and will show quantifiable results within 6 to 8 months. Early successes are vital for gaining commitment and enthusiasm!

Once projects are selected and assigned, the teams get down to work, hard work! It won't be easy. Even finding the time to meet is never a simple task, but positive change doesn't just settle in without messing your hair a little. You have to find ways to support the effort to make it work for you—a little sacrifice today for a greater benefit tomorrow.

Continuing the Journey

After 3 or 4 months tick by, it will be time to turn up the burners. By this time, most teams will still be in the analysis stage of QI problem solving, and people will be talking about Paretos, fishbones, flowcharts, and stratification.

Now that people are feeling more at ease with the process, it's time to invite some interested nonmanagement employees into the world of quality improvement. I suggest making this an event, too, by holding a call for volunteers or applicants. First determine how many lower-level teams you want to form. A half dozen is about right, but try to get about five or six people from a variety of units and form cross-functional teams. Getting the first volunteers should not be difficult if you continued to nurture the interest we generated at the start. At Colonial Penn, 135 people volunteered for 36 team member slots! Later, of course, participating in quality will not be voluntary.

Once you have your volunteers, put them through the same training the managers experienced. Then let them work to select their own projects to recommend to the quality council. This is yet another event. Nonmanagement employees do not usually meet with top management to propose improvement projects. The quality council should be liberal and flexible in approving these first project ideas, but it should not let a meaningless one, or one that is too broad, get by. Then let these new teams get started.

At the same time, it is a good idea to select two or three units to begin the unit-level quality process discussed in Chapter 8. Provide the training needed, and let these quality pioneers start their journey.

Supporting the Test Site

Now that the burners are ignited and turned up, you've got to fan the flames. You've got to support the team effort like crazy! Also, of course, you've got to learn what goes right and what goes wrong. You need to identify what helps and what gets in the way. After all, this is the purpose of the test site.

The quality council, other managers, and your QI advisers, team leaders, and facilitators must be constantly asking team members about how they perceive progress. Issues that trouble the teams have to be analyzed immediately so that adjustments can be recommended. Otherwise, people will flounder and become frustrated. Communications concerning the QI efforts need to flow in all directions so that everyone learns from the experience. Things that go right must be highlighted and celebrated by all. Also, people from different teams need to get together now and then to swap experiences. This candid exchange is very useful.

Finally, don't neglect training. The initial training wears off quickly. So bring people back in small groups or by team for refresher training a few months later. Consider investing in some additional specialized training in the SPC tools provided (possibly) by an outside QI training firm.

What to Expect

Generally, from my experience, here's what you can expect from your first 12 months or so of initiating TQM at a test site. Essentially, the key words are the *process*, the *pain*, and the *gain*.

The process. People will learn the process and will be basically familiar with the SPC tools in less than a year. Their first team assignment will have been a struggle. The second will be much easier because they will know what to expect.

The pain. Some teams will fail to find solutions, or they may find solutions to the wrong problem. Others may get frustrated and disband. Still others may fall apart because of membership turnover. Your leaders and facilitators will not as yet have reached their optimum effectiveness. Their job is a tough one. Some people will strongly resist cooperating and will get away with it for a while. You will need to deal with these resisters and force compliance. Teams will also try to jump from SPC tool to SPC tool rather than follow the logic of the problem-solving process. Major distractions could occur—for example, a management reorganization, which can threaten QI work and push it aside for a short time. Make sure it's a very short time. In addition, the data a team needs may not exist or may not be obtainable from the bureaucrats at headquarters. You will need to smooth the way here.

All in all, you need to realize that it will rain on your golf game. Bring umbrellas and push on!

The gain. Some teams will succeed and deliver results you never could imagine. People who were average will emerge as heroes. Employees and managers will begin to use more facts and data displays (Paretos, and so on) in their daily work. They'll start urging others to speak factually, and they will say the word *customer* in every other sentence. Many will work on their own time to help the team. Communications between levels and units will improve, and a common language will emerge. Employee satisfaction will rise, and customer satisfaction will begin to increase. Management will feel confident that its investment in quality and in people is well made.

Moreover, new problems you never thought you had will be uncovered and brought forward, but you must consider this as a positive long-term development because invisible problems can never be solved. People will make management presentations for the first time and feel like a million dollars afterward. Their self-confidence will soar, and new leaders will be discovered. You'll love it!

Transformation Checkpoints

1. Advantages of a test site:
   - You can focus efforts on a unit of manageable size.
   - Mistakes can be made without distracting the whole company.
   - It is easier to manage communications.
   - It provides a model for success for the rest of the company.
2. Picking the right test site:
   - Pick a site managed by the "right" manager.
   - Select a site physically removed from headquarters if possible.
   - Choose a site where mainstream functions are performed.
   - Choose a site free from other major distractions.
3. Train all managers and select good initial projects.
4. Form the test site's quality council.

5. Build interest by making special events out of training, selecting nonmanagement participants, and so on.
6. Start nonmanagement teams and unit-level quality (see Chapter 8) a few months after the kickoff. Use volunteers at first.
7. Provide training, refresher training, and special training.
8. Support the test like crazy. Plan, do, check, and act, act, act.
9. Know what to expect:
   - The process
   - The pain
   - The gain

11

Beyond the Test Site: Going for Companywide TQM

Ten chapters were needed just to get us this far! This fact illustrates the importance and extent of sound preparations—knowledge building, organizing, planning, stage setting, and testing—prior to turning your TQM process over to the forces at large.

Of course, we've been following our P.D.C.A. cycle. We've planned for TQM, we've done TQM in a test site, we've checked on our process and improved it through our test site experience, and now we are ready to act upon all we have learned by unveiling it to the rest of the organization.

Depending on the actual size and the extent of centralization or regionalization of your company, as well as the extent of available resources for TQM implementation, you may elect either to roll the process out to all units at virtually the same time or to proceed in stages, major unit by major unit. Bite off only what you can comfortably chew. Otherwise, the companywide introduction may be ineffective and frustrating for all involved. For example, if you are not capable of providing the needed training for many employees from a variety of departments within the first 4 to 6 months, then phase in the process over a reasonable time so that people aren't waiting in line.

This chapter will cover the following:

- Packaging and marketing the test site experience
- Organizing for companywide TQM
- Starting a corporate kickoff
- Adding quality planning
- Selecting QI projects
- Forming teams and starting training
- Selecting facilitators
- Promoting communication and awareness
- Sponsoring unit-level quality
- Setting a TQM vision

Packaging and Marketing the Test Site Experience

Before you can package and market your test site experience, you must complete a thorough analysis of lessons learned from the test site, and you must modify or adjust your TQM process to reflect your findings. Was training adequate? Did the test site teams select meaningful, bite-sized QI projects? Were facilitators well trained and effective? These and dozens of other questions must be asked and answered and any issues resolved before going for companywide TQM.

You should also have clear evidence of success or, at the very least, an extremely high level of confidence that you are on a path to success. But, what does TQM success look like and feel like? We'll examine this by looking at the three principal beneficiaries of TQM:

- Customers
- Top management, corporate owners, and shareholders
- Company employees

Customers. Total quality management is a success with customers if QI teams, for example, have found meaningful ways to improve service to customers and if the positive benefits of these improvements can be verified by customer satisfaction research. Have teams been successful at reducing the time it takes to process an order, or have they been successful at reducing complaints? Have teams simplified the billing process? Have they found ways to communicate more quickly and effectively with customers and reduced the number of errors in transactions with customers? Remember, internal customers count too! For example, have units found ways to better support other units—the next process or link in the quality chain of events? If progress is evident in these areas, then customers will benefit.

Top management, corporate owners, and shareholders. Company management, owners, and shareholders are interested in numerical facts and figures. Their language is one which speaks of ROI, levels of productivity, the extent of cost reduction or revenue enhancement, the number of customers, and so on.

Can you show results attributable to TQM or the realistic promise of results that are quantifiable? For example, have some teams proved that their suggested countermeasures will reduce costs or add revenue? Are they finding ways to produce a greater number of widgets or a way to process a greater number of orders in a shorter period of time with no increase in cost, defects, or errors? If so, top management, owners, and shareholders will benefit.

Company employees. Employees are interested in a way to better utilize their skills and abilities in order to make a meaningful contribution to company goals. They are looking to develop their careers. They are looking to find ways to simplify their work processes. They seek recognition for real accomplishment, and they wish to receive better support from other units on which they rely, including vendors.

Can you show that employees are generally more satisfied with their working environment? Can you demonstrate that employees have developed new knowledge and skills that help them do a better job? Has the level of coordination and cooperation—teamwork—improved? Can you identify some employees who used to be so-so performers who now are self-confident, enthusiastic contributors? Have recognition events been focused on real accomplishments, and have people been thrilled with the opportunity to bask in the glow of success? If so, your work force is benefiting from TQM as well.

Colonial Penn's test site, our Tampa, Florida, regional office, achieved a positive financial impact from its first 10 QI team projects of $971,000. About half of this came from cost savings and half from revenue enhancement. Many teams found ways to simplify and shorten internal procedures, which improved service to our customers. In one area, for example, the time needed to respond to a customer's call was cut by 40 percent. In another, the time involved to move an automobile insurance claim from one critical stage of our process to another was reduced from 11 days to less than 3 days. A survey of our involved employees showed an extremely high satisfaction level with TQM, and 83 percent of our people felt that our quality process was having a beneficial effect on our customers.

Generally, the spirit within the Colonial Penn office of more than 300 people is exceptionally high. After a short visit to this site I am on cloud nine for days! Today, I couldn't wrestle the TQM process away from these dedicated TQM professionals—even with a division of infantry!

If your own test site has achieved enough success or the promise of success to warrant a companywide implementation of your tested process, then the experience and the benefits need to be shared with others. There is no better way to incite the rest of the organization than to have people hear it from their peers and to have the facts to back up the message. Here's how you might market your TQM test to the rest of your organization.

Actually, you may see this marketing effort beginning before you, as the corporate TQM architect, can act to stimulate it. We all know that the informal communications channels within a corporation are strong, constant, persistent, and surprisingly accurate. As employees at the test site talk with their friends in other areas of the company, the positive assessment of TQM will leak out. Also, as others outside the test site visit the TQM "laboratory" as a normal course of business, they will personally witness the changing culture.

Aside from the informal network, there are some actions that you will need to orchestrate. First, organize some tours of the test site for other corporate managers. Let them see TQM in action for themselves, and let them hear about it from your quality pioneers. You may also decide to create a quality communications team consisting of nonmanagement and management people from the test site. This team, armed with a message outline and concrete examples, can be sent on a speaking circuit throughout the company to spread the word.

Second, you may wish to produce a video and a brochure that clearly outline what is happening at the test site and the kinds of results achieved or expected. These two strategies, by the way, are also quite useful as you approach your vendors about adopting a quality process of their own from which you could benefit as a customer.

Third, top managers in the form of the quality council must clearly and enthusiastically communicate their delight with what is happening within the test site, and they must pledge their commitment to and personal involvement with TQM as it spreads to other areas of the company.

Tours, communications teams, videos, brochures, top management's involvement, and the informal grapevine combine to infect other corporate areas with the TQM spirit. This is the stage setting needed before TQM is unveiled to the rest of the company. It represents the tilling of the corporate soil to accept the seeds of TQM. From these preparations will spring a bumper crop of QI activities that will be harvested as the evolving QI-oriented corporate culture—your path to a sustainable competitive advantage.

Have some fun with spreading the word. Then buckle up and settle down for the challenge of companywide TQM with renewed commitment.

Organizing for Companywide TQM

It is now time to establish the phase 3 quality organization, which we introduced in Figure 2-1. This phase 3 organization is reproduced here as Figure 11-1. Remember, this is a parallel organization structure, not a new and different one.

Essentially, this organization adds to the corporate responsibility wardrobe of major unit management groups by giving them a quality management hat to wear, the uniform of the quality lead team. These major unit management groups (lead teams) are now responsible for learning the TQM process and for implementing it within their respective areas. It is *their* responsibility, not the responsibility of the corpo-

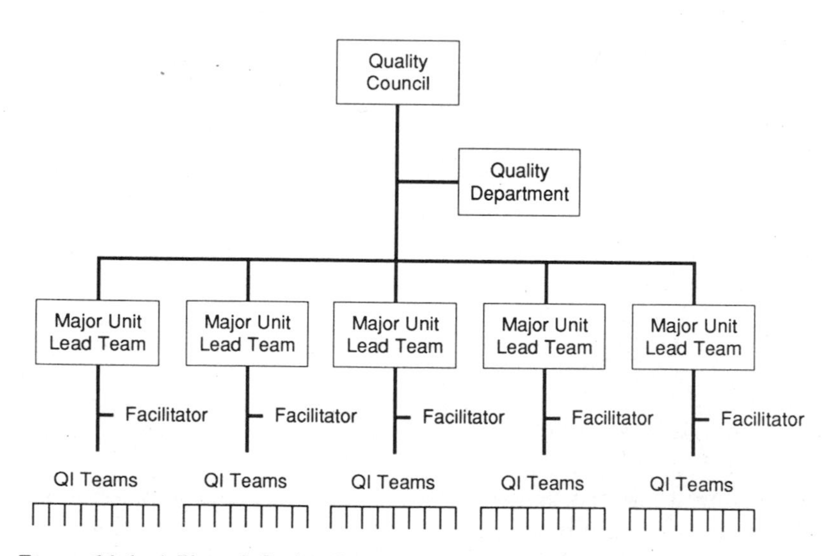

Figure 11-1. A Phase 3 Quality Organization.

rate quality manager. The lead teams are responsible to the top-level quality council.

This "line ownership" is very important. The corporate quality manager and the quality department must not be viewed as ultimately accountable for quality. A dedicated quality department will feel accountable, and that is fine, but the ownership must be with the lead teams—clearly and solidly.

The role of the quality department is that of an internal consultant. The members are most likely selected from your original design team, from the test site, and from the training unit. They must be talented and respected people who possess excellent consulting skills, TQM knowledge, and organizational development abilities. They will organize their own unit to support the lead teams, and in this role they become a vital corporate resource responsible to the quality council. I suggest rotating people in and out of the corporate quality department every 3 years or so because you'll find that members of this unit eventually want to run their own units so that they can apply their extensive TQM knowledge and skills. Also, rotating other talented people into the quality department is an excellent way to develop some of your best people as strong quality advocates. The experience gained as a member of the quality department provides superb consulting and organizational development skills. I suggest, however, that the manager of the quality department remain in place for at least the first 5 years to provide needed continuity during this most critical phase of TQM development. See Figure 11-2 for more on the role of the quality department.

Once the lead teams are formed, they should develop a mission statement and a list of key responsibilities closely resembling those which were established by the quality council (see Figure 2-2). Then the members of the lead team need QI training and a thorough grounding in the company's selected TQM process. Once this is complete, they must settle down and develop a TQM implementation plan that will include goals and timetables. This plan should be presented to the quality council for approval, and the quality department must sign on to support the lead team's goals. Now you're in business—the total quality business. Your company is under new management.

Depending on the size and structure of what I've been calling a major unit, a lead team may decide to form other subordinate lead teams within its area. I particularly recommend this if a major unit includes a remote office or if it is organized into units employing about 100 people or more. These "mini lead teams" will be responsible to the major unit lead team and must operate in the same way. That is, they will need to develop their own implementation plan, arrange for training, and so on.

The Corporate Quality Department

The corporate quality department is responsible to the quality council. Its customers are the lead teams.

Mission:

The quality department exists to directly support the development, implementation, and enhancement of all elements of the TQM process and to provide consulting and training services to lead teams for the successful utilization of the TQM process within their respective areas. The quality department is also responsible for consolidating and reporting companywide results and progress.

Principal Duties:

1. Develop, maintain, communicate, and enhance all elements of the corporate TQM process.
2. Provide TQM consulting services to the lead teams.
3. Develop, coordinate, and provide training and diagnostic support for the pursuit of TQM.
4. Track TQM progress companywide and provide written progress reports.
5. Maintain exceptional, advanced knowledge of TQM procedures, techniques, and so on.
6. Develop and recommend consistent forms and other materials for the pursuit of TQM.
7. Strongly advocate adherence to the principles of quality management and customer satisfaction.
8. Participate in the development of corporate and unit-level business plans to ensure that quality and customers' needs are clearly a driving force.
9. Develop communications and awareness materials to support TQM.
10. Coordinate the submission of applications (if desired) in an attempt to win awards and recognition for the company's TQM efforts, such as the Malcolm Baldrige National Quality Award.
11. Maintain corporate memberships in local and national quality associations, network groups, and so on.
12. Participate in the development of customer surveys, focus groups, and the like.

Figure 11-2. Role of the Corporate Quality Department.

Starting a Corporate Kickoff

Now that your company is well positioned to pursue TQM on a companywide basis, it is time to "jump-start" the organization with a little celebration and hoopla.

In Chapter 3 we discussed complex culture change and the uncertainty people feel when a new way is about to eclipse the old. See Figure 3-2. The corporate kickoff signals that the new way is about to settle in. It also reassures all employees that the new way is needed and that it is totally supported by top management.

If at all possible, the kickoff should take the form of a companywide rally. If this is not feasible, approach it area by area with the obvious involvement of top management. Total quality management and the reasoning behind it should be briefly explained; people should know how they will be involved in the process. The expected benefits should be covered, as should the hard work required. The quality policy or pledge (Figure 2-4) should be communicated, and the quality organization structure should be described.

The test site experience should be declared a success, and the people who participated should be recognized and praised for their pioneering efforts. The next steps for expanding the quality process should be outlined, and ribbons should be cut to signify a breakthrough to TQM.

Finally, as a symbol of the new TQM way, consider providing all employees with some inexpensive gift item with your quality logo to commemorate the installation of TQM—for example, a coffee mug, digital clock, pen, hat, or the like. Be certain that the gift item you provide is of high quality!

Adding Quality Planning

As companywide TQM begins, it is essential that quality business planning (as discussed in Chapter 7) be added at the top of the organization. Although following my recommended model means starting with QI teams as well as starting at the top levels of the company, I pointed out earlier that the planning element must quickly follow in order to guide the QI project selection process toward the company's vital few priorities, CSFs, and customers' needs.

Having chosen these vital few priorities, the quality council and the lead teams now have a corporate goal-oriented context within which to select, approve, and invest in QI projects. With the planning element added, these QI steering groups will naturally focus the TQM energy in the direction that makes the most difference to realizing the corporate vision—its potentially realizable dream.

To ignore this quality planning step is to begin a long, involved trip or tour without a good map or knowledgeable guide. Although you may eventually find your destination, you'll surely waste valuable fuel (energy) as you aimlessly wander the countryside.

This wasted or unfocused energy is one reason why many quality ventures have failed to endure. Total quality management, as described here, however, will endure and contribute precisely because management is involved in QI teams and helps choose projects that are more meaningful because they are aimed at the vital few goals and CSFs of the whole company.

Selecting QI Projects

Once you have organized for the companywide TQM rollout, each lead team needs to begin the QI project selection and team formation process.

Each lead team should be directly involved in this extremely important activity. At this stage, selecting goal-oriented, bite-sized projects becomes a CSF. If good projects are selected, the teams pursuing them will feel meaningfully involved, and the results they achieve will make a significant contribution to the corporate vision. Success will motivate people to continue—to find more good projects and to achieve more positive results. Poor projects, however, can frustrate team members and sour them on the TQM experience.

In Chapter 5, sources of QI project ideas were listed along with some basic criteria for choosing good projects. It was pointed out that a QI project is essentially a problem. The broader definition bears repeating.

Definition of a QI Project

> A QI project is an effort aimed at gaining a lasting breakthrough or revolutionary result that realizes a quantifiable improvement of a process, product, or service. Results typically include the reduction of cost, waste, process cycle time, errors, variation, or rework. In the final analysis, a problem is solved.

Selecting good QI projects is not easy. Your first efforts will probably yield two types of project ideas. These two types and an example of each are as follows:

1. *QI problem-solving project.* For example: Service orders are processed incorrectly. A good "litmus test" for spotting an appropriate QI problem-solving project is to ask: What's the problem? The service orders project definitely identifies a problem that a team can investigate to find the root causes. That is, no solution is presumed in the statement of the project.
2. *Implementation project.* For example: We need to develop a new order processing procedure. This project idea points to something we may need to do—it outlines a task that needs to be accomplished—but the inherent problem and its root causes are not targeted for examination and discovery. Therefore, a solution is presumed, and the project statement orders that specific action be taken.

Having described the two types of projects, I urge that problem-solving projects be the type most often selected. The reason for this recommendation is fairly simple. A QI team that pursues a problem-solving project will, through a careful analysis of the facts, be better able to show that the remedy eventually prescribed by the team will actually solve the problem under study by attacking and neutralizing the root causes. If root causes are validated and treated, the problem is fixed and remains fixed for a long time.

By contrast, an implementation project, such as "we need a new order processing procedure," presumes that the root cause of some unstated problem is a faulty order processing procedure. To develop a new order processing procedure before verifying that this action will adequately address the real problem is a gamble in many instances. For example, the procedure may be just fine, but the people who follow the procedure may not have received adequate training.

Now that I've discredited the value of implementation projects, I will say that they can sometimes play a legitimate role in a TQM process. In reality, there are times when you will be certain that a new order processing procedure *is* needed in order to achieve improved performance. In such cases, the task is clear: Develop a new one, but develop it based on a thorough and accurate understanding of customers' needs.

In most cases it is wiser to discipline your organization to identify problem-solving projects far more often than to identify implementation projects. In fact, during the first 6 months in the life of your TQM process, I suggest that you outlaw implementation projects. After that, problem-solving projects should outnumber implementation projects by 10 to 1.

Forming Teams and Starting Training

As lead teams approve QI projects and communicate them to the quality council, QI problem-solving team members need to be selected and trained. As previously recommended, train team members together as a team once they know what their project is and you'll find the training to be far more effective than if you simply invite a bunch of individuals to the training room. The team's first meeting should occur during the last hour of the scheduled training session. This launches the new projects immediately and ties training and the application of the training closely together.

If you have initially selected good projects and you are taking a top-down approach, as I strongly recommend, you will be selecting management-level personnel for many QI teams, and the team members will come from a variety of functions within the company.

This means that, in many cases, a lead team will not be able to staff a QI team with people only from its own organizational area because most management-level QI projects are cross-functional in nature. Therefore, the team requires representation from several functions. For example, a QI team initiated in the financial area may need a member from data processing and one from customer service if it is going to work on a project that has to do with accurately crediting customers' payments to their accounts in a timely manner. This simply requires close coordination and cooperation among your various lead teams, facilitated by your quality department and your facilitators.

Remember, teams that tackle the larger, more far-reaching projects will more than likely be cross-functional, management-level teams. Putting such teams together is a companywide activity in many instances, not just a department-level activity. Effective communication, coordination, and cooperation across department lines are necessary to form cross-functional teams.

Selecting Facilitators

Facilitators are personal quality consultants to QI team leaders. They provide advice, guidance, support, and additional or remedial instruction for teams. They are instrumental in keeping teams on track and, thereby, minimize wasted time and maximize team results.

Facilitators make a world of difference to the success of QI teams...period! They represent an astute investment that pays significant dividends. This fact is surprisingly difficult to prove until you see it for yourself, and you'll never witness the tremendous benefit unless you make the commitment to use facilitators as you begin TQM. However, your ultimate goal should be to develop your managers as outstanding TQM specialists so that facilitators per se are no longer required.

Select facilitators internally from among your most promising talent and send them for advanced QI problem-solving training. Keep them in the role of facilitator for 2 to 3 years and then rotate them to a regular job within the company. Try to make this new regular job a promotion from the position from which you originally recruited them. Then rotate new talent into the facilitator job.

Facilitators should be selected by lead teams and should report to the lead team that chose them, with a secondary (dotted line) reporting relationship to the quality department for their professional, TQM-related development. As TQM grows, I recommend that each lead team appoint a lead facilitator to whom other facilitators within the lead team's area of responsibility report. The lead facilitator is also helpful in recruiting QI team members from other areas, coordinating training and recognition events, and so on. See Figure 11-3 for a lead team organization structure.

An experienced facilitator can usually handle anywhere from 12 to 16 QI teams, depending on how knowledgeable your QI teams are with the tools and techniques of the QI problem-solving process.

Over time, as you rotate people into and out of the facilitator position, you will be nourishing your organization with more and more ex-

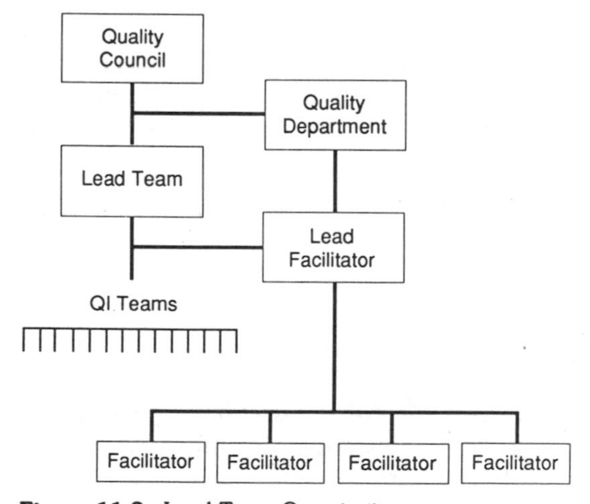

Figure 11-3. Lead Team Organization.

ceptionally qualified TQM talent. You'll be building one of the strongest quality forces around.

Promoting Communication and Awareness

Once TQM begins to settle in on a companywide basis, we see from this chapter alone that there is a lot of activity occurring, with projects being selected, team members being chosen, facilitators being recruited, training being conducted, and so on.

However, even a medium-size organization cannot involve all its people in TQM right away. Consequently, in the early months, more people will be watching from the sidelines than playing in the game. Therefore, it is vitally important to keep everyone aware of what is happening, because a lack of awareness will feed the anxiety many may already feel as a new way begins to eclipse the old.

The quality council and the lead teams need to deal with this communications and awareness issue right away. It is necessary to adopt a communications and awareness strategy that utilizes the most effective and trusted communications channels to explain and to keep people informed as to TQM's progress and future direction. Meetings conducted by management, written communications, and even periodic videos that show what is happening are usually quite effective. I suggest that some form of communications activity take place every 3 to 4 weeks during the first 6 months, and every 8 to 12 weeks thereafter. Also, plan and conduct special quality-related events each October, which is National Quality Month.

In addition, don't forget that faces change every week because of employee turnover. The new employees who are joining your company need to be quickly advised as to the TQM environment, goals, and activities. A brochure or video for new people should be considered, and these items should be worked into your new employee orientation process as soon as possible.

Sponsoring Unit-Level Quality

After 3 or 4 months have passed since the companywide TQM kickoff, the flurry of start-up activities may begin to settle down into a more reasonably managed level of controlled chaos!

You'll know when you've reached this point because you'll make the following observation: We've been working hard to get TQM going and we've got a number of good management-level teams started, but we've only involved 15 percent of our people in TQM!

The response to this observation is unit-level quality, which we covered in Chapter 8. This may be the time to select several in-place departments within the organization to begin the unit-level quality process. This requires training as well, although unit-level quality training is not as technical as QI team training, which includes instruction in Pareto analysis, stratification, cause and effect analysis, and so on.

You'll recall, however, that a department pursuing unit-level quality is likely to identify a chronic problem and, as a result, a QI project that is focused on meeting the needs of either the external customers or the next process (internal customers). When units reach this point, they need to seek their lead team's approval to pursue the project. Then they'll need to train some of their members as a QI team so that their selected project can be analyzed and resolved.

So, after those first few months devoted to QI team formation are over, lead teams should have several departments follow the unit-level quality process, and they should steadily expand this activity. Looking ahead a year or more down the quality road, we'll find virtually all employees off the bench and in the game. At this point, quality start-up will become TQM, for we've now tied the three elements of TQM together: QI teams, quality planning, and unit-level quality.

Setting a TQM Vision

As you continue to nurture and develop your TQM culture, top management will begin to more clearly visualize the ultimate benefits. Here's one way the future may be envisioned and your efforts rewarded.

Not only can a fully developed and effective TQM process improve service to current customers and substantially lower the COPQ, it can also attract new customers by the carload, particularly if you are known for award-winning quality! Management may begin to dream of competing for and winning the Malcolm Baldrige National Quality Award, the American version of the coveted Deming Prize.

The Deming Prize is awarded annually by the Japanese Union of Scientists and Engineers. It is the world's most prestigious award for quality, and it has *never* been won by a company outside Japan...that is, not until November 1989, when Florida Power and Light Company won the Deming! This is an absolutely outstanding accomplishment, and I heartily congratulate all the employees of Florida Power and Light for their diligence and excellence. *Well done*! Your customers are quite fortunate.

As a company deadly serious about the importance of quality, Florida

Power and Light was instrumental in influencing the U.S. Congress to establish the Malcolm Baldrige National Quality Award, the first of which was presented in November 1988. However, no service company was among the winners in either 1988 or 1989.

A company that wins the Baldrige Award and receives the recognition related to this remarkable achievement will be viewed by its current and potential customers as one of the very best in the country when it comes to quality and customer satisfaction. A company that makes the consumer public aware of this achievement will find its customer ranks swelling with more and more delighted customers. Although you don't have to win an award to be recognized as a quality company, studying the application for an award can provide valuable insight into how to improve your TQM process.

Transformation Checkpoints

1. Learn from your test site experience. Did you satisfy your principal audiences?
   - Customers?
   - Top management, corporate owners, or shareholders?
   - Company employees?
2. Communicate the success of the test site through:
   - Tours
   - Communications team from the test site
   - Video programs and brochures
   - Top management's message
3. Establish the phase 3 quality organization. Ensure line ownership.
4. Formalize the role of the quality department.
5. Stage the corporate kickoff. Rally around quality.
6. Fold in quality planning to focus QI projects on the vital few goals and CSFs.
7. Select QI projects, form teams, and provide training.
   - Pick good projects...problem-solving projects
   - Form cross-functional management teams
   - Train team members together
8. Be smart! Make the investment in facilitators.
9. Develop a communications and awareness strategy to keep all employees up to date. Don't forget the new employees joining the company every week.

10. Stir in unit-level quality as the initial flurry of activity settles down.
11. Set a TQM vision. Consider setting your sights on the Malcolm Baldrige National Quality Award or study the award application to improve your TQM process.
12. *Go for it*!

12
For Top Management Only

During one of the many talks I've heard Dr. Joseph M. Juran give, he made this profound statement: "In our experience, no quality improvement effort has ever been successful without top management's involvement." I urge you to consider this statement as a signpost for your TQM development actions.

In Chapter 9 I presented the four CSFs for TQM. Top management's involvement and support is one of those four. In fact, I believe that top management's involvement is the single most CSF because it is top management's behavior and pattern of resource allocation that shape the culture—the attitudes—of the organization. As a result, I'm devoting this chapter entirely to this most vital TQM ingredient.

We'll cover:

- General TQM support tips for top managers
- Ten specific TQM support actions for top managers
- Ten specific TQM involvement actions for top managers

General TQM Support Tips for Top Managers

In my view, most top executives focus their time and energy primarily on business matters that are both pressing and important. Then they focus on matters that are either pressing but not important or important but not pressing. This view would suggest that top managers may spend too much time reacting to situations and dealing with problems after they occur.

Instead, I suggest that the important but not pressing matters bid for the majority of top management's attention. In many cases the pressing matters exist because of some crisis or unexpected event or simply because of ineffective planning and execution somewhere in the organization. Something is out of control and requires top management's attention now!

Important matters for top executives, on the other hand, are not just quantifiable goals. The most important priority for top managers is shaping a corporate team around a strong value system—providing value-driven leadership. This shaping of a corporate team around a strong value system is a long-term and continuous process. On a day-to-day basis, it may not be considered pressing, but it is certainly important in achieving a sustainable competitive advantage. Providing value-driven leadership is also a preventive strategy. As you shape the team and instill the values, the short-term pressing problems diminish as corporate effectiveness improves.

Total quality management is, in fact, a value-driven culture, and top managers must be actively involved in constructing it. As we've said, the TQM value system is centered on continuous project-by-project improvement in company operations, meeting customers' needs, involving employees, subscribing to fact-based decision making, promoting teamwork, and setting a long-term view. If TQM doesn't win its bid for top management's attention, the process of building the winning, value-centered team will be painfully slow and eventually ineffective.

In other words, TQM shapes a value-centered culture that provides an extremely strong base for building a sustainable competitive advantage. Value-driven leadership is essential to developing TQM and must be a top priority for upper management. It cannot be delegated or ignored.

It follows, then, that TQM should be viewed as a new and improved management system and a long-term, permanent one. It is top management's job to convey this attitude and to guard against TQM's being seen as a 1- or 2-year drive for quality, only to be mothballed once the crisis is past or the novelty wears off. To convey this view of TQM as a new management system requires that management send signals to the corporation that are compatible with this view and consistent and regular—a new TQM heartbeat for the organization.

For example, top management must stress the need for high customer-satisfaction levels as a primary indicator of long-term success rather than the usual practice of worshiping at the altar of quarterly earnings per share. After all, customer satisfaction drives earnings per share in the long term. Management should also stress continuous learning in the field of total quality rather than attendance at a few specific training programs. In addition, management must stress continuous, fact-based project-by-project improvements achieved through the identification of root causes of problems rather than quick-fix strategies. It is also necessary to properly balance the short-term interest in having QI teams achieve rapid but potentially short-lived results with the long-term interest in having teams achieve permanent results by following and forever learning a consistent and effective problem-solving process. And the TQM organization must do virtually everything from designing new products or services to deciding on the hours the office will be open for business based on a thorough understanding of customers' needs.

Two more points need to be discussed before I cover the 10 specific support actions and the 10 specific involvement actions I recommend for management.

First, many companies have adopted quality or customer-satisfaction strategies based solely on the need to passionately exhort and support the people in the organization who interact directly with the customer. This is, in fact, an absolutely essential ingredient for any TQM process, but it cannot be the only one. We'll discuss this at some length later in Chapter 15. The point to be made here is simply this: Even the best customer-contact force can keep your customers satisfied only for so long if, for example, your billing process is fundamentally flawed. In reality, it is the large number of underlying and supporting processes of the company that enable your customer-contact employees to delight the customer. Discovering the flaws in your internal processes and procedures from product design to delivery, to billing and involving people in all areas to repairing the damage, is how total quality is really achieved. Once your processes and procedures are effective and efficient, the job of the customer-contact people becomes easier, and they have the opportunity to turn customer satisfaction into customer delight by adding a final touch of professionalism and special caring.

Second, consider adopting a long-term strategy for flattening (reducing the number of levels in) the organizational structure and making greater use of self-managed work teams. Commitment, communication, coordination, and initiative are needed at all levels within the company in order for organizations to be highly effective. The existence of multiple layers of unnecessary managers creates a series of filters and obstacles that dilute or block optimal effectiveness. Seven or more layers of organizational strata are common in most medium to large organizations today, but three, four, or even five can be far more effective.

This suggestion does not mean that middle-level managers should be discarded from the organization. They, in fact, represent a very special resource of talent that can be utilized far more effectively. Middle-level managers are not the problem. The problem is the typical hierarchy style of structure which is a leftover from the early years of the industrial revolution, when the emphasis was on mass production and inspection. The emphasis today must be on quality and on being able to utilize each employee to the maximum extent of his or her potential.

Instead of using managers to interpret corporate strategy, to give direction, and to evaluate results, put them to work on permanent organizational teams to achieve results.

Essentially, self-managed work teams provide employees at all salary levels with a far greater sense of ownership for their work and a much greater opportunity to experience the results of their efforts. Work teams add a greater sense of individual responsibility and accountability and greatly facilitate the task of turning goals into plans and plans into action. All these benefits are directly compatible with the fundamental concepts of TQM and are essential ingredients for a competitive, quality-focused organization.

Ten Specific Support Actions for Top Managers

Top managers need to support TQM, but how is this accomplished? What actions should top managers take to provide the necessary support?

1. *Approve the financial investment in TQM.* It should be no surprise by now that TQM requires both an initial and an ongoing investment of financial resources. It has also been demonstrated that such an investment can yield a significant return both in terms of dollars and cents as well as in terms of customer satisfaction and, eventually, a sustainable competitive advantage.

I cannot quantify the precise amount of the investment required, but I can suggest that it will be modest in relation to the returns gained through a well-planned and well-executed TQM process.

Top management needs to fund the process—to set and approve the TQM budget—and it needs to communicate this act to everyone in the company. Nothing sends a stronger and more positive signal to the organization than the sound of cold, hard cash being put on the table. This is an unmistakable sign of support.

2. *Provide and approve the time for TQM.* In addition to cash, an investment in time is necessary. A commitment to TQM requires the al-

lotment of time necessary for training teams, the allowance for team meetings in daily schedules, celebrations of accomplished quality goals, and so on.

Not only should top managers indicate that it is okay for workers to spend time learning and pursuing TQM, but they themselves must commit some of their own valuable time to these pursuits as well. Later in this chapter I'll cover ways in which top managers should be involved themselves in TQM—how they should spend the time they commit.

If both cash on the table and the actions of management send a strong message of commitment to TQM, they will offer a huge incentive to others to follow suit. Walk like you talk, and others will surely follow.

3. *Require the training and learning in TQM.* Training turns good intentions into good results. Without training, employees continue their old ways; they realize the same results, and attitudes remain unchanged. Top managers should not only encourage people to attend training, they must require it! A key TQM success indicator for top management to track is the number of people attending the various quality training programs. In addition to requiring formal training, management must praise employees for pursuing a path of continuous learning through reading, attending external seminars, joining quality networking groups, practicing TQM, and so on.

4. *Secure consulting help.* Developing a TQM process is a formidable task. It is also large enough, complex enough, and important enough to require the stimulation, instruction, and counsel that a quality management consultant can provide. There are a few good consulting organizations from which to choose. One of these is FPL Group's subsidiary, QualTec, Inc., located in Palm Beach Gardens, Florida. QualTec has incorporated many of the techniques used in Florida Power and Light's QI program into training programs for many of the Fortune 500 companies.

In addition, the most widely renowned quality consulting firm may be The Juran Institute, Inc., of Wilton, Connecticut. The institute's annual conference, IMPRO, regularly attracts approximately 1000 quality professionals from more than 25 countries. The Juran Institute's quality seminars are plentiful and excellent.

Securing a consultant not only helps a company to understand TQM and to chart a QI development process, it also helps stimulate the organization to act. If you are going to pay for TQM, you'd better use it!

5. *Make speeches and appearances supporting TQM.* Visible support by top management is vital. Although signing the checks and meeting with a consultant in the executive suite are essential to a successful TQM process, these are mostly invisible top management activities as

far as the rest of the organization is concerned. Standing face-to-face with the employees of your organization at all levels and in all areas while endorsing TQM exhibits visible, unmistakable support.

This activity will also provide an incentive for top managers to learn TQM and a two-way dialog with the people you are asking to dedicate themselves to learning and adopting TQM.

6. *Join national and local quality associations.* Joining quality associations provides both a learning and a networking opportunity. This involvement by top managers also signals a strong personal commitment to total quality. Once you are involved in such associations, strive for a position of leadership in one or more that you've joined.

Two associations are among the most well known. These are the American Society for Quality Control (ASQC) and the Association for Quality and Participation (AQP).

In addition, you are likely to find local or regional quality groups. In Philadelphia, for example, we have the Philadelphia Area Council for Excellence (PACE), an arm of the Philadelphia Chamber of Commerce. PACE brings companies pursuing total quality together through the sponsorship of seminars that feature such well-known experts as Dr. W. Edwards Deming and Tom Peters. It also provides TQM resources such as books and videos and arranges networking meetings. Colonial Penn's chairman and CEO is a member of the PACE CEO Executive Council, and Colonial Penn is a charter member of this fine organization. Another well-known regional quality organization is the Madison (Wisconsin) Area Quality Improvement Network. There is probably a similar group in your area.

7. *Direct the quality department.* In Chapter 2 we discussed establishing the quality department at the corporate level solidly fixed in a new, parallel structure aligned to support TQM. The quality department should report directly to the top management group as Figure 2-1 illustrates.

This structure provides for an uninterrupted and unfiltered dialog between the day-to-day designers and developers of TQM and top management. Such a structure is not only useful and necessary for practical reasons, but it, too, sends a strong signal of top management's support.

8. *Set a quality policy and vision.* Earlier we discussed the need to develop a corporate quality policy (Chapter 2) and a vision for your TQM commitment (Chapter 11).

The quality policy and vision are top management's responsibility and should be communicated by them personally. Actually taking the time to develop a policy and to create the vision, to write them down, and then to personally communicate them to the employees mean that a strong message of top management's commitment to TQM is established. It is like the power and commitment we attribute to our personal signature. If you're going to take the time to write it down, you're going to believe it, and then you're going to make certain that you back it up!

9. *Deal with resistance.* The rubber really meets the road when top managers face the problem of dealing with resistance, particularly when the resistance is visible and vocal and when it is attributable to those in leadership positions. You'll be fortunate if you never have to deal with this issue. However, I can virtually guarantee you that you will face it, and I urge you to deal with it quickly and firmly.

Resistance from this level that is ignored or not effectively challenged by top management will quickly erode the strong reputation for TQM support which you have earned to this point.

10. *Tie your reward system to TQM.* "What gets rewarded gets done," an old adage advises. There is no stronger signpost for both managers and employees of the organization than the corporate reward system. What gets appraised, recognized, and paid for directs people to the path they will follow.

Top managers must commission and actively support a full review of the reward system to ensure that it explicitly and implicitly channels behavior in the proper direction. A review of the reward system should focus on all aspects of the system, including:

- Performance appraisals
- Compensation practices
- Regular salary increases
- Incentive and bonus payments
- Recognition awards
- Promotion decisions
- Other expressions of "well done"

If the reward system as a whole doesn't clearly support the concepts and principles of total quality, then the troops will be marching relentlessly toward the wrong battlefield.

Ten Specific TQM Involvement Actions for Top Managers

Top management's support is extremely important to the development and fulfillment of an effective TQM process. However, nothing is more critical than top management's hands-on involvement. Involvement is action-oriented and visible to others in the organization. This involvement from the top speaks volumes as to top management's commitment and helps to build a common TQM language. After all, if many people learn and practice the same methods, they will develop a common language. A common language is an extremely beneficial element of a total quality culture.

There are some specific things top managers can do and must do to get meaningfully involved. Here is a list of 10 such involvement actions.

1. *Serve on the quality council or a lead team.* I certainly hope there is little argument over this suggestion. If one believes that TQM represents the shaping of a new and stronger corporate culture, that it will involve virtually everyone in the company, that it requires a significant investment in time and money, that it clearly focuses on meeting the needs of customers, and that it can help to achieve a sustainable competitive advantage, then it certainly follows that the CEO and his or her immediate executive staff must serve personally on the corporate quality council. Delegating this key responsibility to others below the executive staff level diminishes the importance placed on TQM and eliminates the chances for success.

If the CEO chairs the quality council, there will be no question as to who should guide the division or major unit lead teams. It will necessarily follow that the senior executive staffs of these divisions or units will serve in that capacity.

2. *Participate in QI training.* Senior managers need to be the first students in TQM training and learn the concepts, tools, and techniques of TQM. Having accomplished this, senior managers need to find ways to participate meaningfully in the ongoing training sessions. No training session should be considered complete until one or more senior managers has visited the classroom and interacted with the students.

The best way to get senior managers involved here is to have them actually teach part of a TQM training course. Senior managers are particularly well suited to providing an overview of TQM and to explaining why the company is pursuing the development of a TQM process. Senior managers are also well suited to discussing the quality planning element of TQM because this is where they are most deeply and directly involved.

3. *Serve on QI teams.* Quality improvement teams represent the most visible TQM activity and, over time, will involve hundreds of people within the company. Teams are the real guts of TQM because they work to fix the fundamental flaws that prevent customer delight. Specifically, they work to solve chronic problems through the project-by-project approach. Also, as mentioned earlier, management-level QI teams are much more likely to make the more significant problem-

solving, QI contributions, particularly if they are cross-functional management teams.

Therefore, managers at all levels should find ways to involve themselves personally on a QI team. Not only will top management's presence add to the results a team achieves, it will also demonstrate the commitment management truly has for the TQM process. The fact that the CEO of Colonial Penn and his staff served as a QI team did not go unnoticed by the employees of our company! Their work was also noticed on the corporate balance sheet because their team saved a half-million dollars in the first year after their project was completed. Even after his first team involvement experience was completed, the president of Colonial Penn asked for additional TQM "tutoring." He wanted to know the process as well as anyone in the company! As soon as tutoring was complete, he elected to form his own QI team and designated himself team leader. At this writing, this top-level, cross-functional team is making significant progress in pursuing its QI project.

4. *Review QI team presentations.* Managers who know the TQM process well meet a practical need in addition to the need for simply demonstrating personal top-level commitment. Often, senior managers will be asked to hear and evaluate completed team projects and required to approve the implementation of a team's recommended countermeasures. On many occasions, approval will call for funding to implement the changes a team is presenting. The best decisions will be made only if the senior managers fully understand how a team has reached its conclusions and why a specific set of actions is recommended. The team presentation "review board" has to know almost as much about the process as does the team making the presentation in order to reach sound decisions and to assure the presenting team that its work is well understood and appreciated.

If you wish to select some of your QI teams for special corporate recognition, senior managers will want to play a part in the selection. They can do this job well only by being able to identify the strong points and weak points of a team's project presentation. They must know how the teams operate inside and out.

5. *Present QI certificates and awards.* This senior management involvement action is a lot of fun. Almost everyone likes to participate in celebratory events and present awards. Looking into the smiling faces of people who know they have accomplished something significant is quite gratifying.

Senior managers must play lead roles in any and all events at which accomplishment is recognized. And, on an informal basis, they need to actually create such opportunities. For example, just go out into the company and find some people doing things well with respect to quality and administer a few sincere thank-yous and handshakes.

To be more formal, make sure that you present certificates to each employee who completes your TQM training classes, and present the awards to teams when they complete QI projects.

6. *Talk with customers.* Talking with customers is a fundamental and extremely important action for senior managers to take in order to promote and participate in a successful TQM process. Unfortunately, it is also one with which too few senior managers involve themselves today.

Quality means meeting the needs of customers. To meet the needs of customers requires that we have a clear and up-to-date understanding, first, of what customers need or expect and, second, how they perceive what they are currently receiving from the company. This is far too important an activity to be completely reduced to a form or questionnaire, with its interpretation left to subordinates.

Hearing the results of customer surveys, focus groups, and the like is fine, but senior managers must also find ways to interact directly with customers on a regular basis in order to have a genuine feel for what customers are thinking. Managers should visit with customers when feasible and speak with them on the phone. This activity should center on customers who are dissatisfied as well as customers who are delighted, because it is just as important to know what is being done well as it is to know what is being done poorly. Executives should also regularly review correspondence from customers, and this should include letters directed specifically to executives as well as routine correspondence.

Over a period of time, senior managers will build a personal database of customer perceptions that will prove to be particularly useful as their involvement with TQM continues.

7. *Lead the quality planning effort.* Chapter 7 discussed quality planning and reserved this important activity principally for management. In fact, quality planning should be *directed* by top management.

The CEO should lead the meetings that define the corporate vision, the CSFs, the long-term goals, and the competitive, legislative, and economic environment and outlook. He or she should also be weaving the company's assessment of customers' needs throughout this process.

Top management should take the lead to thoroughly communicate the plan throughout the corporation and to require the units of the company to identify ways by which they can support the plan's vital few goals and CSFs.

8. *Approve QI project ideas.* Although approving QI project ideas overlaps the quality council's mission and the quality planning effort, it still deserves separate mention.

As TQM takes hold, people throughout the company will be suggesting QI project ideas for teams to tackle. The obvious involvement for senior managers—specifically for the quality council and for lead teams—is the review and approval of project ideas. This is primarily because projects may need to be funded but also because all projects need to be evaluated to determine how they will contribute to the achievement of the vital few goals, the CSFs, and so on.

Any review and approval process has to be very efficient so as not to delay the formation of QI teams and the training of team members. Consequently, time and effort are saved if top managers are the reviewers, because they will ultimately decide approval of project implementation plans and funding.

9. *Visit team meetings and visit departments.* "Management by wandering around" has become a familiar phrase to many senior executives. This means touring the organization and interacting with the employees on an informal basis. The technique is quite valuable for demonstrating interest in and commitment to TQM.

Have your quality department or facilitators keep you advised as to where TQM activities are taking place. Specifically, make yourself aware of where QI team meetings are being held and which departments are pursuing unit-level quality. Then, drop by and get involved for a while. Ask questions and offer advice and assistance. This show of interest will be well received and not soon forgotten.

10. *Speak the language.* As your TQM process takes root within the company, a quality language will develop. If you have been actively involved through training and team participation, you will be quite conversant. Words and phrases like *vital few, cause-and-effect analysis, data gathering, customers' needs, root cause,* and many others will be spoken throughout all levels of the company.

It is important that senior managers speak this language, too, in order to nurture the TQM environment. This common language is a powerful force in organizational effectiveness. It breaks down barriers between the higher levels in a company and the lower levels, and it greatly facilitates communications and understanding. Some day you may hear the CEO having a conversation with an application order clerk in the hallway that goes something like this:

CEO: Sounds like a broad problem. How did you stratify it?

CLERK: We stratified the issue in at least five ways and couldn't find a Pareto effect for several weeks. But we did eventually find that 72 percent of the orders we process beyond our 6-day indicator came from 12 percent of our customer base.

CEO: So I guess you could then develop a good problem statement.

CLERK: That's right, and it helped us greatly in our cause-and-effect analysis. We isolated and verified three root causes.

CEO: Did you choose to treat all three root causes?

CLERK: No. We are now developing actions on two of them. The third was judged to be something we couldn't affect in our own unit, so we referred it to our lead team and they'll discuss it with the marketing lead team.

CEO: Sounds like you are doing very well. What outcome do you expect?

CLERK: By the end of the year we should be processing all orders within our indicator target level of 6 days.

CEO: That's great! Wasn't your goal for order processing set at 14 days last year?

CLERK: [*Beaming*] Yes. But our customers really need a response in 7 or 8 days according to the research we did.

CEO: So the customers must be delighted!

CLERK: Delighted today, but we think we can hit 4 or 5 days within the next 12 to 18 months!

CEO: That's terrific! See you at the TQM awards luncheon.

Support and involvement are keys to success. Plan for it, and get on with it.

Transformation Checkpoints

1. A TQM effort will not be successful without the involvement of upper management.
2. Be a value-driven leader.
3. Stress customer satisfaction levels as a primary indicator of long-term success. Don't worship only at the altar of quarterly earnings per share.
4. Even the best customer-contact force can keep customers satisfied for only so long if, for example, other processes like billing are fundamentally flawed.
5. Consider "flattening" the organizational structure through the use of self-managed work teams.
6. The 10 specific TQM support actions for top managers are:

- Approve the financial investment in TQM.
- Make and approve the time for TQM.
- Require formal training and continuous learning in TQM.
- Secure consulting help.
- Make speeches and appearances supporting TQM.
- Join national and local quality associations.
- Direct the quality department.
- Set a quality policy and vision.
- Deal with resistance.
- Tie your reward system to TQM.

7. The 10 specific TQM involvement actions for top managers are:
   - Serve on the quality council or lead team.
   - Participate in QI training.
   - Serve on QI teams.
   - Review QI team presentations.
   - Present QI certificates and awards.
   - Talk with customers.
   - Lead the quality planning effort.
   - Approve QI project ideas.
   - Visit team meetings and visit departments.
   - Speak the language.

8. Get on with it.

13 Celebrating Quality

A TQM process that doesn't include periodic doses of celebration and recognition is like eating tasteless food. It may continue to ensure good health, but it sure "ain't special or all that much fun." At this point in the process you need to stir in the spices and flavorings and to add the garnish that can make your TQM efforts more enjoyable and rewarding. You want to nourish the quality spirit so that it will propel everyone to the crest of the next hill on the horizon of competitive advantage.

In this chapter we'll cover:

- The roles of celebration, recognition, and rewards
- The guiding principles
- The development of a celebration, recognition, and reward process

What Are the Roles of Celebration, Recognition, and Rewards?

Celebration, recognition, and rewards, whether meant to reinforce a TQM process or any other important activity, first need to rest on a solid base—competitive base pay. Employees who feel underpaid in relation to those in similar jobs in other companies or in other departments within their own company will view celebration, recognition, and supplementary rewards with skepticism at best and hostility at worst.

The employee opinion survey we discussed earlier can help management determine whether it has built a sound foundation upon which to erect a celebration, recognition, and reward process. If the base pay foundation is found to be weak, then it must be strengthened. This can be a difficult judgment to make, because many people, when asked about their satisfaction with base pay and with regular or "normal" increases in pay, may express some level of dissatisfaction in hopes of winning more dollars. Or so we tend to think. However, I believe that employee responses to the pay questions generally reflect their true perception when it comes to pay, and I've done a great amount of work with employee surveys over the years.

In any event, the consultant you retain to help you design, administer, and interpret your employee opinion survey can be particularly helpful and objective when it comes to analyzing responses to pay questions. Listen carefully to what you hear, and don't underestimate the veracity of the data. Then take whatever reasonable action is necessary. To ignore reality at this point of implementing a TQM process is to venture upon a bridge that cannot handle the stress to which it will be subjected.

Another mistake to avoid is to assume that fair, equitable base pay rates are enough to ensure the special dedication and enthusiasm that are necessary to really make a difference to the key corporate goals. Pay will bring the body to the office each day, but it will not provide or sustain the spirit needed for that above-and-beyond-the-call-of-duty performance, or at least not for very long.

In addition, pay and pay increases must be linked closely to performance. Results are always better when people can really see a cause-and-effect relationship between their performance and key goals and their rate of pay. Study upon study has shown this to be true. Attempt after attempt to provide this critical linking has shown that, although important, it is not easily achieved. Obviously, this whole area of pay and pay for performance is a subject great enough for further research or for another book. However, enough has been said here for our purposes.

I have been using the words *celebration, recognition,* and *rewards* separately, but we really need to string them together so that they can be seen as an integrated system. To simplify what otherwise might turn into a lexicon of sorts, I will use the term *recognition* to refer to this integrated system of celebration, recognition, and rewards.

Webster defines *recognition* as special notice or attention, *celebration* as the demonstration of satisfaction by festivities or other deviation from the routine, and *reward* as something that is given for some service or attainment. For our purposes, we'll define *recognition* as deviations from the routine in order to pay special attention to those who distinguish themselves in the pursuit of quality.

Recognition is important because it reinforces the desired behavior necessary for the achievement of significant results or milestones. The *application* of recognition is also important because we can recognize an individual for a specific achievement, or a group of people such as a QI team for remarkable results, and we can also recognize the entire organization for having reached a notable milestone in terms of either the overall TQM journey or the results it is broadly achieving. The point is, there are lots of opportunities for recognition. And recognition activities are fun, gratifying for all parties involved, and definitely beneficial to the success of your TQM effort.

The role that recognition plays in reinforcing a TQM process is, indeed, an important one. Recognition certainly makes people feel good and provides an incentive and the spirit to press on. This result is valuable, even all by itself; however, recognition does much, much more.

Recognition reinforces the cultural platform—the guiding beliefs and values—of the company. A process that recognizes people for achievements and results directly related to the key priorities and values set by the organization provides a visible demonstration for everyone of the desired behavior. After all, as we know, what gets rewarded and recognized gets done. Therefore, a well-designed recognition process acts as a flashing set of directional arrows or signposts signaling the right roads to follow.

In addition, a recognition process and, specifically, the events of the process itself bring top managers together with others in the company on frequent occasions outside the normal work routine. This added management visibility and communication create a stronger bond among the organizational levels and promote a single team spirit.

Typically, whenever executives think about recognition processes, they tend to get hung up on the role that monetary awards seemingly need to play in a "successful" system. Many feel that cash must physically change hands in order for recognition to be successful. Although recognition activities in the form of plaques, luncheons, certificates, prizes, and the like need to be funded, it is not necessarily true that cash awards are required. Cash can certainly supplement and complement other recognition activities, but many highly successful programs exist just fine without the cash exchange. Conversely, cash-only programs are rarely found to be successful for the long term because they tend to nourish only the pocketbook and not the spirit. Cash has little afterglow. For example, most people have a strong desire to be recognized by their peers, family, and friends. If you award me $100, I'll buy a pair of shoes and be done with it. However, if you give me a nice plaque I can hang on my wall, put my picture in the company newspaper, and shake my hand in front of my fellow employees, then I'm turned on. It is an event I'll remember and an event those around me will remember. In the long run you'll get more value for your money by investing it in plaques, luncheons, certificates, prizes, and the like.

So don't get hung up on the cash question when designing your recognition program. Although you'll find that including cash in your design will certainly please your employees, if you ever discontinue the cash feature, the recognition process in total will be devalued in the minds of your employees far beyond the value that the cash added to your process in the first place. It is always much easier to alter or rearrange the noncash features of your recognition program and not have the overall program devalued than it is to alter a cash feature unless, of course, you are raising the amount of the cash award.

Adopting Principles of Recognition

When designing or redeveloping your recognition process, there are several key principles to keep in mind at all times.

1. *Reality and relevance.* In the long run, employees will respond favorably only to a recognition program that provides rewards for accomplishments which they feel are relevant to key goals or real corporate priorities and values. For example, recognize people for graduating from quality training and serving on a QI team rather than for coming to work each day for 6 months. Recognize a person for going out of his or her way to help a customer with an unusual problem rather than for having the cleanest desk in the office.

In other words, give considerable thought as to why you wish to recognize people. Other employees will be in the audience for recognition events. If they see people being recognized for trivial accomplishments and for acts that don't clearly support the stated corporate priorities and values, both the recognition process and management will lose credibility.

However, don't design your criteria for recognition so that only superhuman effort can qualify. It is far better to try to make many people feel like superheroes. If you make me feel like a winner, I'll continue to act like one. The principle of the self-fulfilling prophecy is strongly at work with recognition processes.

2. *Sincerity.* Recognition activities must be seen as a sincere expression of appreciation. This principle relates closely to the first principle. If we recognize people for real and relevant accomplishments, we are

far more likely to exhibit sincere appreciation for what they've done, and this sincerity will be felt by all.

You can't write the need for sincerity into your program. You have to deliver it on the spot, and only the best actors can feign sincerity time after time. It must be truly felt to be perceived by the audience. If the words *rote, routine, mechanical,* and *listless* are used to describe recognition activities at your company, there is some serious remedial work that needs to be done!

3. *Timeliness.* Recognition events and activities should not be limited to the semiannual or annual grand festival. Just-in-time recognition is far more effective than the gunnysack method, which refers to collecting recognizable accomplishments in a sack and pulling them out under the spotlight months later.

Just-in-time recognition requires a highly responsive and flexible recognition program, but the process will still fall short if those of us who need to spot the acts deserving recognition are asleep in the watchtower. Ideally, recognition should occur within hours or days following a significant and relevant accomplishment, not months later.

You can write this requirement into your process, but it won't happen unless you make it happen through diligence and dedication.

4. *Variety.* There are dozens and maybe hundreds of ways to recognize people. A short list is presented as Figure 13-1. Develop a number of recognition methods rather than only one or two. This variety adds to the flexibility of your program and will spice it up considerably. A program that is entirely predictable gets dull quite quickly. You may

Plaques
Trophies
Certificates
CEO Letter
Honor Roll
Letter to Personnel File
Picture in Company Newspaper
Picture in City Newspaper
Use of Limousine
Savings Bond

Logo Items:
- Hats
- Shirts
- Pens
- Mugs
- Coasters
- Shorts
- Decals
- Paper Weights
- Desk Sets

Banner for Office
Special Parking Space
Introduction to Board
Lapel Pin or Jewelry

Special Luncheon
Dinner with Spouse or Friend
Trip (Local)
Trip (Distant)
Seminar Attendance
Pick-Your-Own-Gift Catalog
Gift Certificate
Day Off
Cash
Tickets to Sporting Events

Figure 13-1. Some Recognition Options for Groups and Individuals.

need a standing committee to keep track of all the options a program with variety has, but you'll find it to be far more effective than the assembly-line method or the "one of these always gets one of those" method.

5. *Management involvement.* No recognition event or presentation should take place without the presence and involvement by one or more members of senior management. Further, no recognition event should ever have to be postponed because a top manager cannot attend.

This principle relates to sincerity as well. If top management is not represented and involved in some meaningful way, or if event after event has to be rescheduled because top managers are too busy, the recognition process and, more important, the values it reinforces will soon be seen as unimportant. Top managers must make recognition involvement a high priority on their busy schedules. This is part of being a value-driven leader, as discussed in Chapter 12.

6. *Employee involvement and publicity.* We've established that recognition events reinforce the priorities and values of the organization. They continuously point the way for others. But if other employees never hear what accomplishments are recognized, they can't very well be influenced by what occurs.

Whenever possible, involve the peers of an employee who is receiving recognition so that they can witness the spotlight treatment and the reason for it. As mentioned earlier, this, in turn, makes recognition all the more meaningful for the person being honored. Try to hold individual recognition presentations in the winner's own work area. Avoid using the senior manager's office. Instead, make management come to the work unit, which is another way to provide visibility for management and to demonstrate management's support for TQM.

In addition, recognition activities should be widely publicized within the company through the use of the most effective and credible means available. This will help to ensure that the message gets to everyone.

7. *A customer focus.* The customers or recipients of the recognition process are the employees of your company. Just as you should research customers' needs before you design and market a new product or service, you must also research employees' needs and preferences before finalizing your recognition process. It is unwise to assume that management knows what the employees want.

In an earlier chapter I promised to relate how Colonial Penn almost went down the wrong road in developing our TQM recognition process. It was this last principle of researching employees' needs that we nearly ignored.

Several members of our original TQM design team were asked to develop a recommendation for the recognition process. They started by researching thoroughly. They went to the library, talked to people in other companies, and discussed the issue extensively among themselves. They developed a proposal that, after review by certain members of top management, was considered to be creative and potentially effective. Everyone wanted to install it right away.

At the last minute, one senior manager asked if we planned to discuss it first with some of our employees. There was momentary silence followed by the sound of several people kicking themselves.

As a result, we conducted numerous employee focus groups with the able assistance of our own market research specialist to determine employee reaction. We included people in the focus groups who were knowledgeable of and involved with our TQM process as well as people who were not yet involved.

At the conclusion of the focus groups our employees had essentially this message for us: Nice try. We appreciate all the creative thought that went into your proposal, but it has too many bells and whistles, it's a little too involved, and, by the way, you've missed some key ingredients.

Our employees—our recognition program customers—went on to outline their needs and preferences as follows:

a. We feel that just being selected as a QI team member is recognition in itself. So don't do anything special at this point other than make sure my top-level manager knows that I was selected, send a note to my personnel file that says I participated on a QI team, and let my friends and coworkers know by listing new team members' names in the company newspaper.
b. When we successfully complete QI training, we'd like a member of senior management to present us with our graduation certificate.
c. We don't deserve further recognition until our team has completed a QI project. Then we'd like our whole team to be recognized together at a luncheon or a reception with top management. Also, communicate our accomplishment in the company newspaper. At this point, we'd also appreciate a plaque that has each team member's name. No individual should be singled out as special. The team as a whole is special.
d. We'd like our bosses to know what we are up to, so it would be nice to have them drop by now and then to visit while the team is meeting.

Not only were we somewhat surprised at these findings, but we are extremely proud of our people for their ability to focus on what are really the essential, vital few ingredients of a successful recognition program. Behavioral scientists take note! Managers, don't sell your people short; treat them as the mature, intelligent adults they are.

To complete the story, we redesigned our recognition program to meet the needs of our customers. The budget for the year to run our newly designed recognition program was set at $17,250 for a total work force of 3000—$5.75 per employee on the payroll.

Developing a Recognition Process

There are seven basic steps to follow in the development of a recognition plan. Obviously, because we are concerned here with developing a process specifically to support our TQM efforts, we'll follow the P.D.C.A. cycle. Of course, we should *plan, do, check,* and *act* when working on tasks or projects that don't relate specifically to the TQM process as well!

The basic steps are listed in Figure 13-2 according to the P.D.C.A. model and briefly described as follows.

Step 1: Determine Priorities and Values. Determining priorities and values is a crucial step, not only because it is important to the design of a recognition program but because it is central to the whole TQM process. With respect to TQM, some of the priorities and values that must be reinforced are:

1. Participating on QI teams
2. Acquiring QI knowledge and skills
3. Completing projects and achieving targeted results
4. Utilizing the team problem-solving process effectively
5. Improving the ability to meet customers' needs—both external and internal customers
6. Determining ways to improve the TQM process by applying the P.D.C.A. concept to the TQM process itself

Step 2: Identify the Criteria or Milestones. Once you have determined the underlying values and priorities that need reinforcement, you must define the basic criteria or the milestones which qualify people for recognition. For example:

- Successful completion of QI training
- Successful completion of a QI project
- A factual demonstration that customer satisfaction has been improved

P.D.C.A.

Plan

1. Determine the principal corporate priorities and values that the recognition activities and events should reinforce.
2. Identify the criteria or milestones to be met by individuals and groups in order to qualify for recognition.
3. Set a preliminary budget for the recognition program.
4. Determine who will have primary accountability for administering the program.

Do

5. Design and describe the features, benefits, and procedures for recognition.

Check

6. Review your proposed program with groups of employees.

Act

7. Modify your process based on the feedback and suggestions you received from employees prior to initial implementation.

Figure 13-2. Developing a Recognition Program.

- Reaching a dollar savings milestone through TQM activities (for example, the first million dollars saved—for corporatewide or divisionwide recognition

Step 3: Set a Budget for Recognition. A rule of thumb for a preliminary budget is from $5 to $10 per employee on the payroll per year. However, once you have some experience with your recognition process, your budget should be reviewed for adequacy and periodically reset.

Step 4: Determine Accountability. I suggest that the division or major unit lead teams be given the accountability for utilizing the recognition program in their respective areas. Essentially, they are the ones who must select the employees or teams to be honored, arrange the recognition event, and so on. The TQM department should serve as the overall coordinator, administrator, and watchdog to ensure adherence to program guidelines.

Step 5: Design and Describe the Features, Benefits, and Procedures. Develop a document that specifically outlines the recognition procedures, the awards and ceremonies to take place, the role of senior management, and any other information lead teams will need to effectively implement and administer the program.

Step 6: Review the Program with Groups of Employees. Once you have assembled the components of what you think you want included in your recognition program, test the ideas on employees. This may be accomplished through a brief written survey of a random sample of people or through focus group–type meetings. Also, don't forget to solicit input from your lead teams, the administrators of the finalized recognition program.

A variation on the approach of checking with employees after a program has been conceived and outlined is to seek employee input even before you outline a program. Typically, however, you will get more useful feedback if you give people something to react to rather than ask them to provide input only to a broad concept.

Step 7: Modify Your Program Based on Employee Feedback. Once you have collected feedback, consider it seriously and use it to modify your approach. Also, don't forget to advise those employees who participated in your survey or focus groups of the outcome of these sessions, in terms of both an outline of all feedback received and a description of how it will be used. Thank them again for their help.

Once you have modified your initially conceived recognition program to reflect the needs of its customers, it must be carefully communicated to those who will be charged with its administration. Then, during the early stages of its implementation, continue to evaluate its effectiveness and make further modifications as needed. After a year or two, you should look to make some basic changes, if only to keep it fresh. In other words, always continue to spin the P.D.C.A. wheel.

Finally, when developing a recognition program, don't hesitate to be creative. There are as many ways to provide meaningful recognition as there are businesses in the United States.

Paul Revere Insurance Company, for example, awards bronze, silver, and gold lapel pins and charms—an Olympic Games theme—along with certificates to employees for reaching certain milestones. By prior arrangement, 50 stores and restaurants in the local Worcester, Massachusetts, area redeem the certificates for products and services.

A major hotel supplies its nonmanagement employees with outstanding service cards, which employees give to fellow employees who do an outstanding job of supporting them. An employee who receives a certain number of these service cards can turn them in for prizes. This process is a very creative way to support the internal customer concept.

Transformation Checkpoints

1. Any recognition program should complement and supplement a sound base pay program. Make sure that your basic salary system is fair and equitable before installing a recognition process.
2. Base pay alone is not enough to ensure dedication to and enthusiasm for the principal priorities and values of the corporation. Base pay brings the body to the office but does not raise the spirit needed for excellence.
3. Base pay and other rewards must be tied closely to performance in order to be meaningful. Rewards must be used to guide behavior along the right path.
4. Recognition reinforces the cultural platform—the guiding beliefs and values of the company. And it's fun!
5. Recognition activities promote management visibility and improve communications among organizational levels.
6. Cash need not change hands in order for a recognition process to be successful. Eliminating a cash feature from a recognition process later can be very difficult.
7. Heed these principles of recognition:
   - Recognition should be perceived as real and relevant. Recognize those acts and results that really make a difference.
   - Sincerity should mark your recognition program.
   - Recognition should be timely or just in time.
   - Variety should be built into your program.
   - Management must be directly and constantly involved in recognition events and activities.
   - The peers (fellow employees) of a person or group being recognized should be involved; and events should be publicized throughout the company.
   - A recognition process should not be implemented before soliciting input from some of the employees who will be its customers.
8. Follow this seven-step P.D.C.A. plan when developing your recognition program:
   - Determine priorities and values to be reinforced.
   - Identify criteria and milestones to be met.

- Set a budget.
- Assign accountability.
- Describe the features, benefits, and procedures of the program.
- Review your program with its customers.
- Modify your program based on feedback received.

9. Be creative!

14
Hitting High Gear

For many companies, after 2 or 3 years the TQM process will leave the rather bumpy and winding road characteristic of the development and introduction phases and will begin to enjoy the smoother and straighter road to delighting customers and achieving a sustainable competitive advantage. This part of the road will be smoother and straighter but not mirror smooth or arrow straight. You'll be able to hit high gear, but don't dare switch to cruise control! There may still be bumps and obstacles ahead, and there may be some unexpected bends in the roadway. Remain alert and in control. As the miles flash by, you'll now begin to see some of your competitors and some old ineffective corporate habits fading from sight in your rearview mirror. However, keep your eyes on the road ahead.

Hitting high gear will present what you should concentrate on as the road smooths and straightens. We'll cover:

- The changing role of the quality department and the quality council
- A week in the life of a quality lead team
- Keeping the "rig" on the road
- The role of your principal vendors
- Considering the Malcolm Baldrige National Quality Award

Understanding the Changing Role of the Quality Department and the Quality Council

During the first couple of years, your quality department will have been extremely busy working with the design team to develop your TQM approach, designing training programs, working with employees at the test site, and developing communications, awareness, recognition, and progress-tracking systems as well as fighting the fires set by the forces of resistance.

As the road becomes smooth and straightens, the quality department's role switches somewhat from a combination of rugged explorer, thoughtful inventor, and visionary to a blend of supporter, manager, and consultant. The change is subtle rather than drastic. The need to continue to explore the road ahead, to invent new ways to negotiate the more widely spaced bumps and bends, and to touch up the vision remains a key role of this group for the duration of the journey.

In the meantime, however, the quality department must maintain support for the caravan of quality vehicles that are running in high gear in order to ensure the quality of the journey. The members of the quality department now need to oversee the entire quality process and to play a lead role in managing the many support systems such as quality training, recognition, communications, and progress tracking as well as in diagnosing the causes of vehicle breakdowns. They need to continue being strong and vocal advocates of the right way, as opposed to the error-prone quick way. If others don't view the quality department as a pain in the neck from time to time, then the department probably isn't doing its job well enough. It must be constantly assessing progress and suggesting adjustments to smoothly negotiate the bumps and bends as the journey continues.

At this stage, the quality department interacts most frequently with the facilitators (who should exist in all divisions and major units), the division lead teams, and the corporate quality council. In other words, the department spends most of its time working closely with top managers and with those quality specialists and ambassadors who are the internal consultants for quality—the facilitators.

The small force of facilitators must be supported like crazy because their role is a critical and difficult one. Facilitators will be closest to the action, and their advanced quality training will permit them to guide, nurture, and enhance all TQM activities in their respective territories. Listen to them, support them, and include them in your plans for recognition. They are the coaches and unsung heroes of the winning team.

The role of the quality council also changes slightly at this stage. Initially, the council was deciding whether or not to begin a TQM effort, how to develop the process, how much to invest, and how best to support the early efforts. Now, with the full model in place, the council plays the lead policy-making role in the quality planning element of TQM, which we discussed in Chapter 7. In addition, it plays an active role in reviewing the QI project themes proposed by the lead teams and plays a continuous role in celebration, recognition, and day-to-day encouragement. The council will continue to be called upon to make some key decisions, such as whether to apply for the Malcolm Baldrige National Quality Award, and must actively take part in the continuing communications and awareness events.

Reviewing a Week in the Life of a Lead Team

Once the road has smoothed, there is no element of the quality organization structure more vital to success than the lead team, assuming that the quality council members are firmly committed to the journey.

Because the quality council consists of the top managers of the organization, they are too removed from the operating level of the company to strongly influence what happens there on a week-to-week basis. The lead teams, however, although also consisting of upper-level managers, are in the best organizational position to directly and continuously influence what is accomplished.

During a typical week, here's what a lead team and its members should find themselves doing:

Monday: The regular weekly lead team meeting takes place, with the division's lead facilitator guiding the meeting through its agenda. The following items are covered:

- A review of newly proposed QI team projects. Do they relate to key corporate goals and priorities? Who will be the members? The leader? The facilitator? When will training take place? How can we help? And so on.
- Status of teams in the early stages.
- Status of teams in the latter stages.
- Are any teams struggling or particularly excelling?
- What's getting in the way?

- How is the planning for the next quality celebration and recognition event proceeding?
- How are our units doing at unit-level quality?
- A review of the division's quality process indicators, such as the number of teams, percent of employees directly involved, and number of completed projects.
- What special opportunities or events will present themselves this week for which lead team members can show support and provide assistance or encouragement?
- A review of the calendar for scheduled times for all team meetings.
- And so on.

Tuesday: Individual lead team members informally visit with a few quality teams or departments engaged in unit-level quality.

Wednesday: Individual lead team members stop by a QI training class in progress even if no members of their division are among the students.

Thursday: Individual lead team members meet with their facilitator to be updated on how their own unit's QI teams and departments engaged in unit-level quality are doing.

Friday: Prepare thoughts and notes for next week's lead team meeting. Go out and catch someone doing something right and say thank-you. Encourage someone who may be struggling, or "sell" someone who may be resisting.

None of these activities takes very long, but the effect on the organization is strong and lasting. The point is: Be a day-by-day, year-after-year quality manager. It's an investment with a payoff!

Keeping the "Rig" on the Road

After 2 years or so, as you hit high gear, you'll probably find that your TQM process is self-propelled. That is, it is proceeding on its own power and momentum. Someone may remark, "We couldn't stop this thing now if we wanted to!" In the first year or two you worked on finding the right propellant. Now you'll work on steering to keep it all on track. This is a challenge too.

Here are some guidelines to consider in order to avoid running off the road or turning onto the wrong side street.

1. *Listen like crazy.* When things are going well, we have a tendency to relax and think we've got it knocked. This is when we may have a tendency to use cruise control. Don't make this mistake. A TQM process is both fragile and dynamic. It needs to be carefully nurtured and constantly managed like an exotic plant.

   Listen like crazy to those people in your company who are directly involved on a day-to-day basis: QI team members, team leaders, your facilitators, members of the quality department, supervisors, and others. Always ask the key question: What can we be doing better?

   A TQM process consists of hundreds of activities, from selecting good projects, training people, supporting teams, and measuring progress to choosing leaders, recognizing winners, researching customers' needs, and the like. As each month goes by, those involved will identify both large and small opportunities for enhancing your process. If you are not asking and listening, you'll miss these process-improvement opportunities.

   If the four elements of the P.D.C.A. cycle can be thought of as a four-speed transmission or gearbox, you always want to be shifting from third to fourth and back again. You want to be checking constantly and acting on what you hear, which can be beneficial to the continuous improvement of your process. When you find something that needs modification, don't forget to shift through all four P.D.C.A. gears in developing your enhancements. Keep spinning the P.D.C.A. cycle to higher and higher levels of improvement.

   Listen like crazy outside the walls of the organization as well as inside. Listen to your customers. Seek feedback constantly on how you are doing at meeting their needs. This feedback will point to what you are doing well and to what you still need to improve. Your customers, of course, can't tell you how you are doing at managing the dozens of QI activities, like selecting QI projects and team leaders, but, more important, they can give you an idea of whether or not the hundreds of activities are making a difference to them. This is the ultimate question: Is our quality process making a positive difference to our customers?
2. *Continue to learn.* I'm an avid sailor. One reason why I love the sport so much is that there is always more to learn. The range of knowledge and skill to be acquired is extensive. For example, a beginner can be taught in a few hours to sail a small boat from point *A* to point *B* and back. This is one end of the range. At the other end, the skills and knowledge are wide-ranging, like those necessary to circumnavigate the world single-handedly in a 48-foot ketch, or

more focused on racing, like those required to skipper an America's Cup yacht in sailing's ultimate competition.

Quality management is like sailing. The basics aren't all that tough to acquire, but there is always more to learn to more effectively and efficiently reach your destination. Just as a sailor is constantly alert to the vagaries of the wind so that he or she may trim the sails to move faster and smoother through the water, you must always be aware of opportunities and events to fine-tune your process to move faster and smoother on the quality journey.

Even though your TQM process is in high gear, I urge you to continue learning. Visit other companies—both within and outside your industry—that are pursuing quality. If you can visit some of the Deming Prize winners in Japan, or if you can visit Florida Power and Light Company, the first and only Deming Prize winner in the United States, do it. In fact, attend the monthly orientation and overview given by its sister company, QualTec, Inc., which is open to those in other organizations. Read more books and articles. Attend seminars and join local and national quality associations for the networking and the other benefits. And periodically invite a quality consultant or some other set of eyes to review what you're up to and to provide feedback and ideas. Never stop learning!

3. *Celebrate regularly.* Once you have hit high gear with your TQM process, the momentum needs to be sustained. Nothing is more effective here than celebrating your successes.

   With a companywide TQM process, it will be a simple task to find success stories and the heroes behind those stories. Regular celebration will ensure that the heartbeat of quality sounds strongly.

4. *Match strides with another company.* Matching strides with another company won't work for everyone, but look around your town or area for another company that is also pursuing a TQM process—preferably not a direct competitor, but one you may consider a vendor.

   Suggest to this company that you form a quality partnership to help each other sustain the drive for quality. From time to time this partnership may even include a little Olympiclike, friendly competition in order to raise the quality spirit. Here are some suggested activities in which your partnership may engage:

   a. Have your respective facilitators and quality departments meet two or three times a year in order to discuss successes, failures, issues, and answers. The purpose is for each company to learn something from its partner that may prove valuable to its own quality process. For example, you may find a better way to arrange recognition events, a more effective process for selecting projects, or a new method for communicating with customers.

b. The quality councils may wish to hold a joint meeting once or twice a year, as well, in order to share experiences and observations at a more strategic level.

c. Consider swapping a key person for 6 months, probably someone in the quality department or a facilitator. This new set of trained eyes and ears may see and hear some things that end up being valuable to both companies.

d. Exchange TQM items such as internal brochures, newsletters, team guidebooks, or training outlines so that each company can build a reference library of other approaches.

e. Arrange tours of your respective companies for QI team leaders and members so that more people can see firsthand the quality process in another company.

f. Pool your resources to take advantage of learning opportunities that may be costly, such as the use of a particularly well-known consultant, a trip to Japan, or a trip to Florida Power and Light Company's headquarters in Miami.

g. Hold a quality partnership festival once a year and split the cost and planning effort. Hire a hall and set up booths with exhibits of some of your TQM successes. Have QI teams manage the booths. Hire some entertainment and invite employees' families and some customers of your respective companies to attend. You'll also find the local press interested in covering such an event. Invite the mayor and members of the chamber of commerce.

h. Establish an Olympic organizing committee consisting of employees from both companies. Have the committee come up with about three events for some friendly competition. The best QI team presentation of a project could be one such event. The medals should go, however, to the teams who pursued the most customer-focused improvement projects and who adhered most closely to a logical, fact-based, problem-solving process to achieve results. Speed and results may count, but don't put these at the top of the list because your partner company may be engaged in a business that inherently yields more easily achievable and quantifiable dollar results.

Another event could be an essay contest for employees on the subject of "How TQM Harnesses the Talent of Employees to Benefit the Customer."

The panel of judges should include two people from each of the partner companies and three outsiders. Outsiders may be quality consultants who volunteer a half day of their time, local business leaders, typical (unbiased) customers from the community, professors from a local university, government officials, and the like.

Medals can be awarded to the winning individuals, and a perpetual trophy can be presented to the winning company. Each company may also wish to put up $1000, with the cash eventually going to a charity selected by the overall winning company.

I'm sure that if this idea of a quality partnership interests you, you'll conceive even more creative quality events. It takes a little time, but it can do a lot to raise spirits and improve your quality efforts, and it will provide meaningful publicity for the participating organizations.

If your city includes a local quality networking organization such as the Philadelphia Area Council for Excellence or the Madison (Wisconsin) Area Quality Improvement Network, these groups may be helpful in arranging such an activity.

The Role of Your Principal Vendors

When you've hit high gear with your TQM process, you've got an effective quality effort working within your company. But, there is still a critical piece missing—the committed involvement of your principal vendors. This is particularly true of manufacturing companies, but it is also true in the service industry.

The basic value-added model is shown in Figure 14-1.

This model, by the way, also depicts the internal working of a company as discussed in Chapter 8, "Unit-Level Quality." In this case the model looks like Figure 14-2.

In manufacturing, vendors or suppliers typically provide raw materials, supplies, or components that are enhanced or completed to form a product which is then sold to customers. In service businesses, vendors may supply "hard" products, such as computers, or they may supply

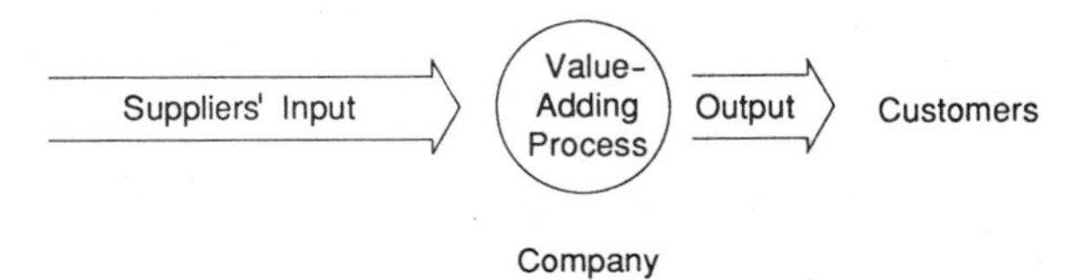

Figure 14-1. Company Value-Adding Process (VAP) Model.

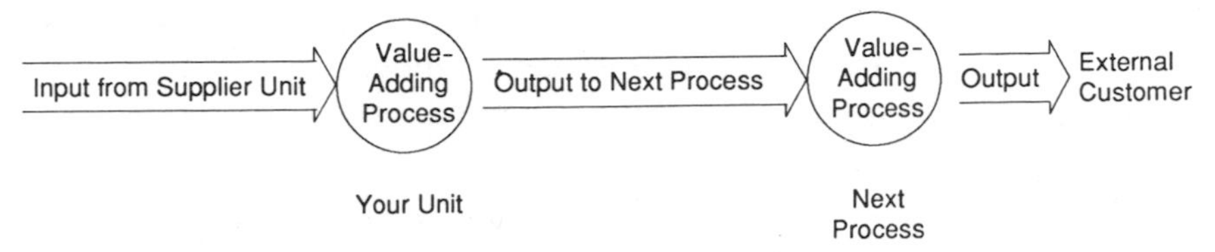

Figure 14-2. Internal Value-Adding Process (VAP) Model.

"soft" materials, or services such as overnight mail delivery, which the service company needs in order to do its job. The input for a hotel, for example, may include many outside firms that supply food services, cleaning services, sight-seeing tours for guests, audiovisual services for conventions, television services for hotel rooms, or computer services for the reservations system.

The point is that you will never be able to fully achieve your goals for customer delight if the input from your suppliers is defective, unreliable, late, or in short supply. Therefore, a *total* quality management system must pay attention to vendor input or your own efforts will be suboptimized.

In the case of any relationship with a vendor, *you* are the customer. At this point, you know a lot about quality. This knowledge, plus your heightened commitment to doing it right the first time and every time in order to delight your customers, makes you far less tolerant of shoddy service.

Because you have a great deal of influence over your vendors, you may be able to cause them to improve, but if they don't deliver a quality product or service, take your money and your business and go elsewhere. At this stage of the quality journey, you need to measure the quality of vendors and encourage them to improve their performance.

First, conduct an analysis similar to the one suggested by the format shown in Figure 14-3 to measure vendor quality.

For example, if you are managing a hotel's conference and convention department and utilize a vendor to supply audiovisual equipment and services, you may develop the following data:

Customer Need	Our Quality Indicators	Our Quality Goals	Vendor Quality Indicators	Vendor Quality Goals

Figure 14-3. Vendor Quality Analysis.

Customer need: Fully defect-free audiovisual performance at trial testing 4 hours prior to conference registration.

Our quality indicators:

1. Number of audiovisual defects.
2. Number of times equipment is not deployed and tested 4 hours prior to conference registration.

Our quality goals:

1. No more than a 2 percent defect rate per year at initial on-site test.
2. 100 percent timeliness.

Vendor quality indicators:

1. Number of audiovisual defects.
2. Number of times equipment is not deployed and tested 4 hours prior to conference registration.

Vendor quality goals:

1. No more than 1 percent per year at initial on-site test.
2. 100 percent timeliness.

This is a very basic model, but it should set the example. Translate researched customer needs to quality goals and indicators and further translate these needs—now your needs as an interim customer—to your vendor or supplier. Use this scale to measure vendor performance and identify key deficiencies, and work with your vendors to gain improvements. Your vendor should be involved in setting the goals and quality indicators, but always begin by stating the needs of the ultimate customer.

It is usually better to work closely with vendors, to turn marginal ones into great ones, than to frequently fire vendors and hope to find a better one. So work with them to set the goals. Monitor measurable performance, share customer feedback with them, and require them to adopt a TQM process like yours over the next 2 to 3 years as a condition of retaining you as a customer.

Ultimately, you may wish to set a long-range goal of reducing the number of vendors to the vital few that demonstrate the ability to constantly meet quality goals through the use of a well-developed TQM process. Be demanding on this point because it makes a big difference over time.

In many cases, it is wise for you to commit time and resources to provide hands-on help to vendors in developing a TQM process. You've learned a lot and can act as their adviser or consultant.

Consider assigning a few people in your own organization to study vendor quality and to provide the assistance to vendors as needed. By doing this, you'll be helping yourself, delighting your customers, and spreading the quality commitment to more and more firms throughout the country.

Considering the Malcolm Baldrige National Quality Award

As I've mentioned, 1988 was the first year that the Malcolm Baldrige National Quality Award was offered to and won by U.S. companies for successfully pursuing TQM. Florida Power and Light Company, Dr. Joseph M. Juran, and others played a significant role in getting the necessary legislation approved. To date, although no service organization has won, several have competed for this distinguished award.

The Baldrige Award is still not widely known. As the next few years pass, I for one hope that the existence of this award sparks a burning fire for the serious pursuit of TQM throughout the United States for both consumers and corporations. As this increasing awareness takes place, companies that win the Baldrige will earn reputations as being the best in the United States when it comes to producing quality goods and services for customers. Winning the award may result in your having improved ability to attract new customers at reduced advertising costs.

When you hit high gear with your TQM process, I suggest that you begin to consider at least applying for this award. You'll reap significant benefits even if you never submit your application or if you file an application but fail to win—the experience of preparing for the review will teach you a great deal about what still needs to be done to fully develop your TQM process.

So I urge you to simply go through the exercise of completing the award application because this can be a helpful and revealing experience and will serve to point out any deficiencies in your TQM process.

For information pertaining to the Malcolm Baldrige National Quality Award, call or write to:

The Malcolm Baldrige National Quality Award Consortium, Inc.
National Institute of Standards and Technology
Gaithersburg, MD 20899
Telephone (301) 975-2036

or

P. O. Box 443
Milwaukee, WI 53201-0443
Telephone (414) 272-8575

Transformation Checkpoints

1. You'll hit high gear in just a few years, but don't switch to cruise control. Keep your eyes on the road ahead.
2. The role of the quality department switches from rugged explorer, thoughtful inventor, and visionary to supporter, manager, and consultant.
3. The quality department must always advocate the right way, not the quick way.
4. It's important to support your facilitators like crazy!
5. The quality council continues to support and drive TQM. The council members also lead the quality planning process.
6. Lead teams are in the best organizational position to directly and continuously influence your TQM efforts.
7. Lead team members and other key personnel must learn to be one-minute quality managers.
8. Guidelines for keeping the TQM rig on the road:
   a. Listen to the people involved and to the customers and continuously spin the P.D.C.A. wheel to make improvements.
   b. Continue to learn.

      Visit other companies, such as Florida Power and Light Company.
      Read books and articles.
      Attend seminars.
      Join quality associations.
      Invite a review by a consultant.

   c. Celebrate regularly.
   d. Match strides with another company.

      Exchange ideas, material, and people.
      Hold a quality Olympics.

9. Examine the critical role your vendors and suppliers play. Work with them to set quality goals and indicators and to help them establish a TQM process.
10. Assign someone to the vendor quality mission.
11. Learn about the Malcolm Baldrige National Quality Award.
12. Apply for the Baldrige, or at least complete the application in order to improve your TQM process.

15
A Thousand Points of Contact

Points of contact between your employees and customers are repeated hundreds or thousands of times a day, every day, and offer the optimum opportunity to build and reinforce a positive company-customer relationship. The employees who normally work in sales or service departments are your front line and, in the eyes of the customer or the potential customer, are in fact the company. To take advantage of each of these vital points of contact requires that your TQM process focus on maintaining a staff that will be exceptionally and continuously responsive to the needs of your customers.

By now you know that even the best customer-contact employee can't keep customers delighted for very long if the fundamental processes or systems of your organization are flawed or hostile toward customers. You have established QI teams whose work it is to constantly improve these internal mechanisms and to continuously solve the problems that prevent you from delighting your customers. At the same time, it is also true that the most effective, efficient, and customer-friendly internal processes can't delight your customers for very long if the front-line, customer-contact employees are not totally and consistently responsive to the needs of customers in areas such as courtesy, promptness, follow-through, accuracy, and professionalism. One discourteous customer-contact employee can unravel or discredit the whole system of TQM.

Because TQM touches every segment of the organization, the focus we must place on those who have regular direct point of contact with external customers is equally applicable to employees in every other department as well. After all, each employee in the company plays an important role in meeting customers' needs through the quality chain of events—the internal provider to the internal customer to the external customer. Think of this chain as the quality partnership that must exist in order to achieve exceptional levels of customer delight. Each and every "partner" in the company must know how his or her efforts affect others within the organization and how his or her work eventually affects customer perceptions. For example, if the order processing clerk doesn't send the correct data to the billing unit, then the customer gets an incorrect statement and the customer service representative receives an angry call. Unit-level quality, discussed earlier, is designed to help build this partnership.

As a former officer in the U.S. Marine Corps, I can tell you that, in their own way, the Marines recognize this concept. Each and every new Marine, regardless of his or her eventual military occupational specialty (MOS), is first trained to be a member of the Marine infantry—the front-line fighting force. All Marines, therefore, whether they are later trained to be a cook, truck driver, artillery specialist, or tank driver, know the job and skills required for enemy contact.

Disney provides a more business-oriented example. New employee training, regardless of the job ultimately assigned, prepares employees to be a member of the "cast" that "entertains" the customer. Customer delight is everyone's job at Disney, and so it must be at your company as well.

The following issues in selecting and maintaining a staff of exceptionally customer-responsive employees will be discussed:

- Selecting the best people
- Training for customer delight
- Managing for customer delight
- Rewarding employees and building spirit

Selecting the Best People

Selecting the best customer-contact employees should not be considered a routine process. Instead it should be viewed as vitally important, and the recruiting and selection process itself should reflect this importance.

Any device you use to attract applicants for customer-contact positions, such as newspaper and radio ads, employment agencies, and employee referral programs, must clearly advise interested applicants that your company is serious about selecting the best, and it should convey the strong commitment you have to delighting your customers. There is no better time to advertise your customer-focused culture than right up front. Remember, too, that your current employees and many customers may see or hear these ads, and this will serve to reinforce to these important audiences your commitment to customer satisfaction.

Once you have attracted a group of eager applicants, screen and evaluate these potential new employees very carefully. Initial interviews must be thorough and should attempt to determine the extent to which each applicant fundamentally believes in the value of satisfied customers. Develop a series of interview questions that may help to reveal *attitudes* about customer service rather than focus only on experience at customer service. Experience may or may not be useful. Bad habits can be hard to break. Remember, it is attitudes that drive behavior. When developing a series of interview questions, include a variety of people from within your organization. For example, include one or two of your best customer-contact people, a personnel representative, the hiring manager, a customer service trainer, and a member of your customer satisfaction research staff, if you have one, or a member of your quality department. Developing the interview questions can be a tricky task. First, it is not easy to determine questions and assess responses when it comes to understanding attitudes or motivation. Second, it can be easy to run afoul of equal employment opportunity laws.

I also suggest that the same group of people who determine the list of interview questions be involved in helping to evaluate responses and draw conclusions. This doesn't mean that each applicant should be interviewed by a group of five or six people, because this could be too intimidating. Instead, divide your question list into two or three smaller lists, and conduct two or three interviews with one but not more than two people serving as interviewers. Afterward, the original group—the selection team—can get together to discuss each applicant.

A useful technique to use in this process is the telephone interview. Many customer service contacts will occur on the phone, so it is logical to witness firsthand the applicant's telephone manner and skills.

You may also wish to explore professionally designed screening instruments for selecting customer-contact people. These tests or assessment centers can be quite helpful, but great care must be exercised to ensure that they are valid predictors of success on the job.

Once you have identified a few applicants who appear to meet your demanding requirements, conduct a second series of interviews as a double check, and begin the process of checking references using some of the same questions developed for the selection interview.

After final selections are made, you will probably end up with very talented and committed employees, and these new staff members will feel that they are indeed special after having survived such a thorough preemployment examination. They will also know that you are extremely serious about providing the best customer service possible.

The recruitment and selection process I've described does take time to plan and follow, but when you consider the critical nature of the customer-contact position and the fact that each person you may hire represents about a half million dollar investment on the average, then considerable care is certainly justified.

Finally, don't neglect the people who are already on the payroll in non-customer-contact jobs when you look to find new people for the customer-interface role. Many of your current employees may have a desire to seek a transfer or promotion to a customer relations position. In most cases, you'll have a much better chance of selecting the right people from among your internal candidates because they have established visible track records with your company. An internal candidate's supervisor can more accurately predict success on the job based on actual experience, whereas a selection team evaluating outside candidates has to rely more heavily on their judgment and questionable reference checking. Also, any internal people applying for the customer-contact job will already have a good understanding of your products, procedures, and, of course, your commitment to quality and customer satisfaction. The devil you know is usually a better gamble than the devil you don't know!

Training for Customer Delight

Training the customer-contact people is one of the most important things any company does, yet too little attention is paid to designing a curriculum that is varied, fun, and effective. Plain vanilla is what usually exists.

Typically, customer service training consists of learning internal procedures, processes, forms, systems, and products with a little "and, oh yeah, be terribly nice too." I challenge you to develop a multifaceted approach to training for customer delight. Consider, for example, these three techniques, which can be woven into the collage for continuous learning in customer delight.

1. *The tools.* It is necessary, of course, that your customer-contact people learn all the internal systems and procedures available for processing customers' orders, answering their questions, and handling their requests. A thorough knowledge of the tools available permits customer-

contact employees to serve as effective guides. They can hear a customer's request and then select the path within the corporate maze that leads most directly to the desired outcome.

When providing this instruction, avoid the urge to have the systems expert, for example, provide the training. This expert will be more concerned with protecting the integrity of the system than with delighting the customer. Instead, select some of your most experienced and effective customer-contact pros, train them as part-time trainers, and have them do the tools training. These experienced "guides" will have great credibility with a class of new people and can serve as role models. They have also learned how to most effectively use the tools available to get the job done. The inside tips they can provide can be quite useful. In other words, no system or process can meet all the demands made of it. Your experienced reps can share special techniques they've learned for avoiding some of the "official path" traps.

This technique also sends what I believe is the right signal to your rookies: the systems and procedures are, in fact, tools, but their personal challenge is to delight the customer even if it means making an end run around the system to do it. In other words, be creative, use your head, and, if the prescribed path is questionable, blaze new trails.

Obviously, management and the reward system must cherish and encourage trailblazers for their customer-focused creativity, not chastise them for their circumvention of the system.

2. *The techniques.* Another phase of your training should concentrate on techniques of the trade for delighting customers. These refer to suggested methods for effectively serving customers when interacting with them directly via the mail, on the telephone, or in person.

There are techniques for greeting customers, soothing ruffled feathers, thanking customers for their business, making them feel special, managing their expectations, and even soliciting business from their friends and neighbors. Some techniques are quite specific and subtle. For example, have you ever talked on the phone with a customer service representative who says good-bye and then breaks the connection (hangs up) almost simultaneously? Some of us have a quick trigger finger if we do a lot of talking on the phone. To customers, it feels like having the door closed on their heels as friends are seeing them from their house. It can leave an uncomfortable last impression. It is better to let the customer break the phone connection first, or at least wait for a count of 3 before you do it.

Some companies provide their customer service representatives with a little mirror by their phone so that they can watch their facial expressions. At the bottom of the mirror are the words, *Are you smiling?* Have you ever tried to be abrupt, discourteous, or confrontational while you're smiling?

3. *The trials and triumphs.* It is necessary to model or to demonstrate highly effective customer contacts for the new employees. They need to build a mental video library of what great customer-contact experiences look like, sound like, and feel like.

Here again, use some of your experienced people, those who have been customer-delight role models. Have them relate stories of excellence in dealing with customers—the triumphs. Pass around letters received from customers that praise representatives for their courtesy, attention, and helpfulness.

Include experiences that went sour (but don't name those responsible), and use these as case studies for learning. How could you have handled this contact more effectively? Such live-fire trials and triumphs exercises can be very effective in teaching your new people how to behave with customers. Also consider using outside speakers or some of Tom Peters's excellent videos.

Once you have developed a multifaceted training program, consider doing these two things:

- Update your three training modules each year, and bring your people back for brief refresher training. This establishes a continuous learning culture.
- Create a half-day or full-day mini version of your training, and require that every person in the company attend, from top managers to entry-level personnel. Take a lesson from the Marines and from Disney. You never know when these support staff persons may find themselves face-to-face with customers. This idea also advises others of the key role the customer-contact people play, and it can create a stronger commitment on everyone's part to support them effectively. Finally, it underscores the importance placed by your company on customer delight.

When it is time to release your new people from their initial training, make their graduation a special event. Certificates, a class photo, a visit from the CEO, and an audience of experienced customer-contact people can create a memorable ceremony. Then, for the first month or so, assign each new graduate to an experienced customer service or sales representative for moral support and friendly guidance. This peer-level coach can supplement and complement the role of the supervisor, but it is not meant to replace it.

Managing for Customer Delight

The role of the manager has changed (or must change) from that of keeper of the rules, auditor, second-guesser, and so on, to coach, adviser, lead blocker, and cheerleader. Once you, as a manager, have hired the right people, trained them effectively, and provided the basic tools needed to get the job done, your role is to have faith in your people and to do everything you can to kick aside any obstacles that may prevent performance excellence. You need to support your people like never before.

This supportive role requires that you establish a reputation as credible, caring, approachable, and effective at pointing the way and clearing the path. To do this, you must be a great communicator and an aggressive problem solver. Without effective communications, you will not learn about what is getting in the way. The hurdles on the path to customer delight will turn into insurmountable walls, and effectiveness will suffer greatly.

You must adopt an aggressive problem-solving style. This requires frequent and regular conversations with your people, during which you constantly ask questions like:

- How's it going?
- What's getting in the way?
- What should we consider changing in order to permit you to do an even better job?
- What can I do to smooth the way?
- What's your greatest frustration?

Ask these questions in one-on-one meetings and in both formal and informal staff meetings or rap sessions. Keep these questions in mind as you simply look around the organization. Then, when you get answers that point out the need for changes, pursue them aggressively and keep your people well informed of your efforts to remove the hurdles. Even if you are not able to solve all the problems, your people will know that you have tried and will know why certain things must remain as they were. Your credibility will soar and so will the effectiveness of your unit.

You may also search out the problems and frustrations by keeping in close touch with representatives from your human resources department. Often these people hear about employee relations issues first. Or, if your company provides an internal consulting unit or permits the use of outside consultants, use them to help uncover opportunities for improvement.

The point is to do all you can to constantly permit your staff to do their jobs free from the restrictions placed in their path by bureaucracy, ineffective procedures, personal or work-related problems, and the like. Only by keeping the path clear can excellence be achieved day after day.

As we discussed in Chapter 8, leading your unit through the process of unit-level quality, particularly if your unit supports customer-contact people directly or indirectly, can be an extremely effective method of isolating the issues that may detract from the performance of excellence. So get on with it!

If you manage a customer-contact unit, there are a few other challenges. Constant customer contact can be a stressful role. Your people are on stage all day, and this demand can wear down even the strongest and most dedicated people.

Attempt to organize the routine so that a few people each day get an hour or two to work on special issues or projects. Get them off center stage for a while, but give them something meaningful to do. One opportunity already mentioned is to get some of your best people trained as customer service trainers and have them influence the new class of rookies. You may also send some people periodically to tour other units that support yours to learn more about how this support is provided.

You also need to be particularly observant in order to quickly spot the person who may be feeling the stress. For example, a person who has a sick child at home and a spouse on a business trip may be distracted and worried. Another person whose mother is in the hospital or whose marriage has just run aground may be finding it difficult to cope. People under stress need relief.

If your company does not have an employee assistance program (EAP), you should fight for one. An EAP that provides free (to the employee) confidential counseling services on a wide range of matters, from substance abuse to getting an elderly parent into a nursing home, can be an extremely valuable resource for your people. And the special training many EAPs provide for supervisors can help them spot employees with problems in the very early stages. You owe it to your employees and to your customers to provide the needed assistance promptly, to resolve the issue, and to welcome the employee back to center stage once the issue is resolved.

An effective EAP can easily pay for itself in reduced absenteeism and health-care costs, not to mention lower employee turnover, higher morale, and greater productivity. It is also wise to consider providing some level of child-care support for your employees. Working parents have a lot on their minds when child-care arrangements are less than ideal.

Rewarding Employees and Building Spirit

As mentioned earlier, a company's reward system is not centered only around rates of pay and salary increases. A reward system consists of all the methods used to say to your people, "You're doing a good job and we appreciate it." Some components of reward systems include:

- Pay raises
- Incentive rewards
- Special recognition programs
- Promotions
- Appointments to special task forces
- Suggestion awards
- Expressions of appreciation
- Appraisal systems
- Time off with pay

A well-designed and effectively administered reward system can add spirit and drive to an organization, and I include spirit-building and morale-building activities in the broadest definition of reward system. Reward systems must take a multifaceted approach similar to that discussed previously for training programs. A company's reward system with only three or four components, which remain unchanged for several years, becomes stale. We need to be constantly stirring the pot to keep the system fresh and exciting. Events that build spirit throughout the company should occur occasionally even if they don't single out individuals or groups for job-related acts of gallantry. At Colonial Penn, for example, we have an employee-run recreation club. The club's officers arrange art contests, photography contests, talent shows, picnics, holiday decorating contests, and casual dress days, and select in-house talent to anchor our monthly video news program. These activities build spirit, bring managers together with the nonmanagement employees, and seem to say that business is not all business—it's okay to have fun.

The important thing to remember about reward systems is that they must clearly support the key goals and values of the organization. Remember: What gets rewarded gets done.

In Chapter 13 we discussed celebration and recognition relating more directly to participation in your TQM system. Here, we'll cover just the basic components of a reward system strategy. I challenge you to develop other incidental but spirit-building components to supplement the basic ones.

Pay. Basic salary systems won't be discussed here, but I will convey my belief that base pay and periodic regular increases should be supplemented by some type of profit sharing. If all employees have an opportunity to share in the success of the business, they play their roles with a stronger motivation. They begin to see themselves as partners in the business, and they take pride in their contributions. The basis for profit sharing, however, must not be limited only to profit. It is necessary to focus on customer-satisfaction goals as well. Therefore, a profit-sharing or gain-sharing system in a TQM-managed company must be driven by goals such as:

- Profitability
- Growth of the customer base
- Reduction of customer complaints

These bonus-related goals must be applied equally to all levels of employees. Otherwise the credibility of the system will deteriorate rapidly, and customer-related measures will take a backseat to profits.

Recognition. Formal recognition, such as an award presentation banquet, is useful because it allows people to enjoy a short time in the spotlight while their peers look on, and it also permits more management involvement. Recognition ceremonies also communicate and reinforce key values to others in the company. As mentioned previously, recognition need not be an expensive proposition. However, it must be prompt, sincere, and relevant.

Promotions and career advancement. Career advancement moves are probably the ultimate expression or most tangible evidence that employees have really contributed to and are highly valued by their organization. Too often salary systems fall far short of conveying this message because most people receive nearly the same level of salary increase. A promotion, however, represents a more long-term commitment on the part of the company awarding it and a greater feeling of commitment on the part of the employee receiving it as well.

Promotions should be made only after careful thought is given to the implications pertaining to corporate values. For example, if your employees observe that people get promoted for taking exceptionally good care of customers, for advocating and acting on ideas to make the company more customer-focused, for participating in the QI efforts, and for being a team player, then you are using this reward system component to further the values of the company. People watch promotions very carefully and adapt their behavior to put themselves in line for advancement too.

Appraisals. Appraisals, too, could be the subject for another book, although for Dr. Deming it would only be a one-line summary: "Toss them out." The fundamental problem with appraisals is that they are often linked directly to pay-raise decisions and force a manager to label people as winners, losers, or so-so types.

I suggest that appraisals be a less formal tool that managers use to provide guidance and feedback (both positive and constructive) for enhancing performance. Completely unhook your appraisal system from the pay system. Discard the long form and go with a "1040EZ" (short-form) approach, which is a collaborative exercise between manager and employee three times a year. Avoid attaching to employees labels such as *superior, satisfactory*, or *distinguished*.

For example, in January have the manager and each employee meet for a two-way conversation. This meeting is to determine:

- The essential mission of the position
- The principal "customers" for that position
- The two or three vital few outcomes for the year
- One personal, developmental objective

In May another meeting should take place. Discuss progress in pursuing the vital few outcomes. Determine what obstacles exist and how the manager can help. Have the manager provide some feedback and suggestions based on his or her observations over the past 3 or 4 months. Discuss progress made on the personal, developmental objective. What help is needed here?

In October repeat the process followed in May.

Then again in January repeat the exchange and see whether the mission, outcomes, or personal, developmental objective should be modified.

A simple form for recording notes can be used and kept by both the manager and the employee. However, nothing is sent to the employee's file, and nothing is sent to the salary department. No salary decisions should be made during the month a 1040EZ discussion is held. Be a coach, not an evaluator!

I know that this system will be hard for many companies to accept.

After all, we've grown up with and operated under formal systems for documenting and justifying personnel actions. We worship at the altar of consistency in order to avoid discrimination claims and so on. But along the way, we have lost our senses when it comes to managing for personal development and performance improvement. Take a chance. Do it right.

Total quality management is a people-intensive process for delighting customers. Therefore, we must intensify our efforts to select the right people for the job, train them well, reward and recognize them, and provide them with the leadership that subscribes to the new role as coach, cheerleader, lead blocker, and adviser. In the final analysis, it is the people of your organization, not the management group, who will delight your customers. At Colonial Penn we say that "employees are the key to customer satisfaction, and customer satisfaction is key."

Transformation Checkpoints

1. To your customers, your customer-contact employees *are* your company. Their actions shape customer perceptions.
2. Take employee recruitment and selection very seriously.
3. Search for the right attitudes first—a customer-delight value system.
4. Use a recruitment team, not just the personnel staff.
5. Promote from within whenever possible.
6. Develop a customer-delight collage for continuous learning:

   The tools
   The techniques
   The trials and triumphs
7. Require that *everyone* attend customer-delight training.
8. Adopt the new managerial role:

Coach	Lead blocker
Adviser	Cheerleader
9. Be a great communicator and an aggressive problem solver.
10. Manage by using the unit-level quality process (Chapter 8).
11. Watch for and help reduce stress in customer-contact people:

    Vary their routine
    Establish an employee assistance program (EAP)
    Provide child-care support

12. Establish a multifaceted reward system.
13. Build spirit into corporate life.
14. Provide for gain sharing or profit sharing tied to key customer-delight measures.
15. Provide celebration and recognition.
16. Promote the right people. Promotions advertise values.
17. Reinvent your approach to appraisals:

    Follow a 1040EZ approach.
    Avoid labels such as *superior, distinguished,* and so on.
    Unhook appraisals from the salary-increase system.

18. Remember that it is your people who delight your customers.

16

Avoiding the Traps

To help you avoid some of the common mistakes, this chapter will review some points for the successful implementation and the continued nurturing of your growing and expanding TQM process.

Like a newborn child, a TQM process is a fragile, complex, and most precious thing. It must be carefully and lovingly raised, and this delicate process, which encompasses infancy to adulthood, must be linked to a strong, positive, and consistent value system. Mistakes can and will be made. In fact, there are a hundred ways a day to foul it up. Some mistakes along the way will not, in and of themselves, completely derail a TQM process. However, others may do precisely that. Plus, a combination of errors, if left uncorrected, will doom your TQM effort to certain failure.

No company can expect to foresee and avoid all the traps along the TQM journey. Careful planning, testing, and use of an experienced consultant will help to chart a course through the sea of possible mistakes. I won't suggest that I am aware of every possible trap, and I certainly cannot boast that I've never seen the inside of one or more. What I will do is describe and discuss many of the common traps and dangers that lie squarely in the path of most developing TQM processes.

One reason why it is difficult to avoid falling into these common traps can be traced to our very nature. It is common to be skeptical of the advice of those who have gone before. Our confidence in our own abilities, our acute powers of observation, and our attitude of self-reliance combine to form a feeling of immortality. Add to this our natural urge to move forward quickly—to capture the flag before time runs out—and we may have a recipe for disaster. Is it true what "they" say of us impetuous Americans: Do we follow the strategy of "Ready, fire, aim"?

The fact is that TQM represents, for most companies, a major change in corporate culture. Hundreds and even thousands of people work in our competitive businesses, and, in many organizations, too many layers of management exist between the captain on the bridge and the sailors on the deck. It takes a long time to change the course of a large vessel as well as of a good-sized company. The more traps we can avoid as we steer the course, the better our opportunity is to maintain our momentum and reach our destination.

As well as points covered earlier, "Avoiding the Traps" will discuss ones that we haven't covered or, at least, haven't covered explicitly. The traps I'll discuss relate to:

- Management behavior
- Some basic TQM concepts
- Training
- Selection of QI projects
- The quality organization
- Customer research
- Culture

Evaluating Management Behavior

Trap 1: Short-Term Focus

If managers believe and then communicate to others that TQM must be able to pay its own way in a matter of a few short months, then they have fallen into the short-term focus trap. Depending on whom you ask, it may take anywhere from 2 to 10 years before TQM is fully institutionalized within a medium- to large-size organization.

A short-term focus is like a crash diet. It will weaken the organization and rarely ensure that the ultimate goal is achieved and sustained. A short-term focus frustrates the people involved with TQM because they quickly realize that it takes time to develop the skills, attitudes, and knowledge required to make a difference to customers and to the bottom line.

Remember, TQM is a journey, not a destination. It is a process, not an annual drive or program. If you imply that it is short-term, it will receive lip service as people lie low to wait it out. A long-term, forever-and-ever focus, however, signals strong, unwavering commitment and eventually wins over the people who must make it all happen.

Falling into the short-term focus trap can be fatal for TQM because it is difficult for the same management team to earn a second chance. Your employees simply won't buy it!

I don't mean to complicate matters, but there is a trap within a trap when avoiding a short-term focus. When I urge you to avoid a short-term focus, I do not mean that management should not convey a sense of urgency. Rather, a long-term focus and a sense of urgency are entirely compatible attitudes and, in fact, are the right ones. We must express a sense of urgency to get on with it, to develop something, to test it, to learn from the test, to modify the process, to try it again and elsewhere within the company, and to keep at it every day while, at the same time, conveying a commitment to long-term results.

In other words, break the long journey into its manageable parts. Express a sense of urgency to get started and to keep pushing through each phase; however, don't push to achieve the ultimate goals by a week from Tuesday!

Trap 2: The Closed Kimono

In the broad sense, TQM is about establishing an attitude of continuous improvement throughout the company. We need to have every person in the organization enthusiastically looking to identify what gets in the way of quality from the perspective of meeting customers' needs. This new attitude prompts us to ask, Where are the confusing forms, the inefficient processes, the incompatible procedures, the ineffective equipment, and so on?

As problems hindering quality are uncovered and brought forward, we need to sincerely and publicly thank those who identified the issues. Then we need to investigate and resolve the root causes of these problems. If we frown at the exposure of the problem and look to place blame rather than seek causes, those who are in the best position to discover problems will quickly learn to keep their kimono closed, instead of "exposing themselves" to discipline.

From beneath the rugs to far up into the rafters, opportunities for quality improvement abound. Many are small, but taken together they have significant impact. The heroes of the company are those who expose these problems. Treat them like heroes, not like messengers of bad news, and involve them in fixing these problems.

If you want the office floor to be abuzz with improvement activity rather than littered with the bodies of dead messengers, you must practice the open kimono approach. A closed kimono attitude is a trap that will shut down your quality system as quickly as anything else. Why does the typical Japanese worker submit more than a hundred suggestions per year? Because the kimono is open.

Trap 3: Quality Improvement Equals Staff Reduction

Quality improvement equals staff reduction is one of the best formulas known for completely destroying your TQM process! Here's how it works. The employees of the billing department see an opportunity for improving the billing process. With approval from the quality council or their lead team, they form a QI team and a few months later implement countermeasures that result in an improved process. The time it takes to issue billing statements for certain services falls from 12 days to 5 days. The new process requires a staff of 14 rather than the previous staffing level of 20 people. Management then lays off six people! Sure, this may reduce salary costs by $120,000, but it also guarantees that far fewer QI teams will be formed, not just in the billing department but companywide! Total quality management will be seen as principally a staff-reduction strategy.

Instead of getting rid of the six people, take advantage of normal staff attrition to find them other jobs, preferably better jobs. Find a way to promote some. Rotate one or two to your quality training department, or make one or two a QI facilitator. Over a short period of time, you'll still be able to reduce the corporatewide staff by six through normal attrition *and* save the $120,000, but you will have protected the integrity of TQM. Later, as a result of continuing TQM successes, you'll be attracting even more customers, and you may again need 20 good people in the billing department. Total quality management should build opportunity for employees. It must not be seen as a staff-reduction program.

Trap 4: A Green Eyeshade Only Attitude

Customers come first. It's not a platitude; it's a fact. Without customers there are no revenues. Without revenues there is no survival. Financial goals are fine, but delighting customers must be first and foremost. Market-share goals are fine too, but delighting customers must be first and foremost.

Put another way, the ultimate act that defines success for a company is the transfer of money from a customer to a company in exchange for a product or service. The number of customers we have, the number of new customers we attract, and the number of customers who are repeat buyers of our products or services represent the greatest opportunity for continued financial success. Customer delight is what drives profitability.

Of course, if we are not able to produce and market our product or service efficiently or effectively serve our customers after the sale, profitability will elude us. Total quality management helps profits in two ways. It can help to ensure that our internal operations are cost-effective, and it can help to ensure that we delight the customers by providing what they need in terms of the product and the service behind the product.

Too many organizations pay attention only to the operational cost-effectiveness benefit of TQM because it is easier to measure. They wear the green eyeshade and use the sharp pencil to track the costs and related benefits. As a result, it is easy to be trapped into paying too much attention to the currently measurable benefits of a QI project and ask only: What will it cost, and how much will it save?

Instead we must pay more attention to how a QI project will affect customer attitudes. In many cases, this question is difficult to answer in a precise manner. Only time may tell. We need to have confidence that improved satisfaction makes a big difference.

It is at this critical point that top management's fundamental belief in and firm commitment to the value of customer delight are tested. If management wears only the green eyeshade and is skeptical of this "customer satisfaction myth," then TQM earns a reputation of being only a cost-cutting program. Few employees are satisfied for very long working in what they may perceive as a cut-cut-cut environment. As a result, your TQM culture–building journey will take a turn down the wrong road.

Management must have the courage of its convictions to prevent this wrong turn. It is probably with this same type of courage of conviction that your company was founded in the first place—the courage a founder had that his or her dream (company) could make a positive and lasting difference to a segment of the consuming public.

Trap 5: Delegation

Although this point has been made strongly already, the subject is important enough to warrant repeating. Top management's involvement and commitment are absolutely essential to the long-term success of any TQM effort. To continuously delegate responsibility is to downplay importance. If TQM really is a matter of survival in the long run, as I've suggested, then it warrants top management's attention both personally and directly.

Understanding Some Basic TQM Concepts

Trap 6: Ignoring the 85/15 Concept

Too many managers believe that most problems related to quality are caused by worker-controllable errors and that, therefore, a QI process is mainly a technique for fixing workers. The 85/15 concept, however, suggests that 85 percent of quality problems are traceable to faulty or fundamentally flawed work processes, procedures, working environments, or systems where workers are more the victims than the root cause. It is really management that holds the key to work processes and the working environment. Therefore, in order to make effective strides in quality improvement, managers need to be personally and continuously involved; and they need to be aware that, on average, only 15 percent of quality problems are attributable to employee error or carelessness.

If we believe the 85/15 concept, then our TQM efforts must involve management and nonmanagement people working together to mend or rebuild any inefficient processes and to adjust the working environment to ensure that all employees have an understanding of what the quality goals are, the means of knowing how they are doing at meeting their quality goals, and the means to adjust their work processes to better meet their goals. This partnership fosters a greater level of trust and cooperation between the organizational levels, builds a common language, and provides a greater return on the company's TQM investment.

If we don't believe the 85/15 concept, then we will end up in the trap promoting "fix the work force" strategies that retain a Theory X management style and produce disappointing or even dismal results.

Trap 7: QI Teams Are the Only Way to Achieve Improvements

In Chapters 5 and 6 we discussed how QI teams should follow a structured problem-solving process to identify, stratify, and analyze problems as well as to isolate root causes, develop countermeasures, and track the effectiveness of the remedial actions implemented.

This is the best way to effectively and permanently resolve chronic issues of poor quality, and it should always be a principal feature of TQM. However, don't fall into the trap of too intensely scrutinizing sporadic problems that may not warrant weeks or months of a QI team's investigation. The QI teams can and should be supplemented by another, related method I call the *implementation project.*

Once the company attitude changes focus toward continuous improvement, people from all over the organization will be identifying problems related to poor quality. By far, most of these quality problems will be deeply rooted, chronic issues that a trained QI team should and must address if lasting improvement is to be achieved. More sporadic problems, however, may have obvious solutions, and implementation projects can be undertaken to resolve them. Implementation project opportunities should not be studied to death, but once we take the necessary remedial action, we need to carefully measure the results of this action to determine whether the desired improvement has been achieved. If it hasn't, then maybe it should be turned over to a trained QI team.

Here again we have a trap within a trap. My implementation project advice should not be viewed as a special permit to circumvent the QI team strategy. The implementation project approach can be very appealing, but we must use it sparingly. As a general rule, I suggest that most QI problems you find are best addressed by trained QI teams and that implementation projects be held to a minimum. The greatest payback over the longest period will come from your QI team efforts. At the same time, you'll be developing a work force that is highly capable of problem analysis and resolution.

Suggestion programs are a source of implementation project ideas. If you have a suggestion program, my advice is to continue its use, but to be careful not to let a suggestion program undermine your QI team effort. Some suggestions, of course, will point toward chronic problems, so use these to feed your QI teams. Remember that a suggestion program is used as a supplement to, and not a replacement for, our TQM approach.

Training

Trap 8: Too Little, Too Soon

A well-planned, formal training curriculum is absolutely essential to building an effective TQM process and culture. Training teaches people to do things differently, which, as you recall, is where we should intervene in the cycle of behavioral change discussed earlier. Doing things differently leads to different results, and different results begin to change attitudes. These changed attitudes are necessary to modify the corporate culture.

Many companies are trapped by the tendency to serve up an appetizer or a small dish of training as TQM is introduced and then fail to provide the full five-course meal—the refresher training and advanced training necessary to sustain progress. As suggested earlier, it is better to design training in modules and provide what is needed at the time it is needed—just-in-time training. This is especially true when training people in a structured problem-solving process that includes SPC tools. For example, don't teach me how to construct a control chart in February if my team won't use it until July or August.

A good formal training curriculum of TQM courses may include:

- Introduction to TQM
- Quality team workshop: phase 1
- Quality team workshop: phase 2
- Quality team workshop: phase 3
- SPC refresher
- Advanced SPC techniques
- Quality leadership (for management)
- Team leader training
- Team facilitator training
- Unit-level quality for supervisors
- Quality planning for managers and product developers
- Training skills for the TQM instructor

Trap 9: Formal Training Only

Although formal training for your employees will be the backbone of their TQM education, it should not be the only source. It must be supplemented by an environment of continuous learning. Create an atmosphere that will stimulate people to learn more.

Set up a quality library that includes books, magazines, and videos. Purchase some of the quality software for PCs, and form a learning center. Invite outside speakers and encourage attendance at outside quality workshops and conferences. If you pursue the idea of establishing a quality partnership with another local company, as suggested in Chapter 14, this collaborative effort will provide greater opportunities for continuous learning.

Selecting QI Projects

Trap 10: Solving World Hunger

Selecting a project the size of solving world hunger is one of the most difficult traps to avoid. There seems to be a natural tendency to select QI projects that are far too broad and complex to be resolved by one QI team. If too broad a project theme is initially identified, have a well-trained QI team first try to stratify it in order to identify a number of smaller projects related to the broader theme. This usually results in enough good, workable projects for maybe 8 to 10 teams. For example, customer complaints is a world hunger–size problem. After some initial investigation, you may need to assign 9 teams to pursue these smaller parts of the problem.

Customer Complaints

1. Complaints relating to product *A*
2. Complaints relating to product *B*
3. Complaints relating to product *C*
4. Complaints relating to product *D*
5. Complaints relating to order delays (shipping)
6. Complaints relating to the eastern region
7. Complaints relating to the western region
8. Complaints relating to billing
9. Complaints relating to order adjustments and refunds

This gang-tackling approach can sometimes be quite effective. However, you need to exercise some caution, judgment, and careful coordination in order to avoid several teams stumbling all over each other.

The more classical TQM approach would be to do enough data gathering and initial analysis to determine where the big payoff may be—the Pareto effect. For example, a first-level Pareto analysis may reveal that 68 percent of customer complaints are traceable to product *C*. Within product *C*, a second-level Pareto may reveal that 60 percent of complaints relating to this product are attributable to billing-related issues.

See Figure 16-1. This analysis suggests that a single QI team assigned to the problem of product *C*'s billing-related complaints may be able to deliver a sizable improvement in the overall problem.

Further review of this multilevel Pareto may suggest that other teams be assigned to investigate shipping complaints related to product *C* as well as complaints related to product *D*—the second-highest bar on the first-level Pareto.

World hunger–size projects send a team off in search of too much data. This causes frustration. Remember to stratify issues and conduct a Pareto analysis in a search for the vital few.

Trap 11: Lack of Focus

Quality improvement teams represent a significant but wise investment. As such, their efforts must be focused on the issues that make the most

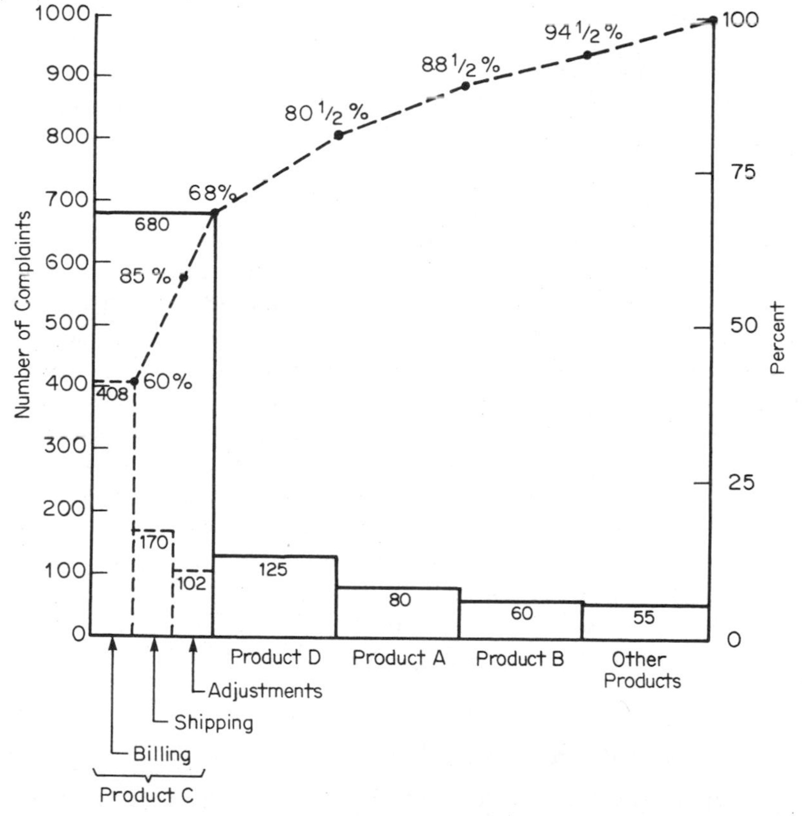

Figure 16-1. First- and Second-Level Pareto Analysis: Customer Complaints.

difference to the organization and its customers. As Chapter 7 on quality planning pointed out, the QI efforts should be focused on the company's principal goals and CSFs to ensure the greatest success.

If the goals were carefully selected to represent areas where breakthroughs in performance can significantly propel the organization to achieve its strategic competitive advantage, then a heavy concentration of QI effort in these areas will provide not only the fuel to get there but also the best return on the investment.

Failure to focus the efforts of QI teams on the key goal areas will result in slower progress toward the company's vision, with a far less effective outcome. Just like any other important investment, an investment in QI teams should be aimed at key corporate goals.

Defining the Quality Organization

Trap 12: A Separate Structure

Chapter 2 discussed a three-phase quality organization. It was pointed out that this organization should be a parallel structure, never a separate one. If a separate structure is put in place for TQM, we fall into another trap—we suggest that quality is not necessarily a day-to-day, forever-and-ever mainstream focus for the company. A separate quality organization structure suggests that only a special group or separate chain of command is responsible for quality and that others who are not in the special group or chain are off the hook. This is a mistake—a very large mistake—that will prevent you from achieving the desired TQM culture.

Instead, a parallel quality organization makes quality everyone's business. The basic organizational structures and chains of command that direct and implement other key corporate strategies also drive the TQM process. It is okay to form special, temporary task forces from time to time in order to develop special enhancements to TQM, but they must be recognized as temporary. Colonial Penn's design team serves as such an example. At no time should anyone wonder or fail to recognize where the real and permanent ownership for TQM lies.

Trap 13: The Quality Department

Although trap 13 is closely related to trap 12, it is stated separately for emphasis. The quality department must be kept small and should never be thought of as the unit ultimately accountable for quality.

Instead, the quality department should be thought of as an internal consulting group that can advise, promote, counsel, and assist in auditing TQM performance. Also, this unit should be seen as a staff group that can propose and develop supporting systems such as training, recognition processes, and communications strategies—which should be somewhat consistent across organizational lines.

As suggested earlier, it is a good idea to rotate people in and out of the quality unit in order to maintain a fresh stream of ideas. For many people, a tour in the quality unit will be a good developmental experience as well.

Finally, because this unit has corporatewide impact, it should always report directly to the quality council—to top management.

Trap 14: Putting the Test Site on a Pedestal

If you do use a test site, you will probably find it to be quite successful. Measurable results will be impressive, and its emerging culture of continuous improvement will be visible at about the time the rest of the organization is beginning to understand TQM. As your quality process is introduced companywide, the test site will continue to develop its own process and will probably remain a few good strides ahead for some time.

Of course, you need to showcase your test site in order to help others understand TQM, and the employees of the test site can be your best quality sales staff. But what we need to avoid at this point is—in an organizational sense—sibling rivalry. If a parent says to a child, "Why can't you be like your sister?" the reaction can be somewhat defensive, and feelings of resentment may result. So don't put the test site on too high a pedestal, and don't try to shove the test site's success down the throats of the rest of the company. Admittedly, there is a fine line between showcasing and shoving. Utilize the success of the test site to its best advantage—as just one success story—to avoid creating feelings of sibling rivalry.

Researching Customers

Trap 15: Researching Customers' Satisfaction

Many companies have conducted customer satisfaction research for years. Surveys typically focus on determining where customer satisfaction and dissatisfaction lie. These data are essential if we are to understand how well we are doing as a company.

However, we also need to know where we should be going. This means that our research should also determine the principal needs of our customers. Examine your current database on customer research to determine whether your studies have supplied the data that will enable you to develop a clear understanding of your customers' needs. You may find that you've fallen short in this area. Or you may think you know the answer to this vital question, but the actual research doesn't support your conclusion or any other for that matter.

If this is the case, consider conducting studies designed to determine customer needs and then communicate the findings widely throughout the company, especially to the product developers. Set indicators to help measure how well you are meeting the needs of customers.

Studies to determine customers' needs are a little more complex than mere satisfaction report cards. A survey question which asks: "How do you rate our billing and payment procedures?" may reveal that 62 percent rate them as good or very good. But how do you discover that a growing number of customers may prefer an electronic funds transfer (EFT) option? Well-designed focus groups (carefully structured group interviews) may be needed to supplement the regular satisfaction report cards.

Understanding the Corporate Culture

Trap 16: The Split Personality

Changing the culture of a company is a complex process, as discussed earlier. We know that culture change by proclamation won't work. The change must come about slowly by having people do things differently. Nothing interrupts the process of culture change more quickly than the existence of a split personality, and it is usually management that exhibits this split.

As you identify the values that will be the cornerstones of the desired culture, particular attention must be paid to how management is living up to these values. Is management practicing what it preaches?

For example, if management says that customer satisfaction is a top priority but the key corporate indicators set by management are earnings per share, revenue growth, and the like, a confusing message is sent. Instead, if we focus heavily on indicators such as customer complaints, customer turnover, the number of repeat buyers, and the number of customers referred by current, satisfied customers, then we are sending a consistent signal. Management must not profess one thing and act on the basis of another. Management must walk like it talks.

Consider carefully if what you measure is in line with the right cultural values. Determine what measures really drive the reward systems because, as we've heard time and time again, "What gets measured and rewarded gets done!" Don't present a split personality.

These 16 traps to be avoided as you develop and nurture your TQM process are just a few of many awaiting an unsuspecting TQM architect. Careful planning and testing will help you to spot the traps that lie in your path, and a strong commitment to quality goals will provide the desire to steer around them. If you find that you've fallen into one or more of the traps, act quickly to free yourself, admit the mistake, and move on.

Transformation Checkpoints

Avoid the traps that can damage or derail your TQM process.

Trap 1: Short-Term Focus. Believe that TQM is a long-term journey, not a destination, and add a sense of urgency.

Trap 2: The Closed Kimono. Don't place blame. Find fame when your employees bring quality problems out into the open.

Trap 3: Quality Improvement Equals Staff Reduction. If quality improvement can result in a reduced staffing level, utilize attrition rather than termination.

Trap 4: A Green Eyeshade Only Attitude. Believe that improved customer satisfaction will bring great benefits. Don't look only at the dollars and decimal points.

Trap 5: Delegation. Total quality management leadership is too important to delegate.

Trap 6: Ignoring the 85/15 Concept. Believe that management must be involved in order to resolve 85 percent of your quality problems. Total quality management is not a "fix the worker" program.

Trap 7: QI Teams Are the Only Way to Achieve Improvements. Use QI teams extensively, but supplement and complement them with other continuous improvement strategies. Minimal and selected use of quick-hit strategies is okay, but be careful.

Trap 8: Training: Too Little, Too Soon. Provide just-in-time training.

Trap 9: Formal Training Only. Build a continuous learning environment.

Trap 10: Solving World Hunger. Break large issues down to those more solvable problems that can make the greatest difference.

Trap 11: Lack of Focus. Focus QI efforts on the key goals and CSFs of the company in order to advance more quickly toward your vision.

Trap 12: A Separate Structure. Build a parallel quality organization, not a separate one.

Trap 13: The Quality Department. Don't make the quality unit accountable for quality either implicitly or explicitly. Keep the unit small—an internal consulting staff group.

Trap 14: Putting the Test Site on a Pedestal. Showcase the test site carefully. Don't flaunt it or shove it down people's throats.

Trap 15: Researching Customers' Satisfaction. Don't just check on how you are doing in the eyes of the customer. Check to see where you should be going in order to meet customers' needs.

Trap 16: The Split Personality. Practice what you preach in order to shape the desired culture. What gets measured and rewarded gets done.

17
A Quality Conclusion

Throughout the United States, there is evidence that a quality revolution is taking shape in both manufacturing and service organizations. In manufacturing, we are beginning to see a transformation from an emphasis on quality inspection to an emphasis on building quality into the product from the outset. In services, we are beginning to realize that limited experimentation with employee involvement techniques and "smile training" is not enough to do the job. Instead, we understand that a totally customer-focused strategy, culture, and management system are needed.

This awakening in the United States probably began in earnest about 10 years ago. *In Search of Excellence*, by Tom Peters and Robert Waterman, was one of the igniting sparks, particularly for service companies. Also, more people began to take notice of the messages brought forth by such experts as Dr. Joseph M. Juran and Dr. W. Edwards Deming. Today it is difficult to get a ticket to hear Peters, Juran, or Deming.

The Malcolm Baldrige National Quality Award has also helped spark attention to quality improvement. However, it needs wider recognition, particularly in the service industry. In its first 2 years, not one service organization was named a winner. I anticipate that service role models will be selected in the near future and that the Baldrige Award will receive the extensive promotion and publicity it deserves. This could be the additional spark necessary to fuel our slowly accelerating quality revolution.

In the final analysis, however, the need for U.S. businesses to achieve exceptional and consistent quality performance must be driven by far more than the attraction of a prize or award. In reality, quality is a matter of long-term survival. The needs of consumers have never been as demanding as they are today, and the competition from other countries has never been so intense and challenging. The Japanese, for example, are not content with competing only in selected manufacturing sectors. They are targeting retail, hotel, restaurant, and financial services sectors as well.

There is absolutely no doubt in my mind that the worker in the United States is more than capable of meeting and turning back this economic challenge from overseas. But inspired and totally committed corporate leadership is required to get the job done. These leaders must realize that the current emphasis on quarterly earnings—a short-term view—is a major enemy of continuous long-term improvement. We must come to grips with this fundamental issue and make the strategic decisions to build quality and value for the long term. Winning the confidence and loyalty of customers by constantly delivering quality products and services is essential to our corporate survival.

Mounting a Quality Revolution in Your Company

This book has been about mounting the quality revolution in your company. It has provided, I hope, a blueprint for building a TQM system. To proceed, you must fully understand this blueprint and have the motivation to carry it through.

Many people in my own company have heard me say that "it's simple but not easy." One need not be some kind of wizard to understand and practice the basic concepts and components of TQM. They are all relatively simple. The difficult task, however, will be to weave all the concepts and features of TQM together to create a lasting quality fabric for your organization. This can't be done overnight. The key to being successful in your quality revolution is a staunch, long-term commitment to making the journey, strong leadership, the courage to take the first steps, and a fundamental belief that the people of your organization can make a real difference. In other words, it will not be just a managerial exercise. It will be a total management-employee team commitment to meeting the needs of customers the first time and every time.

Reviewing the Basic Steps and Key Points

Let's look back at some of the basic steps and key points presented since Chapter 1.

1. Total quality management is a journey, not a destination. If you are looking for an annual, quick-fix, slogan-based strategy, then don't bother with TQM, because TQM is a long-term, customer-focused strategy for achieving a sustainable competitive advantage involving all people of the organization. It is aimed at continuous, fact-based, project-by-project improvement driven by a consistent understanding of the needs of your customers.

   A bonus point of TQM is that delighting customers has bottom-line impact. By improving the quality of what you produce, you will delight customers, retain them, attract more customers, and ultimately reduce your costs—to estimate conservatively, the COPQ amounts to from 20 to 25 percent of sales revenues. Some say that it can be as high as 40 percent. Furthermore, studies show that it costs four to five times more to attract a new customer than it does to retain your current customers.
2. Begin your quality revolution by organizing for quality. Build a parallel structure headed by a top management quality council, and consider the use of a specially appointed design team to build your initial TQM plans. Also consider experimenting with your quality model at a test site.

   Thoroughly research customer satisfaction levels and customer needs. This will identify the challenges ahead and provide a baseline against which you can measure progress.

   Because TQM represents complex organizational change, survey the attitudes of your work force and assess the current corporate culture. Take the action needed to prepare the organizational soil to accept the seeds of your quality revolution. Set a quality policy and communicate it.
3. Select an initial TQM implementation strategy that gets people to do things differently and that secures and models management's commitment and direct involvement. A top-down approach starting with the formation of management-level QI teams is strongly recommended.
4. Be familiar with the total quality model (Figure 4-1) so that you know what lies ahead. Realize that, generally, 2 years of pioneering is needed before you have a basic TQM system in place.
5. When forming QI teams, realize that selecting good projects is an essential ingredient for success. Projects the size of "world hunger" will frustrate teams and lead to disappointing results.

   Eventually, QI teams should exist in all parts of the company and at all levels. Teams represent the guts of quality improvement.
6. Train QI team members in a structured problem-solving process that is in four parts, as follows:
   a. Highlight the issue or problem.

   b. Analyze the problem.
   c. Solve the problem.
   d. Follow up in order to monitor results, hold the gains, standardize new procedures, and replicate good solutions elsewhere in the company.

   Provide strong support for QI teams to particularly include thorough training and an open kimono attitude.

7. Engage in quality planning in three phases:
   a. Quality strategic and business planning
   b. Quality products and services planning
   c. Quality process planning

   Communicate your focused business plan to everyone in the company, and ask each area to identify and commit to pursuing quality projects that relate to key corporate goals and CSFs.

   Quality process planning requires that you see your company through the eyes of the customer and that you create customer-friendly processes, procedures, and systems.

8. Have all corporate departments engage in unit-level quality; that is, have them follow the P.D.C.A. cycle as the routine way to run their units. Unit-level quality includes these steps:

   Plan

   - Set the unit's mission.
   - Identify the unit's products or services.
   - Prioritize products or services.
   - Identify the customers (internal too) of products and services.
   - Determine customers' needs.
   - Translate customers' needs to the unit's language.
   - Set quality indicators to measure performance.
   - Set a unit plan for improvement.

   Do

   - Implement the unit's improvement plan.

   Check

   - Monitor the quality indicators.
   - Check frequently with customers.

   Act

   - Take action, based on indicators and customer feedback, to improve.

9. Pay close attention to the CSFs:
   a. Top management commitment and involvement
   b. A supportive corporate culture

   c. Training and a continuous learning environment
   d. Customer communications
10. Pick the right test site and get started. A good test site should:
   a. Be managed by the "right" person
   b. Be physically removed from headquarters
   c. Perform mainstream company work
   d. Be free of other significant distractions
11. Model the success achieved at the test site, but do so carefully. That is, have the test site's success grow on others. Don't shove it forcefully at the rest of the organization. Kick off TQM for the rest of the organization.
12. Continue to ensure that top management is meaningfully involved in TQM by having top managers:
   a. Serve on the quality council and lead teams.
   b. Participate in QI training.
   c. Serve on problem-solving teams.
   d. Review team project presentations.
   e. Present certificates and awards.
   f. Speak directly with customers.
   g. Lead the quality planning effort.
   h. Approve quality project ideas.
   i. Visit team meetings and departments.
   j. Speak the TQM language.
13. Develop a recognition process, based on sound principles, to support TQM. Recognition should:
   a. Be perceived as real and relevant.
   b. Be sincere.
   c. Be timely.
   d. Have variety.
   e. Include management involvement.
   f. Involve peers of those recognized and be widely communicated.
   g. Be designed on the basis of employees' input.
14. When TQM hits high gear, sustain momentum by listening carefully to all who are involved, and continue to spin the P.D.C.A. wheel to constantly improve the process. In addition:
   a. Continue to learn.
   b. Celebrate regularly.
   c. Create a quality partnership with another company.
   d. Involve your vendors.
   e. Consider applying for the Baldrige Award.
15. Take great care in the selection, training, and management of your customer-contact employees. And consider *every* employee and manager as, potentially, a customer-contact employee.

16. Always attempt to avoid the most common traps that can destroy or derail your TQM process. The common traps are:
    a. Having a short-term focus
    b. Wearing a closed kimono
    c. Believing that quality improvement equals staff reduction
    d. Having a green eyeshade only attitude
    e. Delegating too much TQM leadership
    f. Ignoring the 85/15 rule
    g. Believing that QI teams are the only means to improvement
    h. Conducting too little training too soon
    i. Providing only formal training
    j. Going after world hunger
    k. Lacking a focus on key goals and CSFs
    l. Creating a separate structure
    m. Making the quality department accountable
    n. Putting the test site on a pedestal
    o. Researching customer satisfaction but not customers' needs
    p. Preaching one thing and practicing another

Going Beyond the Quality Horizon

We have traveled quite a distance together. However, the road to quality performance and continuous customer delight does not end; it continues far beyond the horizon now visible.

As you continue down this road, your TQM process will become more and more effective. Eventually, your organization will attain an outstanding record of achieving improvements in everything you do. At this point, the skills and attitudes of your employees will turn more to preventing poor quality than to fixing poor quality. As an organization you'll become excellent at customer-focused quality planning, and your plans for new products or services or for new procedures and systems will lead to better performance from the day they are conceived and put into place.

On the increasingly rare occasions when this improved performance isn't realized, the system of indicators and controls you've established to ensure quality will alert you instantly to any problems. The improvement abilities of the quality teams will be brought to bear immediately to correct the deficiencies. This responsiveness will be the envy of your competitors and will delight your current customers while attracting new customers in record numbers.

The quality mind-set of your employees will move from the QI team conference room to the office floor and positively affect individual performance every day. Quality and a focus on customers will be the new way of life.

Somewhere along the road to TQM excellence, the number of customer complaints you receive may increase. At first this may seem to be a disturbing development. However, it is really a positive sign—a sign that you are on the right path.

As we've said, studies have shown that most dissatisfied customers simply won't take the time or make the effort to complain. To them it just isn't worth the hassle. This silent majority ceases to buy from you and, in addition, relates their poor service story to at least nine other people, which damages your interests further.

Do not despair as complaints increase because, at some critical point, your customers will have perceived that you are taking quality and customer satisfaction more seriously. As a result, when things do go wrong, the affected customers will be more likely to give you a chance to fix it. They are demonstrating their confidence that you care and that their complaints won't fall on deaf ears or get lost in a bureaucratic shuffle. The number of complaints will rise until the point at which your attention to customers' needs combines with your more sophisticated level of TQM abilities to eliminate the root causes of the most common concerns. Then the complaints will drop dramatically. So don't be alarmed if complaints increase, but be delighted and continue to listen like crazy. It is a sure sign that you are on the right road and making visible progress.

In addition, we need to discuss the role that price plays in the customer delight equation. In my opinion, too many business leaders still cling to the notion that the price of a product or service is, by far, the first and foremost concern of the customer.

Price is, of course, very important to customers, but it has become increasingly clear that value is more important. *Value* is the customer's perception of the entire life of the purchase. This includes not only the actual product or service purchased but also the customer's entire experience during the duration of its use. A customer may buy the cheaper product the first time, but if it falls apart, if the customer can't reach the company to ask questions about the product, or if the product is not delivered in a timely fashion, the customer will go elsewhere the next time. Customers are not only buying the product or service per se, they are buying all the features, benefits, backup support, and future reliability as well. A shortfall in any of these areas will affect the customer's next purchase decision. Price must be backed absolutely by responsive and effective service as well as a strong commitment to meeting the price and product-feature needs of the customer. This combination is the right way to build a reputation for your company as the supplier of choice. This long-term view provides the only way to a sustainable competitive advantage.

Many recent studies show that customers are willing to pay a little more for quality (total value). However, don't be sidetracked by this shortcut to short-lived increased profits. Stick with the long-term TQM goal, which is to provide a competitive price, with the quality or total value already built in. A high level of quality will work to lower your costs, thereby permitting you to price your products or services attractively while ensuring that customers return again and again with their friends and neighbors in tow. This strategy will provide value not only for your customers but for your shareholders as well.

Finally, a quote to remember because it says it all. This anonymous note was handwritten on a card and found by the president of Colonial Penn taped to the door of an out-of-business discount furniture store:

> The bitterness of poor quality lingers long after the sweetness of low price is forgotten.

THE BEGINNING

Index

About the Author

Thomas H. Berry is now quality management director for the Vanguard Group of Investment Companies, Valley Forge, Pennsylvania. He is also a member of the board of examiners for the Malcolm Baldrige National Quality Award. At the time of writing, he was vice president of quality management and corporate training for Colonial Penn Group, Inc., whose parent company, Florida Power and Light, won the Deming Prize in 1989 for its quality improvement program. Berry is a former officer in the U.S. Marine Corps and is a graduate of Washington College.